THE CRIMINAL LAW'S PERSON

The state's use of the threat, and imposition, of punishment to regulate conduct is thought (or at least said) by many to be legitimised by the idea that the criminal law's burdens only fall on those who are blameworthy for their conduct. However, the formal concept of 'blameworthiness' needs to be made substantive. This puts various ideas regarding the criminal law's person at the heart of debates about blame, guilt and responsibility. How is the criminal law's person constructed, by whom, and with what disciplinary norms? How is it threatened by new 'knowledge', and how do those threats play out amongst the various stakeholders who claim the criminal law's person as 'theirs'? To address these and cognate questions, this volume brings together an international group of academics to engage with the criminal law's person from a range of disciplinary perspectives.

The Criminal Law's Person

Edited by
Claes Lernestedt
and
Matt Matravers

•HART•
OXFORD • LONDON • NEW YORK • NEW DELHI • SYDNEY

HART PUBLISHING
Bloomsbury Publishing Plc
Kemp House, Chawley Park, Cumnor Hill, Oxford, OX2 9PH, UK
1385 Broadway, New York, NY 10018, USA
29 Earlsfort Terrace, Dublin 2, Ireland

HART PUBLISHING, the Hart/Stag logo, BLOOMSBURY and the Diana logo are trademarks of Bloomsbury Publishing Plc

First published in Great Britain 2022

A catalogue record for this book is available from the British Library.

Library of Congress Cataloging-in-Publication data

Names: Lernestedt, Claes, editor. | Matravers, Matt, editor.

Title: The criminal law's person / edited by Claes Lernestedt and Matt Matravers.

Description: Oxford ; New York : Hart, 2022. | Includes bibliographical references and index.

Identifiers: LCCN 2021044672 (print) | LCCN 2021044673 (ebook) | ISBN 9781509923748 (hardback) | ISBN 9781509956449 (paperback) | ISBN 9781509923762 (pdf) | ISBN 9781509923755 (Epub)

Subjects: LCSH: Criminal liability.

Classification: LCC K5064 .C745 2022 (print) | LCC K5064 (ebook) | DDC 345/.04—dc23/eng/20211006

LC record available at https://lccn.loc.gov/2021044672

LC ebook record available at https://lccn.loc.gov/2021044673

ISBN: HB: 978-1-50992-374-8
ePDF: 978-1-50992-376-2
ePub: 978-1-50992-375-5

Typeset by Compuscript Ltd, Shannon

Acknowledgements

THIS VOLUME HAS taken a long time from conception to publication. First and foremost, we would like to thank the contributors, not just for engaging with the project and for writing such interesting chapters but for their patience, which we know has been stretched exceedingly thin at times.

In the very early days of the project, we benefited from a discussion with Matthew Kramer, Professor of Legal & Political Philosophy in the Faculty of Law at Cambridge. Following that, as the project developed, we were joined by Marianne Kristiansson, Senior Forensic Psychiatric Consultant and Professor of Forensic Psychiatry, Karolinska Institute, Stockholm. Although, in the end, neither Matt nor Marianne contributed a chapter, both shaped the project (in ways for which, of course, they should not be held responsible). We are very grateful to them.

The contributors came together for three workshops: in York, Cambridge and Stockholm. Many thanks go to Alexandra Rodell, who took care of practical matters both great and small in Stockholm. Funding for these meetings was gratefully received from a British Academy/Leverhulme Small Research Grant, a Seminar Award from the *Modern Law Review*, the Centre for Research in the Arts, Social Sciences, and Humanities (CRASSH) at the University of Cambridge, the Morrell Centre for Legal and Political Philosophy at the University of York, Justitierådet Edvard Cassels stiftelse, Stiftelsen Hans Thornstedts minnesfond, and the Karolinska Institute.

We are grateful to Jonathan Fisk for editorial assistance. At Hart/Bloomsbury, we would like to thank Sasha Jawed for his unfailing cheerfulness and patience, and Anne Bevan for the exemplary way in which she pulled it all together in publishable form.

Vilshärad and York
August 2021

Contents

List of Contributors

Kai Hamdorf, Justice at the Federal Court of Justice, Karlsruhe, Germany

Jules Holroyd, Department of Philosophy, University of Sheffield

Claes Lernestedt, Professor of Criminal Law, Stockholm University

Matt Matravers, Professor of Law, York Law School, University of York

Alan Norrie, Professor of Law, School of Law, Warwick University

Federico Picinali, Associate Professor of Law, Department of Law, London School of Economics and Political Science

Craig Reeves, Department of Law, Birkbeck, University of London

Malcolm Thorburn, Professor of Law and Chair, Legal and Ethical Implications of Technological Innovation, Faculty of Law, University of Toronto

Robin Zheng, Department of Philosophy, University of Glasgow

1

Introduction: The Criminal Law's Person

CLAES LERNESTEDT AND MATT MATRAVERS

THIS VOLUME BRINGS together an international group of academics to engage with the criminal law's person from a range of disciplinary perspectives. The main, but not exclusive, focus of the essays that follow is on various aspects of what is described as the criminal law's general part, containing (the more general of) the rules for ascription of responsibility. This is not because there are no interesting issues to be discussed regarding the construction of the individual in the special part of criminal law. On the contrary: the special part's rules, that regulate various parts of life (sexual relations, property, etc), rest on ideas and points of departure regarding how the person functions – what could and should be demanded of him or her, etc – all be it that such ideas are perhaps more visible in some areas of the law than in others. Our focus on the more general issues regarding the ascription of responsibility (and thus the general part) is not because the special part lacks interesting problems in this sense; it is instead because it would be too much for a single volume to try to tackle both.[1]

For the same reason, the volume is mainly concerned with the person as the subject of criminal regulation, as the accused, and sometimes as the convicted. There are of course many other persons in the criminal law – for example, victims, lawyers and judges – and these categories are not mutually exclusive when it comes to actual persons, but they are not the main focus of the essays that follow.

[1] We might add here that where the German tradition in criminal law has emphasised the general part as the most important, in the Anglo-American tradition the discussion, and even the existence (in a relevant sense), of a general part are historically rather new. Moreover, the size of what is considered to belong to the 'general part' differs in the two traditions, with emphasis on its not being large amongst Anglo-Americans. Perhaps the best way to think about such issues is that 'the truth' lies, and must lie, somewhere between the extremes. The (rules that we tend to think of as belonging to the) general part comes to life, existence and shape only through the interaction with the rules of the special part, and the shape that the general takes will vary depending on the part of the special with which it is confronted.

The cover of this volume is of the 'Trial of a sow and pigs at Lavegny'. According to Chambers' *Book of Days*, the sow and her six piglets were put on trial in 1457 for the murder and partial consumption of a child. The sow, it is said, 'was found guilty and condemned to death; but the pig[let]s were acquitted on account of their youth, the bad example of their mother, and the absence of direct proof as to their having been concerned in the eating of the child'.[2]

The picture, of course, is absurd to us and perhaps invokes thoughts of the advance of enlightened, rational, thinking. Today we know, or at least we agree, that it is inappropriate to hold non-human animals criminally responsible.[3] They are deemed to lack something, or perhaps many things, that we believe to be necessary for responsibility. Moreover, when it comes to human beings – to the (criminal law's) *person* – we (or at least most of us) agree that, at least in theory, it is the characteristics, capacities, etc, of this entity that allows society to have a system of criminal law: a system that communicates the message that certain things should not be done; threatens those who break the rules with punishment (ie, with various kinds of burdensome treatment, designed precisely *to be* burdensome);[4] actually inflicts such punishments on concrete individuals of flesh and blood; *blaming* them for what they have done, and furthermore through this, as a kind of by-product, stigmatises not only the *act* but also *the actor* for having committed the crime. Although it is regularly said that criminal law concerns itself with 'acts, not persons', persons are the ones who commit the acts and even if the criminal law, or moral, theorist might say that 'it is not you *qua* person we are blaming, it is what you *did*' such distinctions tend to collapse – particularly in the eyes of the public – when the person is convicted.

Moreover, the stigma brought about by a conviction does not necessarily disappear or even substantially fade away when the individual in question has served his or her sentence. This is particularly true for certain kinds of crimes (such as possession of child pornography). The afterglow of a conviction is often extended, in various formal as well as material senses, for the rest of the life of many of those who have been punished. Even if he or she has served the sentence, something which in the best of worlds would mean that the person 'has paid their debt' to *the criminal law system*,[5] this is not the case regarding other limbs of society, public as well as civil. For example, depending on what (kind of) crime was committed the conviction might effectively prevent

[2] R Chambers (ed), *The Book of Days: A Miscellany of Popular Antiquities in Connection with the Calendar*, vol 1 (W & R Chambers, 1863) 128–29.

[3] For a historical overview, see EP Evans, *The Criminal Prosecution and Capital Punishment of Animals* (Heinemann, 1906).

[4] Proponents of restorative justice and abolitionists would, of course, put these things in a slightly different way.

[5] Even here, in most criminal law systems, the 'payment' is incomplete in that earlier convictions remain relevant should the person reoffend. For doubts about the metaphor of a 'debt to society', see A Levins, B Jarman and T Thomasin Reimer, *False Accounting: Why We Shouldn't ask People Who Commit Crimes to Pay their Debts to Society* (JCFJ: Jesuit Centre for Faith & Justice, 2021).

the person from getting certain kinds of jobs or from accessing certain state services.[6]

Turning to more material sides of the potential afterglow, the 'political forgiveness' that could be said to be part of the communication between society and the convicted and punished individual is a shallow, formal and ritualised one,[7] whereas the reactions of the victim(s) cannot be expected to follow a similar pattern. Furthermore, society has little or no standing to demand from victims of crime that they follow the state in forgiving.

This reflects an important, and more general, point. The state, and society as whole, are not, should not behave like, and should not be looked upon as being, *persons* engaged in interpersonal relations. This means that discussions regarding what the state can, should and may do, ought to be grounded in political not moral philosophy. This means, furthermore, that moral philosophy is of limited application when it comes to how society and the state should behave in relation to certain matters such as the proper moral and emotional attitude to be shown towards someone who has completed his or her punishment.[8] What is required from society and the state is a certain kind of 'shallowness'. We return to this below, as well as to other aspects of what it means for the state to relate to persons in a 'political' way.

We are not claiming that the features of the criminal justice system briefly mentioned above are necessarily unjustified or illegitimate. What we do claim, though, is that being convicted and punished for a crime is not, and should not be, an insignificant thing. A great deal is at stake, both in an individual case concerning a particular person accused of a crime, and when considering the overarching question of the proper (justified, permissible, etc) use of the criminal law in general: its targets, structure, contents, sanctions, etc. What follows is that a great deal is also at stake when it comes to how the system of criminal law sees the person, or to put it another way and for reasons that will be developed shortly, how the criminal law's person is *constructed*.

Putting the criminal law to one side for the moment, the idea of 'a person' is not, of course, uniform across domains of human life any more than it is across academic disciplines. Depending on what area of life and/or society is in focus, and depending on what questions are posed, the conception of the person will differ. In economics we find *homo economicus*, in politics and sociology, the *zoon politikon*, and in psychology a plethora of persons across psychotherapy,

[6] See here (amongst others), Z Hoskins, *Beyond Punishment? A Normative Account of the Collateral Legal Consequences of Conviction* (Oxford University Press, 2019).

[7] We have borrowed what we find an especially useful term, 'political forgiveness', from PE Digeser, *Political Forgiveness* (Cornell University Press, 2001). Digeser uses it in a description and discussion of the work of the South African Truth Commission. We think that it can also be related to the way that the regular criminal law communicates with offenders.

[8] *cf* JG Murphy and J Hampton, *Forgiveness and Mercy* (Cambridge University Press, 1988). This wonderful book should be read as focusing on the individuals involved and not on society or the state.

cognitive and evolutionary psychology, and so on. There is also, of course, the law's well-known, and well-contested, *reasonable person* (formerly known as the *reasonable man*).[9]

Perhaps with sufficient thought we might agree that there is some kind of *core* to be found when we discuss what a person is, but such a shared core will most likely not be able to move much beyond basic distinctions such as (1) distinguishing persons from other kinds of entities, and (2) defining when and where one 'person-entity' spatially ends and another one starts. The further one moves into sub-areas of life, society, science and law, the greater the differences between their 'persons' will often turn out to be. Moreover, as the conception of the person becomes more complex, so it also becomes more contested, and many of those involved in such contests are unlikely to be disinterested 'truth-seekers'.

Returning to the criminal law and the construction of its (responsible and non-responsible) person, there is perhaps a deceptive sense in which it might be claimed that there is an agreed 'core'. For a start, the criminal law's person is not a pig, but an entity that possesses particular rational capacities, etc. However, even if there were such a core – something denied, for example, by moral responsibility sceptics – it requires a great deal of fleshing out: which rational capacities, possessed to what degree, being only two of the issues that need to be resolved.

In reality, the fleshing out of various aspects of the criminal law's person is to a large extent shaped by varying interests. Above, we said that a great deal is 'at stake' in the criminal law and, indeed, it is not unreasonable to think of the advocates of various competing interests revolving around the construction of the criminal law's person as 'stakeholders' both in the sense that the issues are tremendously important, and that many of the stakeholders are agenda-driven: their interests lie not in the discovery of the 'truth', but instead in trying to get (for one reason or another) their *desired outcomes* in relation to the criminal law. Such ambitions are not necessarily bad (we return to this below). The point is just that the outcome of the battles between various stakeholders' views is, to a large extent, what in practice shapes the criminal law's person as that person comes to life in, for example, legislation, enforcement, policing and court practice.

I. CRIMINAL JUSTICE: POLITICAL NOT METAPHYSICAL

Criminal law is a social construction embedded in wider social practices of criminal justice and public policy. These practices rely on institutions. Thus, the subject (in all senses) of the criminal law is a matter of choice. One society

[9] See, amongst others, M Moran, *Rethinking the Reasonable Person: An Egalitarian Reconstruction of the Objective Standard* (Oxford University Press, 2003).

might choose to criminalise conduct that significantly contributes to climate change, and another might not. One society might choose to allow the criminal prosecution of corporations, and another might not, and so on.

The fact that these things are matters of choice raises at least two questions. First, who gets to choose or to influence the choice? Second, what constrains or shapes that choice not in the social science sense of understanding the processes by which decisions are made, but in terms of the underlying theoretical and normative legitimacy and coherence of the enterprise? Who should get to choose, and based on what might those choices be made?

These questions will recur in this Introduction and in the chapters that follow. Our interest in both is not that of the descriptive political scientist. That is, 'who gets to choose?' might be addressed by looking at the legislature of a given society, its lobbying rules, campaign financing regulations, at the ownership and influence of the media, at who votes in elections, and at other factors of this kind. Such an enquiry would be interesting and important, but it is not the one pursued here. Rather, the issue for us is to understand what follows from the fact that the criminal law's person is formed as a theoretical and practical construction. As we note above, one might think of the criminal law's person in its various aspects as an artificial entity surrounded by, and indeed *created* by, various stakeholders – amongst whom are politicians, judges and the legal profession, academics and their respective disciplines – all vying for influence in shaping the criminal law's person and in excluding, or diminishing, the powers of others to do the same (or joining forces – creating alliances, unholy or otherwise – all in the quest for influence).

This 'battle' is reflected in addressing the second question. If one society can choose to demarcate a corporation as a legal person that can stand trial, what is to stop another doing the same for a pig? Again, our interest is not in answering this question as political scientists – 'the legislature would never pass the Bill to criminalise swine' – but as (in various ways) criminal law theorists concerned with the justification, legitimacy and coherence of the practice(s).

That is, if someone were to propose reintroducing non-human animal trials, consider the types of arguments that would follow in response. They would not just, or even primarily, be of the kind that the proposal will not be successful because Parliament would not permit it. Rather, they would encompass arguments about the nature and purpose(s) of criminal law and of its justification and legitimacy. Those arguments would be made by, and (whether intentionally or not) on behalf of interests guarded by the various stakeholders mentioned above. Legal theorists with a moral philosophy background, philosophers of action, political philosophers, lawyers, judges, forensic psychiatrists, psychologists, metaphysicians and others, will make certain types of arguments and try to exclude (or, in some matters, align with) other types.

In other words, the construction of the criminal law's person is intimately related to the arguments that justify and set limits on the criminal law itself and these arguments, too, reflect the vying of stakeholders to secure their views and influence. In the next section, we turn to this issue and to the ways in which the concepts of *blameworthiness* and *responsibility* frame, and obscure, the debate.

II. THE CRIMINAL LAW AND THE CRIMINAL LAW'S PERSON(S)

One – perhaps the primary – function of the criminal law is to regulate the conduct of persons. Moreover, the criminal law does not merely regulate but is part of the apparatus of the state the job of which is to shape the ways in which people behave in 'pro-social' ways.[10] In this, human beings and human communities are not unique. For example, great apes have systems of 'punishment' to reinforce communal behaviour.[11] However, human systems of regulation are subject to a distinctively human demand: that they can be justified. That is, insofar as we use deliberately imposed burdens – so-called 'hard treatment' – we need a justificatory structure and for the most part that structure currently depends on *blameworthiness*. 'Blaming' is key to the distinctive way in which the criminal law is said, at least in theory, to shape behaviour.[12] But, for the practice of blaming to be acceptable – to meet the demands of justification – we may blame, in the criminal law, only those who are *blameworthy*; only those who, in some sense, *deserve to be blamed*.[13]

Before considering this further, it is worth saying three things about this overarching justificatory claim. First, there is a danger in taking it at face value. It is far too easy to become complacent in the face of the burdens of punishment and the idea that only those who are blameworthy are punished can sustain that complacency. This is in part because the claim is ambiguous between blameworthiness as ordinarily understood and blameworthiness as understood in the criminal law. For example, we impose criminal sanctions on people whom many would not regard as blameworthy when using strict liability, although some in the legal and criminal law professions may disagree.[14] Second, blame can be understood

[10] On the 'civilising' function of the criminal law, see L Farmer, *Making the Modern Criminal Law: Criminalization and Civil Order* (Oxford University Press, 2016).

[11] See, eg, FBM de Waal, *Good Natured: The Origins of Right and Wrong in Humans and Other Animals* (Harvard University Press, 1996).

[12] The centrality of blame to the criminal law is standard across the literature. For example: RA Duff, *The Realm of Criminal Law* (Oxford University Press, 2018); MS Moore, *Placing Blame: A Theory of the Criminal Law* (Oxford University Press, 1997). For a recent challenge to this centrality see V Chiao, *Criminal Law in the Age of the Administrative State* (Oxford University Press, 2019), and the collection of papers on criminal law exceptionalism in *Criminal Law and Philosophy*, forthcoming.

[13] Some would say that it is (conceptually) impossible to 'blame' someone who is not blameworthy: we *can* only blame those who are blameworthy. Otherwise, they would say, we are doing something else; something that just *looks like* blaming.

[14] See, eg, T Honoré, *Responsibility and Fault* (Hart Publishing, 1999).

in several ways – instrumental,[15] therapeutic,[16] censuring[17] and others – and the relation of blame to blame*worthiness* is not straightforward. Third, and as discussed below, the idea of 'blameworthiness' can be understood in a variety of ways some of which are very shallow and others much deeper. Thus, some versions would be satisfied with the objective requirements of a crime description being met (A killed B), whereas others would invoke several elements of an elaborated general part. That is, we can define the elements of blameworthiness to 'capture' – and in the end convict – more or fewer individuals.

In short, the justificatory project seems to rest on the idea that the criminal law system reflects an idea of blameworthiness defined independently. However, it is just as – if not, even more – likely that we adjust our definition of 'blameworthiness' to suit what is deemed to be the needs of the criminal law system. To give just one example, we can define the legal concept of *intent* in such a way as to designate certain persons legally blameworthy in circumstances in which they would not be held morally blameworthy (at least not for having done something '*intentionally*'). In other words, the idea of blameworthiness needs to be given substance when we approach the criminal law's person, and it is to that matter that we now turn.

Who, then, can (and thus may) be blamed, and who gets to decide, formally and materially? Here, we need to separate two different kinds of discussion. On one side of the *first* discussion are those who for various reasons argue that human beings cannot be – do not possess the characteristics to be held – 'responsible' in a way that would legitimate blame, punishment, etc. On the other, are those who argue that human beings have, in principle, the necessary characteristics for responsibility and blame. Proponents of the first view find inspiration in the view that all human conduct has antecedent causes – for some, all such conduct is determined – in a way that is incompatible with a sense of responsibility deep enough to warrant blame and punishment.[18] Proponents of the

[15] See, eg, JJC Smart, 'Freewill, Praise, and Blame' (1961) 70 *Mind* 291.

[16] See, eg, N Lacey and H Pickard, 'From the Consulting Room to the Court Room? Taking the Clinical Model of Responsibility Without Blame into the Legal Realm' (2013) 33 *Oxford Journal of Legal Studies* 1. Although, as the title suggests, Lacey and Pickard write of a system 'without blame', what they wish to expunge is what they call 'affective blame'. It is critical to their argument that people are held 'responsible and indeed accountable for their blameworthy conduct'.

[17] See, eg, RA Duff, *Answering for Crime: Responsibility and Liability in the Criminal Law* (Hart Publishing, 2007).

[18] See, eg, D Pereboom, 'Free Will Skepticism and Criminal Punishment' in T Nadelhoffer (ed), *The Future of Punishment* (Oxford University Press, 2013); G Strawson, 'The Impossibility of Moral Responsibility' (1994) 75 *Philosophical Studies* 5; and GD Caruso, *Rejecting Retributivism: Free Will, Punishment, and Criminal Justice* (Cambridge University Press, 2021). This debate has a long history in which very little has changed other than the basis for the challenge. In the mid-twentieth century it appears between Barbara Wootton – pressing the claims of behavioural and social scientific explanations of human action – and HLA Hart resisting the same in the name of the independence of the law. Now, in the twenty-first century, the drive to rethink criminal responsibility is being led by neuroscientists, but the legal response remains the same.

second view defend the aptness of responsibility and blame in one of two ways. Some argue that human beings have the kind of profound freedom of will that is needed. Others insist that no such profound freedom is needed because 'blaming' is a social practice in a (smaller or larger) group – and 'blameworthiness' is a social construction within that group – meaning that there cannot be any external yardsticks used to question the construction in the particular group; the group is master.[19]

It is a *second* discussion that interests us the most in this volume. This takes as an unquestioned point of departure that human beings possess the characteristics needed for society to be able to consider them potentially blameworthy in having done what they have done. The pressing issue then is relatively small (although that is not saying much when compared with fundamental issues of free will): how – that is, on what grounds – can we make distinctions between persons *within* the system, all of whom are assumed by default to be capable of being held responsible, when it comes to blameworthiness in particular (kinds of) situations, circumstances, and so on? This is where the rules of the general part, the rules for ascription of responsibility (and its opposite), come into play. In short, *given* the general capacity for responsible agency and blameworthiness, how can we make distinctions *within* the (criminal law) practice of regulating and shaping conduct?[20]

Finally, for this section, we should note that the criminal law's persons, and proposals from the various stakeholders as to their construction, come in (at least) three ontologically different varieties when it comes to how the criminal law ought to conceive of the person in specific circumstances, with respect to certain issues, and so on. Moreover, which kind of proposal is being made may sometimes be unclear (perhaps even for the stakeholder proposing it).[21] The varieties we have in mind can be captured as follows: it is proposed that the criminal law should conceive of its person in a certain way in a particular matter or situation because,

1. The person actually *is* that way, or
2. The person *should* be that way, or
3. Even if the person *is not* that way, it is proper/desirable/necessary to engage in the fiction that s/he is.[22]

[19] See, eg, SJ Morse, 'Compatibilist Criminal Law' in T Nadelhoffer (ed), *The Future of Punishment* (Oxford University Press, 2013); Honoré (n 14).

[20] Although the chapters in this volume are in the main concerned with the second discussion, the relation between it and the first is not uncomplicated. In making the distinctions needed *within* the criminal law (the second discussion), one partly needs – or, as we will argue below, ought – to draw on material from, and of relevance to, the first.

[21] This was one important general point made in the Liberal–Communitarian debate in political philosophy in the 1980s and 1990s. For an overview, see S Mulhall and A Swift, *Liberals and Communitarians* (Blackwell, 1996).

[22] There can of course be made combinations, sub-groups, etc. See C Lernestedt, 'The Sounds of Silence. Some Reflections from Elsewhere' in U Kindhäuser et al (eds), *Strafrecht und Gesellschaft: Ein kritischer Kommentar zum Werk von Günther Jakobs*, 1st edn (Mohr Siebeck, 2019).

Consider by way of example (many others could be given), the English laws governing those who kill their partners as a response to long-term domestic abuse. Initially, it seemed as if such persons might be able to appeal to self-defence or to the (now abolished) partial defence of provocation.[23] The cases and doctrinal issues need not concern us. What is important are the ways in which 'Provocation', and its successor 'Loss of Control', reflect the distinctions above.

Take (1): in *R v Duffy*, Devlin J. provided the classic definition of provocation as,

> some act, or series of acts, done by the dead man to the accused, which would cause in any reasonable person, *and actually causes in the accused*, a sudden and temporary loss of self-control, rendering the accused so subject to passion as to make him or her for the moment not master of his mind.[24]

As is clear from the emphasised passage, the test was a question of fact: was this particular defendant at this particular time actually not the master of his or her mind? However, before considering this the jury needed to have decided that the triggers for the loss of control were such as to 'cause in any reasonable person' the relevant response. That is, the jury must consider first a question of the type (2): *should* a person have been provoked by these triggers before asking whether this concrete person was in fact provoked?

This twin approach reappeared when the law was revised, and the defence of Provocation replaced by that of Loss of Control. That change was in part motivated by information from psychology, that loss of control – not being the master of one's mind – need not be immediate but can be more like a 'slow burn'. That is, the law tried to reflect better the best account we have of how people work.[25] However, at the same time, the revised law explicitly removed the trigger of adultery. Common law had recognised as an example of provocation 'a husband discovering his wife in an act of adultery' and this continued to be a recognised trigger until it was explicitly removed in the revised Loss of Control defence. Thus, the revised law is clear that persons *should* not lose control in the face of adultery whether or not they might actually do so.

'Fictions' (the third category) are commonplace in the criminal law both in policy terms and in the ways in which the criminal law treats particular

[23] s 3 of the Homicide Act 1957: 'Where on a charge of murder there is evidence on which the jury can find that the person charged was provoked (whether by things done or by things said or by both together) to lose his self-control, the question whether the provocation was enough to make a reasonable man do as he did shall be left to be determined by the jury; and in determining that question the jury shall take into account everything both done and said according to the effect which, in their opinion, it would have on a reasonable man'. Women who killed their abusive partners having, for example, waited for the partner to go to sleep were precluded from successfully using these defences because of the 'gap' between the threat/provocation and their action.

[24] *R v Duffy* [1949] 1 All ER 932 (emphasis added).

[25] For an overview of the new defence, see A Norrie, 'The Coroners and Justice Act 2009 – Partial Defences to Murder (1) Loss of Control' (2010) 4 *Criminal Law Review* 275.

individuals. For example, in England and Wales, the presumption is that children aged 10 and above are criminally responsible for their conduct (whereas other countries set the bar later, at 15, 16 or 18). At trial, defendants are treated as if they are fully sane unless they meet a very high bar of insanity and, for the most part, evidence of partial responsibility that more accurately reflects the fact that people's capacities for reason vary across both populations and situations is excluded.

The explanation of this tripartite approach is complex. What we have called the 'stakeholders' in debates over the criminal law's person drive the choices between the three for a variety of reasons. One might be to respect how human beings 'really' work, physically and psychologically, another to use the criminal law to change people, and a third to treat persons as if they are a certain way as, for example, a matter of respect. Yet, the prevalence of the second and third approaches invites a question. Insofar as the justificatory demand is, as we put it above, that 'we may blame, in the criminal law, only those who are *blameworthy*', to what degree and for what reasons may we justifiably stray from (1) to (2) and (3) without undermining the system as a whole?

III. CONTESTED SOURCES, CONTESTED PURPOSES

The questions posed above – to what degree and for what reasons can, and may, we stray from the 'truth' about blameworthiness – seem deceptively simple. However, for reasons discussed earlier this is far from correct because what it is to be blameworthy – to be (rightly) deserving of blame – is itself contested. And, as we have seen, a legal practitioner or theorist could insist that within the system of criminal law only legal facts matter and so to be blameworthy is simply whatever the law says it is. But this begs the justificatory question. For *that* question to gain any traction, then, the criminal law must in some sense be answerable to critical claims: either in terms of its internal coherence or in terms of its fidelity to what is said 'outside' the criminal law (such as, eg, the psychology of 'losing control'). At the same time, given the law's dependence on blaming as a social practice – and its making equivalent 'blame' and 'blameworthiness' – these 'outside' claims need to make a case for their relevance 'on the inside'; that is, *within* the system.

This in turn raises two important questions: first, what is the source of the formal decision as to what are the legal facts? Second, whose knowledge, disciplinary approach, expertise, etc, has material influence on the decision?

In formal terms, there are actors in the criminal justice system with designated roles when it comes to deciding what is (not) relevant, and what is the 'legal truth'. Legislators determine some things as, for example, when they expressly rule out adultery as a trigger for provocation or decide that this or that offence is 'strict' and does not require a particular associated mental state. Judges in the higher courts have powers in effect to give precedential content to the meaning of legislation in, for example, ruling on what counts as 'reasonable' or 'reckless'.[26] Moreover, at the level of the individual every criminal law court, in every criminal case, through its evaluation of the case and its decision-making, produces its own specific construction out of the pieces of the mosaic of the criminal law's person.

These kinds of decisions are not taken in a vacuum. That is, although they are made by actors with the formal powers of decision-making, those actors are influenced in various ways by the discussions that surround criminal justice, and in many cases they explicitly call upon evidence (or 'evidence') from outside the law in justifying what they do. This is most obviously the case for legislators who argue, for example, that 'the public' demands *x* or *y* ('greater protection for children', 'harsher penalties for drug users', or whatever). But it also applies to other actors with formal roles, and that of course invites the critical question of *whose* knowledge is deemed relevant and in what ways.

It is to that question – the question of which people and disciplines, which stakeholders, are recognised as relevant – that we turn next. However, before doing so it is worth connecting the parts of the discussion above. The justificatory story of criminal law is one of (capacity for) blameworthiness. The system that regulates through threatening and deliberately imposing burdens on people is legitimised (at least in large part), by the idea that its burdens only fall on the blameworthy. We have pointed out various ways in which, taken at face value, that is problematic. Here, however, our concern is specific. The criminal law's person needs to be constituted in a substantive way – the very thin 'core' we described earlier needs to be filled out as much as is possible, and not only (as we have mainly done above) with views on what the person *is not* – and that requires decisions to be made about who and what is to count. We have already touched upon the idea of 'stakeholders', and we will return to them.

As a point of departure, consider the judge (eg, in Sweden) in a case and his or her world.[27] There are things that a judge, and every person, knows and is assumed to know. Amongst these are what we might call 'ordinary facts about the world' that are uncontested: for example, the sun rises in the east and sets in the west; water is wet; there are 24 hours in a day. Then, there are things where no assumption of knowledge can be made and where evidence is needed. In a trial regarding murder, or assault and battery, an external expert may be invited to testify regarding the wounds and what inferences can validly be drawn as to how the purported crime was committed. In such matters, the judge would not trust his or her own opinion on what conclusions to draw. More rarely, and more controversially, an expert in human sexual behaviour might be called as a witness in a case of alleged rape to testify about relevant matters regarding

[26] See, amongst others, F Stark, *Culpable Carelessness: Recklessness and Negligence in the Criminal Law* (Cambridge University Press, 2016).

[27] What follows would be relevant to the jury in common law systems.

human sexuality. Of course, this distinction is fluid. For example, the information about wounds is set against a background of shared 'ordinary facts about the world' such as that human beings are mortal, their blood is pumped around their bodies by their hearts, and that if sufficient blood is lost they will die.

The place of these 'ordinary facts about the world' and of some kinds of expert testimony in the law is uncontested.[28] Moreover, they need to be for the justificatory project to succeed because, as noted above, that project must manifest some fidelity to the world as it is thought to be. However, there are other aspects of the person that are not visible in the way that stab wounds are, but that nevertheless seem to be 'truth-apt' (ie, that would seem to admit of factual statements about them that are either true or false) in that they are part of the best explanation of how human beings – and the particular human being on trial – 'work' physically and psychologically. Not only are these aspects of the person 'truth-apt', but they may also have a bearing on the clearly normative issue of conviction (or not) in the individual case.

One such aspect of the person, as touched on above, is when and in what ways she or he might 'lose control'. Another is what she or he might perceive as reasonable or proportionate given his or her particular psychological arousal level. A third, relevant in common law countries that deploy the McNaughton rule for insanity, is whether the person understood the 'nature and quality' of his or her acts and, if not, whether the deficit could be traced to a 'disease of the mind' or 'recognised medical condition'.

For some legal commentators, the claim that statements such as the above can be 'true or false' is correct, but misleading. This is because whether a statement such as 'the defendant is suffering from a disease of the mind' is true does *not* depend on whether it corresponds to an 'ordinary fact about the world', or even to 'a fact as determined by the consensus of medical experts', but on whether it corresponds to the definition of what it is to suffer from a disease of the mind *within* the criminal law. James Fitzjames Stephen put this robustly when declaring the irrelevance of the nascent discipline of psychiatry to questions of criminal responsibility. Criminal responsibility, he wrote, 'is, and must be, a legal question'.[29] More recently, Stephen J Morse has echoed Stephen in claiming that to think that a legal test such as insanity answers to facts from

[28] Hence, the point of the court scene described in CM Sevilla, *Disorder in the Court: Great Fractured Moments in Courtroom History* (WW Norton & Company, 1999) is to be funny; it is not to illustrate some arcane legal meaning of the word 'alive'. The scene unfolds as follows: 'ATTORNEY: So, then it is possible that the patient was alive when you began the autopsy? WITNESS: No. ATTORNEY: How can you be so sure, Doctor? WITNESS: Because his brain was sitting on my desk in a jar. ATTORNEY: I see, but could the patient have still been alive, nevertheless?' Nobody in or outside the law seriously considers that someone who has had his brain removed could be alive, notwithstanding the witness's reported response: 'Yes, it is possible that he could have been alive and practicing law'.

[29] Sir James Fitzjames Stephen, *A History of the Criminal Law of England*, vol II (Macmillan, 1883) 183.

outside the criminal law is to make 'a category mistake' because 'legal insanity is a legal and moral issue, not a medical, psychiatric, or psychological issue'.[30]

Both Stephen and Morse overstate the case for (at least) two reasons. First, the justificatory project depends on legal categories making sense to those who are governed by them. If the law were to declare that all and only people with red hair could experience loss of control or mental disorder, the resulting controversy would not just be because this would be unfair or internally inconsistent, but because it violates ordinary ideas of how people 'work' (it would not only be unfair, but it would also not make sense). Second, the ways in which these terms were, and are, defined by the law is intimately connected to wider social developments including developments in the sciences. In that sense, legal and non-legal ideas have interacted from the beginning. In other words, different ideas, advanced by different stakeholders, compete – and have always competed – in constructing the criminal law's person, and recognising that invites again the question of who should decide and how the different claims should be balanced. This is not a question we seek to answer – and no 'fixed' answer can be given as the interplay between the claims is inevitably dynamic – but it worth making four comments.

First, the formal decision over this or that defendant resides in most countries with, and within, the criminal law. In a sense, this follows from the law being a rules-based system, and although it is far from perfect in its application, the formal decision being within the law is required to satisfy demands of consistency and the meeting of legitimate expectations.

Second, this formal position does not warrant the kind of closed-mind approach epitomised in the quotation from Stephen above. As we have already said, a great deal of the criminal law's 'knowledge' of the person came initially from elsewhere. The criminal law has imported and absorbed ideas from outside its boundaries for decades (or perhaps even centuries). The danger is that these ideas become fixed and fossilised in the criminal law while the disciplines from which they came have moved on, often discarding the very ideas that the law has now incorporated as definitive. Indeed, it would be interesting to subject the law to the equivalent of 'carbon dating': to ask representatives from the sciences that initially 'exported' their ideas to the criminal law to 'date' them and to explain how, outside the law, they have changed in the meantime.

Thus, third, the formal position ought not to blind us to questions regarding the extent to which non-legal 'knowledge' – including that from areas of philosophy other than moral philosophy and the philosophy of action, and from the social and hard sciences – ought to continue materially to influence the criminal law. Most importantly, this is not a binary question of 'legal knowledge *or* non-legal knowledge', but rather an issue of how to incorporate developments

[30] SJ Morse, 'Mental Disorder and Criminal Law' (2011) 101 *Journal of Criminal Law & Criminology* 885, 926.

outside the law within the law. One starting point might be to say that if there is a shared scientific consensus on a certain issue regarding the person outside the criminal law (in our terms, as to how the person *is*), then the 'burden of proof' should lie with those who argue that the person should be understood otherwise (as they *should* be, or as they *fictitiously* are).

Fourth, and finally, we should attend closely to the ways in which what is proposed by the various stakeholders with respect to what the criminal law 'absorbs' relate to the purposes of the criminal law and, in particular, to the backward-looking need to respond appropriately to what this particular defendant did in these particular circumstances, and the forward-looking need to regulate conduct and, to put it brutally, to secure convictions. That is, while we have argued for the criminal law to be open to findings in other disciplines, we are not naive about 'the fact/value distinction', or unaware that the choice of what to attend to is a deeply normative one.

In conclusion, before we turn to brief descriptions of the contributions that follow, the criminal law's person is not a single coherent entity deployed in legislation, policing, trials, and so on. Rather, this multifaceted, semi-coherent being comes to life in the (doings of) the criminal law system, and this raises many important and complex questions. Our aim here has not been to propose 'solutions' as to how that person should be conceived, but to cast light on the mechanisms (and stakeholders) potentially involved. In the end, a weighing of competing interests of varying kinds must be made.

The criminal law, *qua* tool of the state, cannot (and ought not) engage with each person in his or her entirety. In that sense, 'shallowness' is not a fault so much as a practical and normative necessity.[31] The process needs to be efficient and consistent, and it needs to respect the boundaries of what is appropriate in terms of how deeply to enquire into the lives and minds of its citizens (as we have noted, what is appropriate in interpersonal morality is not always – indeed, it is seldom – appropriate in state–citizen relations).

Nevertheless, we need to attend carefully to how to balance the interests of the various stakeholders surrounding the construction of (the criminal law system and) the criminal law's person. There, the most important question is how to strike a decent balance between forward-looking and backward-looking interests, respectively; how many backward-looking concerns may be negotiated away in order to reach forward-looking aims. These are, in the end, political questions, *but* they subject to important limits set by a substantial, not only nominal, demand for appropriate 'blameworthiness'. What are these limits? The answer will depend on the extent to which one believes that the 'practice of blaming' in the criminal law must be supported by what we know of the person from disciplines outside the law.

[31] Just as in private law, the invention of the legal subject as a being with reduced characteristics is related to the need efficiently to handle various kinds of business transactions.

IV. OUTLINE OF THE VOLUME

The chapters that follow pick up the key themes of the constructed nature of the criminal law's person, and the interplay between criminal law and other disciplines; other sources of 'knowledge'. In chapter two, 'The Criminal Law's Various Persons', Matt Matravers notes that scholarship on 'criminal law and neuroscience' – like its predecessors 'criminal law and psychiatry' and 'criminal law and social-science' – has tended to focus on the question of *responsibility* and on when and in what ways those who break the criminal law may (or may not) be responsible for their actions and so liable to punishment. While he argues that this is understandable given that punishment is the most visible, and most morally troubling, aspect of the criminal justice systems, focusing only on the question of liability to punishment risks missing the fact that criminal justice systems make assumptions and posit different 'persons' at various stages: when opting to criminalise or to regulate or prevent potentially criminal actions by other means; investigating; prosecuting; in determinations of guilt and innocence; and in sentencing. Having briefly considered the ways in which the different 'persons' who appear prior to trial reflect the different – and not always consistent – purposes of criminal justice, he goes on to focus on the significance of this broader context for the interaction of criminal law scholarship and the behavioural sciences.

In chapter three, 'The Criminal Law's Person and Normative Elements in the Legal Definition of Excusing Circumstances', Kai Hamdorf examines the relation of two different approaches to the concept of the criminal law's person: the internal normative perspective of law itself; and the external, empirical scientific perspective of criminologists, sociologists, psychologists or psychiatrists. The focus lies on the allocation of professional roles in criminal proceedings and on the disparate concepts of a person in the various professional disciplines involved. The first section of this chapter discusses constitutional, historical and philosophical aspects of the normative concept of the criminal law's person and presents some provisions of the German Criminal Code relevant to this concept. The second section analyses to what extent empirical facts are taken into account by law and legal practice in the process of determining the guilt of a perpetrator. In other words: who decides and why? The chapter argues that we sometimes have too strong a tendency to emphasise the normative character of guilt and individual criminal responsibility, and thereby pay too little respect to the fundamental rule of individual guilt as the basis for any kind of criminal sanction.

Claes Lernestedt, in 'Standard-Setting versus Tracking "Profound" Blameworthiness: What should be the Role of the Rules for Ascription of Responsibility?' (chapter four) picks up the theme of the 'shallowness' (or otherwise) of the person and the tension between it and the depth needed for judgements of blameworthiness. His focus is on the rules for ascription of responsibility in the criminal law's general part. The making and application of these rules, he argues, reflects a variety of goals not all of which are consistent. Importantly, one ambition is a mainly *backward*-looking one, where the basic idea is that the rules for ascription of responsibility are there to help identify what might be called 'real' or 'true' blameworthiness in the particular individual defendant (in his or her concrete situation as it actually was). A second ambition is a mainly *forward*-looking one, where the central idea is that these rules should be used (at least mainly) to set 'objective' behavioural standards for the future. The chapter argues that the backward-looking ambitions need to be given considerable weight, even though this might give far from optimal outcomes when it comes to forward-looking ambitions.

Chapters five and six examine accounts of responsibility and the ways in which they interact with the criminal law's person. In chapter five, 'Attributability and Accountability in the Criminal Law', Robin Zheng draws on an extant distinction from the moral responsibility literature to distinguish between theories of criminal responsibility as attributability and as accountability. She argues that questions of attributability and accountability arise from two distinct sources of philosophical concern: problems of metaphysics and action theory on the conditions under which our actions reflect our agency, on the one hand, and problems of moral and political philosophy on the fair and just distribution of duties and burdens across a moral community, on the other. She goes on to defend an accountability approach to criminal responsibility on the grounds that (1) the law is fundamentally and foremost a social and political institution; and (2) such an approach unifies instrumentalist and moralist conceptions of criminal law by accommodating its pluralistic aims and purposes. Finally, she considers the ways in which an accountability approach can fend off the standard challenges from neuroscience while remaining sensitive to newer worries raised by social psychology.

In chapter six, 'In Search of Criminal Law's Person', Malcolm Thorburn discusses two aspects of the criminal law's person. First, the idea of 'legal personality' generally, and second the class of things capable of committing criminal wrongs. As Thorburn notes, both of these are controversial. There is considerable debate over who or what is a legal person, and similar disagreements about the proper objects of criminal responsibility. In both cases, Thorburn argues we have reason to reject both moralistic accounts (such as that advanced by Michael Moore), and instrumental theories (such as those associated with legal realists and utilitarians). In their place, Thorburn argues for a 'rule of law' conception of criminal law that incorporates a distinctive account of legal personality and criminal responsibility. On this conception, the law ensures the independence of all moral persons through its claim exclusively to determine the legal rights of citizens and its granting legal personality to all moral persons to enable them to vindicate their rights should they come under attack. This account, Thorburn argues, not only fits better with legal practice, but it also provides an explanation of the particular wrongs that are the appropriate subject of criminal law.

Chapters seven and eight return the focus to judgements of blame and the associated phenomenon of guilt. In chapter seven, 'Victims Who Victimise: Guilt in Political Theory and Moral Psychology', Alan Norrie begins with the specific question of 'the moral guilt of perpetrators viewed as victims who victimise others in settings of structural social injustice', and from this widens his focus to what it means to feel guilty for committing a crime. With respect to the latter, Norrie is concerned that there is a danger of fusing a political philosophical issue of justified state punishment and our understanding of what he calls 'the moral psychology of guilt'. The result, he argues, is that we are unable to deal with the former, with the guilt of perpetrators who are themselves victims.

In pursuing this, Norrie considers classical formulations of the 'perpetrator–victim' issue, and then takes up a modern account in the work of Antony Duff where he finds moves in the direction of a moral psychology of guilt. The argument is then pursued through the work of two psychoanalytic thinkers, Melanie Klein and Jessica Benjamin, to put together an analysis of what it means in the terms of moral psychology to talk about guilt and feeling guilty. In moving from normative political theory to moral psychology, Norrie's purpose is to suggest that we gain a better understanding of what is at stake in just punishment by combining the two approaches. It allows us to address what he calls the 'moral grammar' of guilt in a different way.

Craig Reeves, in 'Responsibility Beyond Blame: Unfree Agency and the Moral Psychology of Criminal Law's Persons' (chapter eight) engages with recent work by Nicola Lacey and Hanna Pickard that attempts to reconcile rehabilitative therapeutic criminal justice with retributive criminal justice – 'the justice model' – in light of clinical work with psychopathology. Although he finds their account richly suggestive, he argues that it fails because at its heart is an unstable compromise rather than a reconciliation. The source of this instability, Reeves argues, is Lacey and Pickard's concession that respect requires (acknowledging) responsibility. Instead, Reeves suggests that Lacey and Pickard's insights should move us away from the theory of agency and moral psychology implicit in our existing practices of holding responsible. 'The real psychology of persons', he claims requires a radical rethinking of those practices and a recognition that 'taking responsibility' is dialogical. In 'asking someone to take responsibility', the community itself must be willing to do the same.

Finally, in chapter nine, 'Implicit Bias, Self-Defence and the Reasonable Person', Jules Holroyd and Federico Picinali consider the implications of research on implicit bias for the reasonable person standard in criminal law. As they say, the criminal law's person sometimes appears as the reasonable person. The example, on which they focus is use of the reasonable person standard in adjudicating claims of self-defence. In US law, an individual may use defensive force if her beliefs are that a threat is imminent, and that force is required, are beliefs a reasonable person would have. In English law, it is sufficient that beliefs in imminence and necessity are genuinely held; but the reasonableness of so believing has an evidential role in establishing the genuineness of the beliefs.

In their chapter, Holroyd and Picinali identify the distinctive issues that arise when we consider that implicit racial bias might be implicated in the beliefs in imminence and necessity. Having first outlined their 'test case', they go on to consider two interpretations of the reasonable person standard. The 'reasonable basis for belief' standard is, they argue, problematic both because it renders individuals with bias-based beliefs unreasonable even when they may non-culpably harbour bias, and because it sets out a standard that, given implicit bias, citizens may have little control over whether they meet. The 'non-culpable reasonable belief' standard does better in terms of fairness to those who non-culpably harbour bias, but Holroyd and Picinali argue that it embeds racist stereotypes. While there are formulations of the defence that may serve to mitigate these problems, and arguments for refashioning criminal justice so that it does not perpetuate racist stereotypes, ultimately Holroyd and Picinali are pessimistic about their prospects in the presence of racist social structures.

2

The Criminal Law's Various Persons

MATT MATRAVERS*

RECENT SCHOLARSHIP ON 'criminal law and neuroscience' – like its predecessors 'criminal law and psychiatry' and 'criminal law and social-science' – has tended to focus on the question of responsibility and, in particular, when and in what ways those who break the criminal law may (or may not) be responsible for their actions and so liable to conviction and punishment. This is understandable given that punishment is the most visible, and most morally troubling, aspect of the criminal justice systems under which we live. However, focusing only on the question of liability to punishment risks missing the fact that criminal justice systems make assumptions and posit different 'persons' at various stages. For example, when opting to criminalise rather than to regulate or to prevent potentially criminal actions by other means; investigating; prosecuting; in determinations of guilt and innocence; and in sentencing. This chapter briefly considers the many and various different 'persons' who appear in the criminal justice system before asking to what degree the construction of these persons is influenced by explanatory and behavioural sciences.

I. INTRODUCTION

The focus on conviction and punishment in criminal law theory is particularly acute when thinking about the criminal law's person and the 'threats' or 'opportunities' that arise in relation to that idea when it is confronted by causal or behavioural accounts of human behaviour. Again, this is understandable. Given the seriousness of punishment, we wonder if the imposition of sanctions is

* I am grateful to the participants in the criminal law's person project, and in particular to my co-editor Claes Lernestedt, for comments on various drafts of the chapter. Versions of some of the thoughts here have been given in various places and I am particularly grateful for conversations with Antony Duff, Andreas von Hirsch and Andrew Simester. From each I have learned a great deal (though needless to say, not enough). Finally, I would like to thank Chelsie Brandrick and Lucy Jackson for research assistance.

warranted or whether naturalistic explanations of behaviour render the judgement of responsibility, and blameworthiness, fundamentally suspect. The questions, 'Did he really deserve that?' and 'Was he really responsible?' readily slide into 'Are we really entitled to do that?'

However, the focus on punishment threatens both to suggest that there is a way of getting that person 'right' and to obscure other appearances of persons in criminal law. That is, it suggests that there is a single conception of the criminal law's person that, once got right, will fit in a neat and seamless whole both with our other normative commitments and with our general picture of the criminal justice system. In what, for the sake of brevity, I will call 'a liberal theory' this person is an autonomous, reasons-responsive being who commands equal respect as a matter of status. Central to liberal thought is a vision of persons as 'free and equal'.[1] In Berlin's celebrated passage (from the first person point of view): 'I wish, above all, to be conscious of myself as a thinking, willing, active being, bearing responsibility for my choices and able to explain them by reference to my own ideas and purposes'.[2] Such a conception of the person is fundamental to contemporary (and not only contemporary) liberal political philosophy, and to the theories of freedom, equality and justice that constitute it.[3]

The rest of this section provides a very rough sketch of this neat picture. The remainder of the chapter then engages with the many and various ways in which the picture does not reflect reality (sometimes in theory, sometimes in practice, and sometimes both). Finally, I ask to what degree the explanatory and behavioural sciences have established their relevance in criminal justice while our attention has been on the core liberal theory and the question of legal responsibility at conviction.

The idea of the autonomous person (or citizen) acts as part of the normative *justification* of, a *constraint* on, and a *source* for, criminal law. With respect to the first, part of the justification of the criminal law is that a complex society of autonomous persons will need rules of coordination and it will need to mark certain things as serious public wrongs that ought not to be done. This is not least because my choices may conflict with yours and if we are to be free to choose, and to live our lives in accordance with our choices, then we will need rules to guide – and, indeed, compel – us.[4]

[1] J Rawls, *A Theory of Justice* (Harvard University Press, 1971) 13.

[2] I Berlin, *Four Essays on Liberty* (Oxford University Press, 1969) 131.

[3] That is not to say that it is uncontroversial as is demonstrated by the various debates between 'liberals', 'communitarians', 'critical theorists' and so on. In using the term 'autonomy', I do not mean to invoke any particular deep theory of the kind developed by, eg, Gerald Dworkin. In what follows, I will use it synonymously with 'liberty' and like terms. On theories of autonomy, more strictly interpreted, see JP Christman (ed), *The Inner Citadel: Essays on Individual Autonomy* (Oxford University Press, 1989).

[4] Of course, this explains the need for law generally. There is a further question of which among those regulations should be 'criminal'.

As a constraint, respect for autonomy requires what Andrew Ashworth identifies as general '"rule of law" principles (notably fair warning and certainty of definition), and the protections of criminal procedure (including the presumption of innocence and the right to a fair trial)'.[5] The rationale being that if the criminal law is to guide behaviour (to provide, or point to, reasons not to do something), then its rules need to be known, clear, not retrospective, and so on. If it is to regulate without tyranny, and to blame people for their choices or conduct, it also needs to allow people the chance to act freely until they break the rules, to be sure of its case, and so on. Second, insofar as one point of criminal law is to protect the space in which people can exercise their individual liberty and choose freely, its justified use is limited. The onus is, or ought to be, on those who wish to criminalise some conduct to show that it is necessary to protect or enhance liberty. As Ashworth puts it, 'the decision to criminalise certain conduct should only be taken for strong reasons and with assurance that no restraining principle applies'.[6]

As a source, the idea of the person gives some content to the criminal law. To shape one's own life in accordance with one's choices requires a certain context and certain capabilities. Thus, the law protects personal integrity, property rights of various kinds, and reflects the fact that human beings are 'vulnerable … to bodily attack'.[7] Moreover, and importantly for the rest of this chapter, central principles of the general part governing responsibility, excuses and other defences, flow from the model of the liberal (criminal law's) person. Consider, for example, the following passage from Stephen Morse:

> Law … views human action as almost entirely reason-governed. Law conceives of the person as a practical-reasoning, rule-following being, most of whose legally relevant movements must be understood in terms of beliefs, desires, and intentions … For the law, then, a person is a practical reasoner.
>
> …
>
> *The law's concept of responsibility follows logically from its conception of the person* … Rule followers must be creatures who are generally capable of properly using the rules as premises in practical reasoning. It follows that a legally responsible agent is a person who is generally capable of rationality, according to some contingent, normative notion both of rationality itself and of how much capability is required.[8]

[5] A Ashworth, 'Attempts' in J Deigh and D Dolinko (eds), *The Oxford Handbook of Philosophy of Criminal Law* (Oxford University Press, 2011) 129.

[6] ibid. On 'criminalisation', see J Schonsheck, *On Criminalization: An Essay in the Philosophy of the Criminal Law* (Kluwer, 1994). On 'over-criminalisation', see DN Husak, *Overcriminalization: The Limits of the Criminal Law* (Oxford University Press, 2008). It is worth noting that the danger of being concerned only with criminal law is that it can blind one to things that the state can do under other headings.

[7] HLA Hart, *The Concept of Law*, 2nd edn (Clarendon Press, 1994) 195.

[8] SJ Morse, 'Deprivation and Desert' in WC Heffernan and J Kleinig (eds), *From Social Justice to Criminal Justice* (Oxford University Press, 2000) 117–18 (emphasis mine).

Thus, on this neat picture, there is – or ought to be – a coherence between the liberal vision of personhood, as captured in the criminal law's person, and the criminal law.[9] Where this is not the case – when, for example, the criminal law fails to allow the person fair opportunity to use her reason by failing in its duties of fair warning or fair labelling, or where it overuses strict liability and so is insufficiently sensitive to the agent's relevant mental state – then the criminal law's person, at least as presented here, provides the critical basis from which to object.[10]

The idea that there is such a unifying conception of the person in the criminal law is in tension with many aspects of both criminal law theory and practice. Moreover, these tensions are not always the result of there being competing accounts of the same thing, but rather reflect distinct 'moments' in criminal justice: the decision to criminalise; the investigating, policing and prevention of criminal conduct; prosecution; determinations of guilt and innocence; and sentencing.[11] These moments, in turn, relate to the profound tension between the 'forward-looking' and 'backward-looking' looking purposes of criminal law.

The rest of the chapter picks up on some – but by no means all – of these tensions. The point is not to try to convict liberal theory of inconsistency or incoherence, but rather to investigate the gap between the theory and its application in some particular instances of the practice of criminal justice. Given the scope of that ambition, the argument is indicative rather than comprehensive. It also does not try to deal with each and every stage of criminal justice separately (let alone completely), but rather follows Andrew Simester, et al, in grouping these in 'two dimensions to the operation of criminal law: *ex ante* and *ex post*'.[12]

[9] See, eg, Morse's claim that 'Criminal law criteria exemplify the foregoing analysis [of the person]'. ibid 118. Morse is of course aware that the precise content of adequate practical reasoning or rationality is a matter of normative (and political) controversy. It is the formal, rather than the substantive, shape that is dictated by the conception of the person. The account sketched glides over important distinctions between choice, fair opportunity, and character theories of responsibility. This is deliberate in that the hope is that what follows in the chapter may be of interest (with some tweaks) to adherents of each of those positions. After all, contemporary character theory, too, is aimed at 'a reasoning being responsible for his or her beliefs, desires, emotions, and values' (N Lacey, *In Search of Criminal Responsibility: Ideas, Interests, and Institutions* (Oxford University Press, 2016) 36).

[10] See, eg, A Ashworth, 'Is the Criminal Law a Lost Cause?' (2000) 116 *Law Quarterly Review* 225.

[11] *cf* Lacey (n 9) 26: 'practices of responsibility-attribution must be interpreted in the light of the whole process of criminalization, from law-making through prosecution and law-application at trial to punishment – hence opening up the possibility that multiple and even inconsistent approaches to responsibility are operating not only at different times within a single system but over different institutional spaces of the criminal process at any one time'.

[12] AP Simester et al, *Simester and Sullivan's Criminal Law: Theory and Doctrine* (Hart Publishing, 2019) 6.

II. *EX ANTE:* CRIMINALISATION, POLICING AND PROSECUTION

In criminalising conduct, the liberal account holds that at its core the criminal law prohibits the intentional (or sometimes reckless or negligent) doing of wrongful harms that are (in some sense) public. It does this both to protect and enhance autonomy in that it protects those whose autonomy would otherwise be violated, and it provides a system of rules that enables us to live together (relatively) peacefully. Given rule of law principles, the criminal law gives us, or points us to, reasons not to engage in the prohibited conduct and punishes us, for the most part, when we do so in a manner that is blameworthy (when we have intentionally done wrong or manifested a disregard for others through reckless or negligent conduct).[13]

The idea of a criminal law that says, 'do not do this, *or else*', is compatible with the liberal model of the choosing person: as reason-responsive choosers we are not thought, or required, to be flawless. Sometimes we act on the wrong reasons; sometimes our wills are weak in the face of temptation and the right reasons fail to move us; sometimes we ignore that to which we should pay attention. We are, as Andrew von Hirsch has it, 'neither saints nor sinners', but rather fallible human beings who need to be reminded of what not to do and, perhaps, given an additional prudential reason not to do it (ie, the threat of punishment).[14] Thus, according to Simester and von Hirsch, criminalisation is an instance of 'rational coercion [that] operates via, and appeals to, the subject's responsible agency'.[15]

The liberal theory sketched above works well for core crimes such as murder and for those in which the harm is either legally defined (such as embezzlement) or at a brief remove (such as crimes of endangerment). It works, too, in providing a critical standpoint to assess criminal prohibitions. A 'crime' of, say, consensual oral sex between consenting adults sacrifices a freedom that some people value as part of the way in which they wish to lead their lives in return for no associated, weighty, gain to those who find the idea of others practising this activity abhorrent. Other areas of human conduct may be more difficult to assess; racist speech, for example, may very well damage the victim and, in certain circumstances, that damage may outweigh the value we place on freedom of speech more generally.[16]

[13] It is important to note that this is a depiction of what I have called a liberal theory of the criminal law rather than a description of criminalisation or the criminal law historically or in the present. It is also partial. There are many aspects of the criminal law – for example, crimes not against persons, but against the state – that are not accurately captured in the account.

[14] A von Hirsch, 'Proportionality in the Philosophy of Punishment' (1992) 16 *Crime and Justice* 55. See also A von Hirsch, *Censure and Sanctions* (Oxford University Press, 1993).

[15] AP Simester and A von Hirsch, *Crimes, Harms, and Wrongs: On the Principles of Criminalisation* (Hart Publishing, 2011) 6–7.

[16] For a particularly strong defence of regulating hate speech, see J Waldron, *The Harm in Hate Speech* (Harvard University Press, 2012).

However, as Vincent Chiao has recently reminded those working in criminal law theory, this hardly captures the many and various current uses to which the criminal law is put. These have extended into a vast number of areas concerned with the environment, health and safety and, in general, the prevention of harm.[17] Moreover, in expanding the criminal law to regulate our common life, many states have moved away from the 'core' picture painted above through the use of 'strict liability', 'possession' and 'preparatory' offences, which can allow the conviction and punishment of the blameless.

The explanation of states' uses of the criminal law outside the 'core' lies in part in the public policy goals they seek to achieve. For example, strict liability offences are often used as an effective means of enforcing certain standards necessary for public protection. Thus, the liability of the holder of a licence to sell alcohol for the actions of their staff in serving those under the age at which it is legally permissible to buy alcohol is explained by its being the most efficient way to ensure that publicans train and 'police' their staff, and the same will be true of many environmental and health and safety regulations. In taking this shape, strict liability offences also speak to a concern with responding to the results of conduct; to the desire to see that 'something must be done'.

In the case of inchoate offences – including perhaps general inchoate offences such as the Swedish 'preparation for crime' – some might be argued to be compatible with the liberal model. Someone who prepares to commit a crime makes choices in response to reasons; the issue lies over when those choices ought to be taken to be decisive and thus sufficient for blameworthiness. In other cases, where criminalisation is pushed back earlier in time, the criminal law reflects what Lacey calls 'responsibility as founded in the apprehension of risk'.[18] In such cases, these offences do not treat individuals as tools of public policy, but as potential dangers (to the state or other citizens). Consider, for example, section 58 of the UK Terrorism Act 2000 (as amended by the Counter-Terrorism and Border Security Act 2019):

> Collection of information.
>
> (1) A person commits an offence if –
>
> (a) he collects or makes a record of information of a kind likely to be useful to a person committing or preparing an act of terrorism,
>
> (b) he possesses a document or record containing information of that kind, or
>
> (c) the person views, or otherwise accesses, by means of the internet a document or record containing information of that kind.[19]

[17] V Chiao, *Criminal Law in the Age of the Administrative State* (Oxford University Press, 2019) § 5.3.

[18] Lacey (n 9) 46.

[19] Terrorism Act 2000.

Although the section provides for a defence of 'reasonable excuse', such as being an academic or journalist, the offence nevertheless would seem to encompass the merely curious – someone who downloads a 'bomb-making manual' just to see what it looks like – and the inadvertent – someone who downloads a map of the area around the MI6 building in London when preparing for their holiday – in a way that goes beyond the liberal model.

On the one hand, legislation of this kind reflects a concern with risk that is inherent in a criminal justice system that is in part concerned with the prevention of harm. On the other, in criminalising conduct that is not wrongful, in a way that is insensitive to the agent's intentions, the state seems to leave behind the picture of the criminal law as responding to the blameworthy voluntary choices and acts of free citizens in favour of a vision of (some) persons as *threats*.

Finally, in England and Wales (and in different ways in other states), the state has adopted various measures of preventive justice such as two-stage civil/criminal prohibitions that regulate individuals' conduct by explicitly constraining where they might go, with whom they might socialise, when they might be on the internet, and so on. These 'preventive orders' are handed down by a civil court, but breach attracts a criminal sentence. Far from offering reasons to free and equal citizens who have yet to fail to live up to the demands of the *criminal law*, they promise the offer of management of those thought otherwise incapable of self-management.[20]

Hybrid measures and the expansion of the criminal law enable police and prosecutorial discretion to play a role in *ex ante* criminal justice. Such discretion is inevitable and need not in itself be problematic. Liberal theories of justice envisage and apply in conditions of moderate scarcity. One defining feature of such scarcity is that policy choices have 'opportunity costs'. In such circumstances, the state and its officials have to make choices to use resources efficiently by, for example, applying 'public interest' tests.

However, discretion can be misused. The police, for example, might treat a group of ethnic minority youths as 'dangers to be managed' rather than as free and equal citizens.[21] Similarly, they can use then policing of minor (potential) offences as pretexts for further investigation of persons perceived as dangerous or as threats.[22] Prosecutors, too, can and do act in ways that reflect an image of the person as a danger as when, for example, they make the choice to charge for the most significant offence because of a belief that the person is a habitual criminal beyond mending his ways. While the topics of policing and prosecutorial discretion have become more important in criminology, they are yet to command the attention they deserve from philosophers and criminal law

[20] A Ashworth and L Zedner, *Preventive Justice* (Oxford University Press, 2014) ch 3.

[21] D Fassin, *The Will to Punish* (The Berkeley Tanner Lectures, Oxford University Press, 2018).

[22] See, eg, I Kohler-Hausmann, 'Managerial Justice and Mass Misdemeanors' (2014) 66 *Stanford Law Review* 611; A Geller and J Fagan, 'Pot as Pretext: Marijuana, Race and the New Disorder in New York City Street Policing' (2010) 7 *Journal of Empirical Legal Studies* 591.

theorists. Yet, in the ordinary lives of many citizens – particularly those from disadvantaged backgrounds – these are the agents and institutions of *ex ante* criminal justice that most impinge on their lives.[23]

In short, in criminalisation, policing and prosecution, the criminal law's person is often far from the assumption of free, equal citizens who are 'generally capable of properly using the rules as premises in practical reasoning'. Rather, it resembles what Andrew von Hirsch has called 'tiger control'.[24]

III. *EX POST:* CONVICTION AND SENTENCING

Above I noted that it was in punishing that the threat of explanatory accounts of human behaviour is most felt. In this section, I want to consider two *ex post* elements of criminal justice: conviction and sentencing. The direction of argument is that liberal theories (as I have called them) attempt to combine a 'thin' liberal conception of the person immune to the threat of causality at the stage of conviction with a thick, causally sensitive account, of the person in sentencing. This thick account acts as a 'pressure relief valve'. Such valves control the pressure in a system by allowing a 'path of least resistance' for whatever is causing the strain (in this case causal threats to the fairness of punishing individual offenders each with a history).

When it comes to conviction, the liberal view of criminal liability is that causal stories are largely irrelevant in determining liability as the latter holds that it is fair to hold people responsible, to blame them, and to express our blame through sanctioning responses, when:

(a) The agent has voluntarily violated a legal norm;
(b) With the appropriate *mens rea*;
(c) Is not acting under duress (or 'hard choice');
(d) Is rational (such that he is 'has the general capacity to understand and to be guided by reasons … or the general capacity to understand the law's commands and the consequences for violating them') and not non-culpably irrational such that 'the agent is unable rationally to comprehend the facts that bear on the morality of his action or is unable rationally to comprehend the applicable moral or legal code that provides the good reason not to breach'.[25]

[23] This is particularly true where being arrested can have significant implications even if the person arrested is never subsequently charged or convicted of a crime. Arrest records can influence whether one is cleared for some kinds of employment. As Rachel Harmon puts it (notes omitted): 'Arrestees lose income during the arrest, and sometimes their jobs when they do not show up for work. They pay arrest fees, booking fees … An arrest can affect child custody rights, it can trigger deportation, and it can get a suspect kicked out of public housing. Over the long term, individuals with arrest records may have worse employment and financial prospects'. R Harmon, 'Why Arrest?' (2016) 115 *Michigan Law Review* 307, 313–14.

[24] von Hirsch, *Censure and Sanctions* (n 14).

[25] Morse, 'Deprivation and Desert' (n 8) 121.

On this account, the criminal law need not assume some radical idea of 'free will'.[26] The voluntariness requirement (a) is weak, so as to rule out automatism, sleep walking and the like. In general, causes matter only if they explain that the agent faced a hard choice (c) or if they can be shown to undermine (d), the rationality of the actor at the time of acting. But note, in these circumstances it is not the causes that do the work, but the hard choice or irrationality. The account thus reflects the thin conception of the person with which we started: a choosing, reasons-responsive being (and so of a non-responsible person as someone who does not choose, cannot be expected to act in accordance with her reasons in certain circumstances, or cannot understand or be guided by reasons at all).

It is this conception of the person that generally insulates criminal law from the pull of proposed new defences such as 'drug and alcohol addiction, gambling addiction, brainwashing (undue influence); battered woman; premenstrual syndrome; post-traumatic stress disorder; genetic disorder; alien cultural beliefs; rotten social background [and] being a sex addict'.[27] These defences derive what intuitive power they have from being *explanations* of behaviour. However, unless they undermine one or more of (a) to (d), they do not speak to the liability of the agent to conviction. As Morse puts it:

> A related confusion is the belief that if science or common sense identifies a cause for human action, including mental or physical disorders or developmental variables, then the conduct is necessarily excused. I refer to this mistaken belief as the 'fundamental psycholegal error': Causation is neither an excuse per se nor the equivalent of hard choice (so-called compulsion), which is an excusing condition.[28]

Whether or not the belief that causes excuse is 'the fundamental psycholegal error', Morse is right that they do not usually do so in the criminal law. Explaining to a police officer that one is, unfortunately, 'just the murdering type' is unlikely to work no matter how much you or the police officer know about social and genetic influences on personality.

All of the above is familiar territory for criminal lawyers and criminal law theorists. Conviction presupposes only a thin sense of the responsible person that encompasses almost all of us almost all of the time (and that of course serves the forward-looking goal of regulating people's behaviour). For the most

[26] Of course, there are those who think that absent some idea of 'basic desert', criminal law could hold to account only in a weak sense, and criminal punishment could not be retributive. See, eg, D Pereboom, 'Free Will Skepticism and Criminal Punishment' in T Nadelhoffer (ed), *The Future of Punishment* (Oxford University Press, 2013).

[27] MP Golding, 'Responsibility' in MP Golding and WA Edmundson (eds), *The Blackwell Guide to the Philosophy of Law and Legal Theory* (Blackwell Publishing, 2005) 222. For a provocative denunciation of such proposals, see AM Dershowitz, *The Abuse Excuse: and other Cop-outs, Sob Stories, and Evasions of Responsibility* (Little, Brown and Company, 1994).

[28] Morse, 'Deprivation and Desert' (n 8) 130.

part, it does not matter how we came to be the people we are, what our inner thoughts were at the time of acting, how we feel about what we did, and so on. What matters is that we had the capacity to respond to appropriate reasons and we failed to exercise that capacity without any standard excusing conditions applying. Yet, when it comes to sentencing this thin conception of the person is jettisoned in favour of a much thicker one: remorse, previous good character, mental disorders that are excluded from relevance in conviction, background and opportunities, can all enter the picture in determining the offender's punishment.

We might make philosophical sense of the different ways in which the criminal law's person is constructed in conviction and sentencing by distinguishing two senses – 'faces' – of responsibility. One is the idea of 'attributability': the relevant conduct is attributable to the agent. She is, so to speak, its author.[29] Or, as Tim Scanlon puts it, 'to make an attributive judgement is to make a judgement as to whether the person is responsible for a given action in the sense that it is appropriate to take [that action] as a basis of moral appraisal of the person'.[30] The second is an idea of 'accountability', which is to make a substantive judgement of responsibility is to make a judgement about what that person is required (or not required) to do as a result.[31]

To understand the ways in which these aspects of responsibility work, and how they speak to the discussion of conviction and sentencing, consider the following from Gary Watson:

> The distinction between aretaic [attributive] and accountability blame helps to explain our ambivalence toward the vicious criminal who is himself a victim of an abusive childhood. His deliberate and remorseless murders characterize him as malicious and cruel in a sense that no nonreflective being could be. The fact that life gave him a rotten deal, that his squalid circumstances made it overwhelmingly difficult to develop a respect for the standards to which we would hold him accountable, does not impugn these aretaic appraisals. His conduct is attributable to him as an exercise of his 'moral capacities'. It expresses and constitutes his practical identity, what he stands for, what he has made of his life as he found it.
>
> At the same time, there is an inclination to doubt that such a person can rightly be held accountable, at least fully, that while he might 'deserve pity' … he 'does not deserve blame'. This ambivalence mirrors the two faces of responsibility. What gives rise to our 'pity' are concerns about fairness. Facts about his formative years give rise to the thought that the individual has already suffered too much and that we too

[29] G Watson, 'Two Faces of Responsibility' in G Watson (ed), *Agency and Answerability: Selected Essays* (Oxford University Press, 2004) 263.

[30] TM Scanlon, *What We Owe to Each Other* (Harvard University Press, 1998) 148.

[31] Watson, 'Two Faces of Responsibility' (n 29); Scanlon (n 30). There are important differences between Watson's and Scanlon's accounts, but they are not relevant to the argument here.

> would probably have been morally ruined by such a childhood. What is inhibited by these concerns is accountability blame.[32]

We need not dwell on whether Watson is right that the vicious criminal in the example does not deserve the kind of blame relevant to the criminal law. Rather, what matters is the claim that our judgements of accountability blame are 'inhibited'. That is, to many people it seems *unfair* to hold such a person equally culpable when compared, say, with a similar criminal whose past was entirely favourable. This matters in sentencing because sentencing is not only about the crime, but about the comparative *blameworthiness* of the particular offender.

It might seem, then, as if we have reached a stable conclusion. Very roughly, issues of conviction speak to whether we are dealing with the kind of being that can be held responsible (ie, a being with certain capacities), and whether that being performed the prohibited action in the absence of any of the standard excusing conditions. The conception of the person is thin, and the answer is (usually) binary: guilty or not guilty. Issues of sentencing speak to the degree of blameworthiness of the particular offender and the ways in which that translates into a proportionate sentencing scheme. The conception of the person is much thicker, and the answer lies on a spectrum. One can be 'more blameworthy', but one cannot (at conviction) be 'more guilty'.

One great advantage of this account is that relieves the pressure created by the ambivalence Watson describes with respect to 'the vicious criminal who is himself a victim of an abusive childhood'. Put differently, consider again some of the proposed new defences listed above. What motivates them is the claim that it seems *unfair* for someone who, for example, acts from addiction or from a personality disorder to face the same consequences as someone who acts in a calculated fashion to further his self-interest. The account above allows us to say that both are 'agents' – they are the kinds of beings who can be held responsible – and in virtue of that might be convicted of the same offence, but that need not mean that they face the same consequences. Their differing degrees of blameworthiness can be reflected in their sentences.

Yet, sentencing regimes seldom work like this. In England and Wales, for example, the Sentencing Council lists five purposes of punishment: punishment, crime reduction, reform and rehabilitation, public protection, and 'making the offender give something back'.[33] Such a pluralistic account may make sense in terms of public policy, but the aims clearly do not pull in the same direction.

[32] Watson, 'Two Faces of Responsibility' (n 29) 280–81 (fns omitted). Watson's example recalls his famous discussion of Robert Harris: G Watson, 'Responsibility and the Limits of Evil: Reflections on a Strawsonian Theme' in G Watson (ed), *Agency and Answerability: Selected Essays* (Oxford University Press, 2004).

[33] See: www.sentencingcouncil.org.uk/about-sentencing/sentencing-basics/.

Consider the following report of the sentencing remarks in the case of a young man, Che Ambe, found guilty of causing grievous bodily harm with intent (Ambe had attacked his victim with a machete entirely severing one of his hands). Ambe had lived in 'squalor' in a 'world of drugs and alcohol' before being taken into care. Expelled from school, he had himself been a victim of knife crime.

Addressing Ambe, the Judge remarked that the 'sins of previous generations have been visited upon you … It is not society that is at fault. It is your parents and family, the way you have been brought up and accustomed to as a young man, which is chaos and violence'.[34] On the account above, then, one might expect leniency. Ambe's formative years 'inhibit' accountability blame (it is his 'parents and family' and his circumstances that have been 'visited upon' him). Yet, this is not how the judge (correctly following the sentencing guidelines) responded. Referring to a Probation Service report, the judge concluded that Ambe posed 'a high risk of harm to others and the risk of further offences is imminent'. The explanation was that Ambe knew of 'no other world' and, given that, the judge passed a very serious public protection sentence of 15 years with an extended licence period of five years.

Interestingly, just such a result is anticipated by Watson in his discussion of the 'vicious criminal'. Directly after the passage quoted above, he writes:

> To be sure, this inhibition does not shield victim-criminals from legal sanctions. We still protect ourselves against their murderous assaults; we hunt them down, lock them up, shoot them. Hence our scruples about fairness are of no consolation (or compensation) to them. Nevertheless, these concerns affect our sense of what we're doing. Seeing the criminal as himself a victim will not prevent us from shutting the cage or pulling the trigger. But these responses will then tend to seem regulative rather than retributive. In a disconcerting way, they lose their normal expressive function.[35]

In other words, sentencing in this case prioritises forward-looking goals of protecting the public, and perhaps reform and rehabilitation over the backward-looking expression of blame and punishment.

IV. 'SCIENCE' AND THE CRIMINAL LAW'S VARIOUS PERSONS

The chapter began by noting the focus of criminal law theorising on conviction and punishment, and the way in which that fits together with a thin, 'compatibilist' liberal theory of the choosing person. On this account, as we have seen,

[34] David Brown, 'Your parents are to blame, judge tells machete thug' *The Times* (5 September 2019) 1.

[35] Watson, 'Two Faces of Responsibility' (n 29) 281.

explanatory accounts of human behaviour are largely irrelevant. As Morse puts it, recent neuroscientific findings are a 'non-challenge' to criminal law.[36]

As noted in the Introduction to this volume, this dismissiveness is not new. Encounters between criminal law scholars and those working in 'explanatory' and 'behavioural' sciences have often been characterised by mutual distrust and defensiveness. In 1883, James Fitzjames Stephen robustly declared the irrelevance of the nascent discipline of psychiatry to questions of criminal responsibility. Criminal responsibility, he wrote, 'is, and must be, a legal question'.[37] Fast forward to the mid-twentieth century and the same debate appears between Barbara Wootton – pressing the claims of behavioural and social scientific explanations of human action – and HLA Hart resisting the same in the name of the independence of the law. Now, in the twenty-first century, the drive to rethink criminal responsibility is being led by neuroscientists, but the legal response remains much the same.

However, just as widening our gaze from conviction and punishment allows us to see the many and various conceptions of the criminal law's person that appear at different, and sometimes at the same, stages of the criminal justice process from criminalisation, through policing and prosecution, to conviction and sentencing, so too does it reveal the many ways in which 'science' and even 'junk sciences' have entered the field of criminal justice. While it is probably true that neuro- and other behavioural sciences have had little impact on the legal doctrine of the adult, reason-responsive agent, that is definitely not the case in almost all the other ways in which the criminal law's person can and has been constructed. For example, in criminalisation, including hybrid orders, and in much of policing, policy is led by a conception of actuarially assessed 'types' and resources are spent on those thought most likely to offend.

It is in sentencing and, although it is not considered here, in the management of prisoners including questions of early release that the effects of predictive and explanatory sciences have been most felt. Pre-sentencing reports, categories like 'dangerousness', and assessments of future risk, can play significant roles in the outcomes for individual prisoners. And yet, at the moment, that fact is seldom fully appreciated by criminal law theorists with the result that it remains under theorised.

One example, with which I will end the chapter, makes the point. Questions of insanity, diminished and partial, responsibility are core to a great deal of criminal law theory scholarship and the literature on these questions includes material by lawyers and philosophers and is enormous. Within that, issues of

[36] SJ Morse, 'The Neuroscientific Non-Challenge to Meaning, Morals, and Purpose' in G Caruso and O Flanagan (eds), *Neuroexistentialism: Meaning, Morals, and Purpose in the Age of Neuroscience* (Oxford University Press, 2018).

[37] Sir James Fitzjames Stephen, *A History of the Criminal Law of England*, vol II (Macmillan, 1883) 183.

how properly to include personality disorders such as Post-Traumatic Stress Disorder and Anti-Social Personality Disorder take a rightful place in the debates. The aspiration, at least, is to provide a theory of the general part that will resolve these issues.

Yet consider how a diagnosis of, say, Anti-Social Personality Disorder – or, perhaps even more dramatically, a high score on the Psychopathy Checklist-Revised[38] – might affect sentencing. In one jurisdiction, and under one of the purposes of sentencing, it might provide a reason for the judge to divert the offender towards a therapeutic setting. In another, and under a different purpose, it might provide a reason to increase the sentence even to the point of imposing the death penalty.[39] In short, while criminal law theorists have, by and large, remained fairly dismissive of the claims of explanatory and behavioural sciences, these sciences are to be found in almost every other domain of criminal justice. That is, of course, not necessarily problematic but it is worthy of more attention from criminal law theorists than it has so far garnered.

[38] RD Hare, *The Hare Psychopathy Checklist – Revised manual*, 2nd edn (Multi-Health Systems, 2003).

[39] eg, the PCL-R has been used to establish that a defendant poses a continuing threat to society, which is a prerequisite for imposing a death sentence in Texas. On the dangers of using predictive mechanisms of this kind, see TMS Neal et al, 'Psychological Assessments in Legal Contexts: Are Courts Keeping "Junk Science" Out of the Courtroom?' (2019) 20 *Psychological Science in the Public Interest* 135; and D DeMatteo et al, 'Statement of Concerned Experts on the Use of the Hare Psychopathy Checklist – Revised in Capital Sentencing to Assess Risk for Institutional Violence' (2020) 26 *Psychology, Public Policy, and Law* 133.

3

The Criminal Law's Person and Normative Elements in the Legal Definition of Excusing Circumstances

KAI HAMDORF

WHEN I WAS invited to contribute to a volume on the criminal law's person, I had to give myself answers to some questions before I could decide whether or not to accept the invitation: what is the purpose of a book on the criminal law's person? What is my role in this project? Is there – and if so: why is there – anything at all that I have to or even want to say about the criminal law's person? I also feel that I have to give these answers to the reader as well before I can say what I have to say about the criminal law's person.

The first question is very open but ultimately relatively easy to answer. Of course there is a large variety of possible perspectives on the criminal law's person, for example, how human beings are treated by the court system in practice, how legal institutions in fact construct the person they deal with and so on. But being a lawyer I am not competent to answer sociological questions, nor would anyone want to read my philosophical treatise on human agency and the human mind. My perspective will rather be one from inside the legal system: I want to take a closer look at the normative concept of the criminal law's person and the legal implications of this concept. What are the prerequisites for a human being to be a 'full' person in law, a person with, for example, the capacity to conclude a contract or make a will (civil law), to vote, to be elected or to be a civil servant (public law) or to be fully criminally liable (criminal law)?[1] My focus throughout will be on the criminal law.[2]

[1] In some jurisdictions even the civil liability under tort law only applies to fully accountable persons, see eg, the German Civil Code (Bürgerliches Gesetzbuch – BGB) s 827 – Exclusion and reduction of responsibility: 'A person who, in a state of unconsciousness or in a state of pathological

The second question is not so easy to answer. Shall I write this chapter as a judge in a national court system with his practical experience and knowledge of the criminal law in his own national jurisdiction? Or am I just someone interested in (criminal) law in general with a view across the borders of national jurisdictions and with some interest in more abstract, maybe even theoretical questions? With regard to the context of this volume, the composition of the group of authors and the discussions at the workshops that led to this volume, I have come to the conclusion that this chapter will be more useful for the overall project if I take the role of a generally interested jurist with a German background. Although quite a bit will be said about German law in this chapter, it is not about German law as such. National law will only serve as a starting point for my observations. The aim is to reach general conclusions, to show underlying ideas and concepts, that is, 'the big picture', not to discuss details that are relevant for one jurisdiction only.

I. INTRODUCTION

So, is there anything interesting to say about the concept of the person in criminal law? I think there is. The concept of the person is in my view the starting point for all reflections about criminal law. If we ask ourselves what kind of function criminal law fulfils or is expected to fulfil in society and how, we have to acknowledge that any tool applied by criminal law is applied on a person, be it in the forward-looking perspective of setting up conduct rules that shall be followed or in the backward-looking perspective when applying a decision rule on a person who is accused of having breached such a conduct rule.

My chapter will therefore ask – and try to answer – exactly these questions: if criminal law is to fulfil its functions 'through' real human beings, what does this mean for the concept of the person in criminal law, that is, the generalised, abstract human being as addressee of the conduct rules contained in criminal provisions? And do we consistently stick to this concept when applying decision rules?

In the first section I will try to outline the concept of the criminal law's person in the light of criminal law's function as well as some constitutional, historical and philosophical aspects. In the second section I first want to show

mental disturbance precluding free exercise of will, inflicts damage on another person is not responsible for such damage. If he has temporarily induced such a state in himself with alcoholic beverages or similar means, he is then responsible for damage that he unlawfully causes in this state as if he were responsible because of negligence; responsibility does not ensue if he came into this state without fault'.

[2] All translations of statutory provisions in this chapter are taken from, 'Laws on the Internet' ('Bundesministerium der Justiz und für Verbraucherschutz'), available at: www.gesetze-im-internet.de, a webpage hosted by the Federal Department of Justice and Juris, a legal database.

how the German Criminal Code (Strafgesetzbuch – StGB) reflects this concept in the provisions regarding serious mental disorders and other abnormalities. After that I will give some examples from German court cases for an application of these provisions that are – according to my opinion – inconsistent with the concept of the criminal law's person that follows from criminal law's function. My argument is that it is not justifiable to apply different concepts of the person in the forward-looking perspective of sending out messages on legal and illegal conduct and the backward-looking perspective that we take when we ask whether a person shall be convicted and sentenced for having breached these rules.

II. THE PRESUMPTION OF GUILT IN THE NORMATIVE CONCEPT OF THE CRIMINAL LAW'S PERSON

In German law, as well as in most other jurisdictions I assume, there is no statutory provision defining the concept of the person in criminal law. There are many hidden or obvious indications in the law though that may – like the pieces of a jigsaw puzzle – allow us to see a picture if we put them together. I would like to take a deductive approach and move from more general to more specific concepts. Therefore I will start with the German Constitution and its history and with the philosophical background for German criminal law (the frame of the puzzle) to then move on to some of the statutory criminal law provisions in the StGB that may be relevant in the context (the puzzle's core or centre).

A. Constitutional Law: The Idea of Man as a Spiritual and Moral Human Being

The rule of *nulla poena sine culpa* (as well as *nulla poena sine lege*)[3] is a constitutional right of every accused person in every criminal trial in Germany.[4] Not only are courts bound by this rule, the legislator also has to abide by it when

[3] Art 103.2 German Constitution and s 1 StGB, have the same wording: 'An act may only be punished if criminal liability had been established by law before the act was committed'. The StGB is in fact much older (1871) than the Constitution (1949), but it has a lower ranking in the hierarchy of norms. Provisions in the StGB (as well as all other statutes) can be declared void by the Constitutional Court if they are in breach of the Constitution. The *nulla poena sine lege* rule is also stipulated in Art 7.1 of the European Convention on Human Rights (ECHR) and Art 49.1 of the Charter of Fundamental Rights of the European Union (CFREU).

[4] HA Wolff, 'Der Grundsatz "nulla poena sine culpa" als Verfassungsrechtssatz' (1999) 124 *AöR* 55 (English summary at 85–86); see also T Hörnle, 'Die verfassungsrechtliche Begründung des Schuldprinzips' in U Sieber et al (eds), *Festschrift für Klaus Tiedemann* (Heymanns Verlag GmbH, 2008).

drafting criminal legislation. Punishment requires blameworthiness,[5] and the amount of blameworthiness is the main factor for the determination of the criminal sanction (sentencing). According to the German Federal Constitutional Court (BVerfG) the principle of guilt or blameworthiness – *nulla poena sine culpa* (*Schuldprinzip*) – is fundamental for criminal law. The Court has based this principle first on Article 1.1 of the German Constitution[6] and some aspects of the principle of blameworthiness that are relevant for the concept of the person as addressee of criminal law have been developed in the BVerfG's case law.

In its decision on the Lisbon Treaty of the European Union the Court ruled, inter alia, that the principle of guilt on which criminal law is built presupposes a human being's own responsibility, that is: 'it presupposes human beings who themselves determine their actions and can decide in favour of right or wrong by virtue of their freedom of will'. According to this judgment the protection of human dignity is 'based on the idea of Man as a spiritual and moral being which has the capabilities of defining himself, and of developing, in freedom'.[7]

In 2013, the BVerfG gave a judgment concerning plea bargaining in criminal proceedings. 'Deals' between the court, the prosecution and the defendant had at least since the 1970s become a more and more regular practice in German courts, namely in complex and lengthy trials, when the legislator in 2009 enacted the Plea Bargaining Act in order to give this practice a legal basis and set up standards.[8] The Court held that '[P]unishment sanctions the offender for having violated social ethics' and that 'such a reaction by the criminal justice system would violate the guarantee of human dignity and the principle of the rule of law if individual blame had not previously been established'. It also argued that the rule of law is one of the guiding ideas of the German Constitution, which also 'encompasses the requirement of substantive justice, and includes the principle of equality before the law as one of the fundamental axioms of justice' and that 'according to the concept of justice, crimes must be punished fairly and punishments must match the crime'.[9]

[5] The German word '*Schuld*' can mean 'guilt' or 'blameworthiness'. I have deemed it more appropriate in the context of this chapter to translate it as 'blameworthiness'.

[6] 'Human dignity shall be inviolable. To respect and protect it shall be the duty of all state authority'.

[7] Judgment of 30 June 2009, BVerfGE, 123, 267, 413; an English translation is available at: www.bundesverfassungsgericht.de/SharedDocs/Entscheidungen/EN/2009/06/es20090630_2bve000208en.html.

[8] The Code of Criminal Procedure (StPO) s 257c.

[9] Judgment of 19 March 2013, BVerfGE, 133, 168, 197; an English translation is available at: www.bundesverfassungsgericht.de/SharedDocs/Entscheidungen/EN/2013/03/rs20130319_2bvr262810en.html.

This latter aspect, the principle of proportionality between the criminal sanction and the individual blameworthiness, as a composition of the severity of the crime and the degree of the offender's individual contribution and personal liability,[10] was also emphasised in a judgment of the BVerfG of 2011 regarding the distinction between prison sentences and preventive detention. According to this judgment:

> The authorisation for the state to impose and execute prison sentences is essentially based on the culpable commission of the criminal offence. The offender may only be sentenced to imprisonment and subjected to its execution for the culpable commission of a wrong. This is based on the [German Constitution]'s image of humanity, which is of a person capable of free self-determination; consideration is to be given to this image in the principle of blameworthiness rooted in human dignity ... In its function of controlling the determination of penalties, the principle of blameworthiness restricts the duration of imprisonment to what is appropriate to the blameworthiness of the offence. Blameworthiness is one of the legitimating factors and the extreme limit of the imposition and execution of prison sentences. The authorisation to impose and to execute custodial measures such as preventive detention, on the other hand, follows from the principle of predominant interest.[11]

We can summarise that the image the German Constitution has of the person as addressee of criminal law's norms and sanctions is the image of a human being responsible for himself or herself, capable of determining his or her actions and able to decide in favour of right or wrong by virtue of his or her freedom of will. In constitutional law this concept sets boundaries for criminalisation by the legislator and the courts. Criminal law is not allowed to treat its addressees as tools for achieving a certain goal. It has to respect them as moral human beings. I want to argue here though, that there is another side to this coin. The concept, idealistic as it is, makes assumptions that real people may not always live up to. It contains a 'presumption of guilt' that can be contrasted to the general procedural rule which demands us to presume the opposite: the accused's innocence.[12]

B. Criminal Law's Person as Addressee of Behaviour Rules

The 'presumption of guilt', understood as the assumption that a person normally has full mental capacities, is not only a result of constitutional law

[10] See also CFREU [2000] OJ C364/1, Art 49.3.

[11] Judgment of 4 May 2011, BVerfGE, 128, 326, 376; an English translation is available at: www.bundesverfassungsgericht.de/SharedDocs/Entscheidungen/EN/2011/05/rs20110504_2bvr236509en.html.

[12] The presumption of innocence is of course a general rule throughout the entire European Union; see CFREU (n 10) Art 48.1.

and its concepts of the spiritual and moral human being. In fact it is inevitably connected to criminal law as such, if it is supposed to fulfil any function at all.

Criminal law consists of conduct rules that guide human behaviour and of sanction rules that apply when a person does not comply with a conduct rule. If criminal law's purpose is to guide human behaviour, this will only be possible if the conduct rules are understood by their addressees. This implies that they have to be formulated in a way that a normal citizen has at least a chance to understand them, and it also implies that they can only be addressed to persons who have the mental capacity to understand them and adapt their behaviour accordingly. In other words, the model of the legal person (in criminal law as well as in other areas of law) implies a certain kind of responsible agency: persons are capable of being guided by norms and may accordingly be answerable for their conduct when they breach those norms.[13] In a different terminology Lindsay Farmer speaks of 'prospective responsibility' – the imposition of obligations and duties on a person who is deemed capable of adapting their conduct to norms and planning their conduct over time – and of 'retrospective liability' – being held responsible for past conduct (answerability or accountability).[14]

From a sociological perspective, behaviour rules are communicated normative expectations.[15] In this respect a criminal act is a communicative act, an act by which the perpetrator disappoints the normative expectation communicated in a behaviour rule and sets a smaller or bigger question mark behind society's (and the legislator's) statement that this rule is valid. By punishing the perpetrator society deletes this question mark and confirms that the rule is still valid – the expectation is being stabilised.[16] The size of the question mark depends on the significance of the act and its consequences for society. Of course burning down a large building sets a bigger question mark behind the rule 'you shall not set fire to somebody else's property' than using someone else's newspaper to light the fireplace. The significance will also vary depending on the attitude that the perpetrator has shown towards the rule. Intentional acts are generally more severe than negligent acts if the consequences are equal. And, finally, the significance – here pictured as a question mark – will depend on the blameworthiness of the person. A person who is mentally ill and does not understand the rule as such cannot question the validity of the rule. The reason why we do not punish a small child is that children under a certain age cannot take what we see as a rational decision for or against a rule, even if the rule itself is simple enough for them to grasp, for example, 'you shall not steal'.

[13] L Farmer, *Making the Modern Criminal Law: Criminalization and Civil Order* (Oxford University Press, 2016) 168.

[14] ibid 169.

[15] As opposed to cognitive expectations, eg, that gravity will make an apple fall from the tree.

[16] G Jakobs, *Strafrecht Allgemeiner Teil* (De Gruyter, 1991) 5–14.

This is what we mean when we say that the child understood the rule but was unable to follow it.[17]

III. THE PRESUMPTION OF GUILT AND EXCUSING CIRCUMSTANCES IN CRIMINAL LAW

Let us now turn our focus to guilt as a prerequisite for a conviction. If the responsible and moral human being according to constitutional and criminal law is the addressee of conduct rules, then excusing circumstances must be an exception. Can we see this presumption of guilt in statutory criminal provisions and court cases? I think we can.

According to the three-step model for the ascription of responsibility in German criminal law[18] a person can only be convicted of a crime if he (a) fulfils all elements of the description of the criminal offence in the StGB and has the required criminal intent or – where applicable – negligence with regard to all of these elements;[19] (b) his action was not justified, for example, because of self-defence, necessity or consent; and (c) there are no circumstances 'excusing' the person, for example, insanity, duress or unavoidable mistake of law. I will deal here with cases touching upon (c), but I do want to mention that guilt – in the form of blameworthiness – is also the general guideline for sentencing.[20] Additionally, a 'reduced' form of guilt/blameworthiness may constitute a mitigating factor and lead to a (mandatory or facultative) reduction of the sentencing scale, for example, in cases of diminished responsibility or if a mistake of law was avoidable, the perpetrator will be convicted, but the sentence may be mitigated.[21]

According to section 20 StGB, any person who at the time of the commission of the offence is incapable of appreciating the unlawfulness of his or her actions or of acting in accordance with any such appreciation due to a pathological mental disorder, a profound consciousness disorder, debility or any other serious mental abnormality, shall be deemed to act without guilt.

The underlying concept is apparently a two-level-model.[22] The first level is a list of abnormal 'biological' features. On the second level such a feature will

[17] ibid 10.

[18] The so-called '*dreistufiger Deliktsaufbau*' (three-step model of crime) with (a) *Tatbestand* (objective and subjective elements of crime); (b) *Rechtfertigung* (justification); and (c) *Schuld* (guilt) is the leading theory in Germany. Some scholars prefer a two-step model ('*zweistufiger Deliktsaufbau*'). According to this concept, the objective and subjective elements of crime include the (lack of) justifying circumstances.

[19] Or was negligent in cases where the negligent form of the crime exists, ie, is criminalised.

[20] See StGB, s 46 'Principles of sentencing'.

[21] ibid ss 17 and 21.

[22] German legal terminology speaks of two 'floors' or 'storeys' (*erstes und zweites Stockwerk*).

only result in lack of guilt under the 'psychological' condition that it made the person incapable of appreciating the unlawfulness of his or her actions or of acting in accordance with any such appreciation. This is called the 'biological-psychological' or the 'psychological-normative' method of establishing guilt or lack of guilt.[23]

For the biological prerequisite one may as a general rule or classification say that:

(1) 'Pathological mental disorders' are the forms of defects that usually have been regarded as medical conditions, ie, the so called exogenic psychosis (eg, tumours, Alzheimer, alcohol or drug intoxication) or endogenic psychosis (eg, schizophrenia, depressive, manic or manic-depressive [bipolar] psychosis).
(2) 'Profound consciousness disorder' are conditions that may occur even for 'normal' or 'healthy' people; they are not organically induced (eg, affective emotional reactions, extreme fatigue or exhaustion or likewise).
(3) 'Debility' is a form of inherent lack of intelligence without any known organic explanation.
(4) 'Other serious mental abnormality' covers all forms of psychological abnormalities that – according to today's scientific knowledge – are not caused by any organic process and do not fall under category (2) or (3). These may be personality disorders ('psychopaths' with severe abnormal, mostly dissocial behaviour patterns), neurosis, stress disorders, sexual deviance, addictions or delusional disorders.[24]

On the second level the person will always be acquitted if the condition made him or her incapable of appreciating the unlawfulness of his or her actions, regardless of whether or not the condition was permanent or temporary and whether it generally excluded or merely reduced the person's capability of appreciating the unlawfulness.[25] On the other hand, the person will be convicted despite any given form of disorder, if he or she in the moment of the crime was capable of appreciating the unlawfulness of his or her actions and of acting in accordance with this appreciation. In such cases a mitigation of the sentence under section 21 StGB (diminished responsibility) can apply.[26]

[23] See, eg, W Perron and B Weißer, *Schönke/Schröder StGB*, 30th edn (CH Beck, 2014) s. 20 Rn 1.

[24] See, eg, H Schöch, 'Schuldfähigkeitsbeurteilung und strafrechtliche Sanktionen bei psychisch Gestörten' in M Dudek et al (eds), *Verantwortung und Zurechnung im Spiegel von Strafrecht und Psychiatrie* (Nomos, 2014) 11.

[25] As mentioned above, in such a case other measures may apply, eg, the mental hospital order according to s 63 StGB: 'If a person has committed an unlawful act in a state of insanity (section 20) or diminished responsibility (section 21) the court shall make a mental hospital order if a comprehensive evaluation of the offender and the act leads to the conclusion that as a result of his condition, future serious unlawful acts can be expected of him and that he therefore presents a danger to the general public'.

[26] StGB, s 21 reads: 'If the capacity of the offender to appreciate the unlawfulness of his actions or to act in accordance with any such appreciation is substantially diminished at the time of the

A. The 'Presumption of Guilt'

We can see that section 20 StGB contains an exception from the general rule that a person over 18 years of age is to be regarded as fully responsible and liable for his or her actions as long as there are no indications for an exclusion or reduction of his or her ability to appreciate the unlawfulness of a certain behaviour and to act accordingly. The law does not require that the court positively establishes the 'guilt' of the accused person: it only asks the court to examine whether there are any disorders that might result in an excuse under section 20 or in a diminished responsibility under section 21 StGB. Moreover, this examination is only necessary if there are any indications for such a disorder, whether they are shown by the accused or by the prosecution or follow from the files or the act itself.[27] Hassemer[28] has given a practical explanation for this:

> According to section 20 StGB the judge is not obliged to ask himself questions that he cannot answer, to gather knowledge that he cannot find, and to produce evidence that he cannot handle. His programme is limited to and complies with his cognitive abilities. This is what I call a mature form of rationality: such a procedure of taking evidence requires fact-finding only in so far as it categorically complies with the possibilities of human knowledge.[29]

This is what I would like to call a 'presumption of guilt' in an untechnical sense. Under German law the burden of proof always lies with the prosecution. The prosecutor has to present evidence for all prerequisites of the crime and the court may only convict the accused if the (majority of the) judges are convinced that all elements of the crime have been fully established on the basis of all evidence and/or a credible confession. Regarding the mental capacities of the accused person it is sufficient though that there are no indications for a lack of guilt. The burden of proof still lies with the prosecution: it is not up to the accused to provide evidence for his own mental disorders, but due to the 'presumption of guilt' it is in his own interest to show indications for any lack of guilt. Moreover, the '*in dubio*' rule is applied restrictively: if there are not enough facts for the forensic expert to draw any reliable conclusion about the mental state of the accused, for example, because the accused is not willing to cooperate and to be explored by the expert, then the accused will not be acquitted '*in dubio*'. Instead the 'presumption of guilt' will apply because the '*in dubio*' rule applies

commission of the offence due to one of the reasons indicated in section 20, the sentence may be mitigated pursuant to section 49(1)'.

[27] Schöch, 'Schuldfähigkeitsbeurteilung und strafrechtliche Sanktionen bei psychisch Gestörten' (n 24).

[28] Winfried Hassemer was professor of criminal law and legal theory and Vice President of the German Federal Constitutional Court.

[29] W Hassemer, 'Verantwortlichkeit im Strafrecht' in G Roth, S Hubig and H-G Bamberger (eds), *Schuld und Strafe* (CH Beck, 2012) 16. Translated here by K Hamdorf.

only to facts, not to the normative assessment of these facts, and if there are no facts to be assessed, the rule does not help the accused.[30] We have to bear this in mind when we take a closer look at how the specific elements of sections 20 and 21 StGB are interpreted by the German Federal Court (BGH).

B. Disorders and Abnormalities as Medical and Normative Elements

The BGH has always stressed that ultimately the question of whether or not a person is guilty according to section 20 StGB is a question of law, not of fact. The judge has to decide on this question on her own authority without being bound by the expert opinion given. The question of law shall be decided by the judge on a basis of an overall assessment (*Gesamtwürdigung*) of the crime and the perpetrator.[31] We see here a 'two-step model': in the first step, all facts about the mental status of the accused at the time of the crime have to be established with the help of forensic experts. In the second step, the courts have to make a normative assessment of these – empirical, medical – facts and determine whether or not they reach the level of a disorder with exculpatory effect under section 20 StGB or at least result in a diminished responsibility under section 21 StGB.[32]

The list of disorders in section 20 StGB is rather long and open and the main problem in most criminal proceedings therefore lies not in the first step, but in the second step: the assessment of the disorder's effect on the perpetrator. A classification of the perpetrator's disorder under ICD-10 or DSM-IV is always required but not sufficient. According to the BGH, the judge has to assess the severity of the disorder with the help of a forensic expert, but the final decision is up to the judge and she is not allowed to simply refer to the oral or written expert opinion. If the judge follows the expert's opinion in the verdict, the expert opinion has to be summarised and discussed in the written reasons of the judgment.[33] For example, in cases of paranoid schizophrenia the diagnosis of this illness is not sufficient for the conclusion that the perpetrator has acted without guilt. An acquitting judgment has to show that the perpetrator had an acute schizophrenic episode, and the written reasons of the judgment have to explain in what way this disorder actually affected the capabilities of the perpetrator in the actual situation of the crime.[34]

[30] Schöch, 'Schuldfähigkeitsbeurteilung und strafrechtliche Sanktionen bei psychisch Gestörten' (n 24) 36. According to Schöch it is therefore generally favourable for the accused to cooperate with the forensic expert.

[31] See, eg, BGH, decision of 7 April 2010 – 4 StR 644/09 – juris, Rn 6.

[32] Lernestedt has called the similar Swedish system a 'two leg model', see C Lernestedt, 'Norge efter Breivik: nytt förslag till ändringar rörande (o)tillräknelighet' *Blendow Lexnova Expertkommentar – Straffrätt* (December 2014).

[33] See, eg, BGH, decision of 17 June 2014 – 4 StR 171/14, NStZ-RR 2014, 305, 306.

[34] See BGH, decision of 27 January 2016 – 2 StR 314/15 – juris, Rn 6.

It is obvious that in these cases it is not always easy to draw the line between questions of fact (where the rule '*in dubio pro reo*' applies) and questions of law. If we say – and in fact we do – that it is up to the judge to decide whether or not the mental disorder described by a forensic psychiatrist in the expert opinion on the perpetrator is severe enough to (a) fall under one of the groups of disorders in section 20 StGB and (b) to make this person incapable of appreciating the unlawfulness of his or her actions, then this allows for a number of normative aspects to be taken into account in this assessment, namely 'standard setting', the necessity of deterrence, of sending out signals to the population and so on.[35]

According to Ulfried Neumann, the BGH applies sections 20 and 21 StGB in a way which enables that the lack of actual capacities of the perpetrator can at least partially be compensated by a past or present duty (of conduct), and this allows for a normative cushioning of the severe consequences that a strict application of the principle of guilt would have.[36]

Now, let us take a look at how courts in practice shift from a psychological, empirical and understanding approach to a more abstract, normative, standard-setting approach. In fact, normative reasoning can come in at two levels: first, it can influence the definition of the mental disorders that are regarded sufficient for an application of section 20 or 21 StGB; second, if the disorder clearly falls under the definition, we can ask whether the person can be held responsible for having (caused) this disorder. I would like to give some examples for both 'strategies'.

i. The Necessary Degree of Illness

The problem with personality disorders is that, obviously, simply a bad character can neither be the basis for punishment[37] nor can it be an excuse. There has to be something more, something about the person's mind and attitude that

[35] This criticism is not at all new: it has been argued by many scholars and even former Supreme Court judges (see, eg, W Theune, 'Die Beurteilung der schweren anderen seelischen Abartigkeit in der Rechtsprechung und ihre Vereinbarkeit mit dem Schuldprinzip' (2002) 114 *ZStW* 300) that the current concept of the assessment of mental disorders in court proceedings is in some cases not compatible with the concept of individual guilt or blameworthiness and the concept of the person in our Constitution.

[36] U Neumann, 'Die Schuldlehre des Bundesgerichtshofs' in CW Canaris et al (eds), *Festgabe 50 Jahre Bundesgerichtshof* (CH Beck, 2000) 83–84.

[37] There are many reasons for this, one being that the person cannot be held liable for the development of his or her character up to a certain age and later developments will often be a result of such an early deformation. The behavioural consequences of a bad character will of course often be an aggravating factor in sentencing. According to the central German provision on sentencing (s 46 StGB), 'the motives and aims of the offender, the attitude reflected in the offence and the degree of force of will involved in its commission' can be taken into account. And persons with such a bad character will quite often have a prior history of convictions, which may also be taken into account and will often exclude the possibility of probation.

goes beyond deviance, beyond a lack of moral development (lack of rules), beyond a criminal tendency or a habit to commit crimes, but without any organic, pathological explanation (such disorders are covered by the three other categories). But how do we define this 'something'?

The courts have said for a long time – and sometimes still say – that the disorder must reach the level of an illness (*Krankheitswert*). But how do we define illness? One criterion is that the mental defect is permanent or at least long-lasting, another is the severity of the defect. The BGH has, for example, accepted the application of section 21 (diminished responsibility) by the district court in a case where the diagnosis was a severe form of debility (*Imbezilität*) that had already lasted for years, combined with a 'highly reduced ability of criticism and judgement' and a very weak own will. The Court stated that the explanation of these conditions given by the district court left no doubt that the perpetrator's deficiencies were not just character deficiencies but amounted to a form of illness.[38]

In many cases though, the BGH has not accepted the lower court's assessment. In the 1950s the district court in Berlin applied the former provision on diminished responsibility on a perpetrator, stating that according to the forensic expert's opinion he was a psychopath. His personality disorder implied that he had no feelings for personal relations with other people (no empathy), he hardly had any emotions at all, did not feel bound by ethical rules, had no sense of duty or obligation and was highly egocentric. The forensic expert saw and the court regarded these character deficiencies as a form of illness due to their degree and the impact they had on the daily life of the accused. According to the expert, the consequences of these character deficiencies, namely the person's inability to subordinate himself to others and to arrange himself in a group were the real reason for his tendency to commit crimes. The Supreme Court disagreed with this assessment, saying that even if the accused had severe character deficiencies, such deficiencies were not seldom in the normal population and could be found frequently amongst lawbreakers. Defective characters were quite often the internal reason for their crimes, but this could not be an acceptable reason for diminished responsibility. The legal order asked of these people as much as of all others to control themselves. Provisions of the StGB were in fact directed also – if not mainly – against such people in order to protect society. Such protection would be needed especially with regard to perpetrators of the accused's kind because such people were a threat to the social order in which we live.[39]

It is quite clear that this decision values the effect of a punishment in this case on and for society higher than the results of the expert opinion that would have spoken for the classification as an illness. The relevant question for the

[38] BGH, decision of 9 January 1986 – 4 StR 616/85 – NStZ 1986, 427, juris, Rn 5.

[39] BGH, decision of 17 April 1958 – 5 StR 80/58 – NJW 1958, 2123. This decision was made under the former StGB, s 51, that had a slightly different wording from today's StGB, s 20.

court is not whether the accused could have controlled himself, but whether he should have controlled himself.

Similar decisions were made later. In a 1966 judgment a district court held that the accused was a neurotic over-sensitive querulous person with very low self-esteem. He was a soft person with no self-confidence, very hard-headed, self-centred and self-opinionated. Whilst he always expected understanding, consideration and mildness for himself, he would act ruthlessly and recklessly against others. When he was told that he would be arrested (for another crime), the feeling of unfair treatment became so strong that his ability to control himself when he attacked the policeman was severely reduced. The BGH overruled this judgment and declared that the neurotic over-sensitivity of the accused may in fact amount to an illness that may have a relevant impact on his capability to control himself in cases of typical querulous crimes like defamation, false statements or likewise. But when it came to an attempted murder on a policeman who was just doing his duty when arresting the accused, the loss of control was – according to the court – merely a result of his defective character. With regard to such crimes, the legal order could not ask less of a person like the accused than of any normal human being.[40]

Again, the question is not whether the accused actually was able to control himself; it is rather that society demands that he should – or did – control himself, regardless of whether or not he could.

ii. Abnormalities as 'Variations of the Normal'

Although the qualification of the disorder as an illness is still relevant today, the focus has slightly shifted. Nowadays the BGH asks judges in the lower courts first to make an overall assessment of all relevant circumstances, including the personality of the accused and this personality's development, the history that led to the crime, its immediate cause, how the criminal act was carried out and the way the accused acted after the crime.[41] The first instance judge[42] has to check whether the personality disorder is not in the end just composed of characteristics or forms of conduct that lie within the range of 'fully responsible' persons and is more than just the usual cause for criminal behaviour.[43]

[40] BGH, decision of 7 June 1966 – 5 StR 190/66 – NJW 1966, 1871.

[41] BGH, decision of 31 March 2004 – 5 StR 351/03 – juris, Rn 7.

[42] 'First instance judge' shall here stand for the judge establishing the facts of the case ('*Tatrichter*'). In Germany this is the first instance judge at the district court (or at the High Court in exceptional cases, eg, terrorism) for severe cases that may be repealed on grounds of law to the Supreme Court. Smaller crimes start in local courts and may be repealed to the district court where the facts of the cases can be questioned in second instance. My point here is: the Supreme Court only rules on legal questions, not on questions of fact; it does normally not hear witnesses or experts. If questions of fact are validly challenged with the repeal, the case will be referred to the first instance court for a (limited) retrial.

[43] This is of course a circular definition since the aim is to find out whether the person is responsible for his or her actions or not. 'Fully responsible' can in fact only mean 'normal' here.

The judge has to show that the personality disorder is not just a form of deviant character or behaviour that lies 'within the range of normality'.[44]

In a judgment of 2000, the BGH said that normative aspects may be relevant in the judge's assessment of psychiatric facts and that the legal relevance of a lack of control was first of all dependent on what the legal order demands of a person with reduced self-control. Whilst an expert opinion may be needed for the medical-psychiatric facts, the normative question is for the judge to decide.[45]

Moreover, the Court said that the more severe the crimes, the higher the demands of the legal order.[46] This means that we ask a person to have better capabilities (control over his actions) when the crime committed is more severe. In a murder case the BGH stated that the high ranking of the legal good protected by the provisions on murder (ie, life) gave reason not to take into account the causal effect of (the history of) the relation between the offender and the victim too much or too readily. In general a sound human being had to be asked to control himself and his emotions.[47]

In a 1998 case the BGH had to deal with a murder case where the perpetrator had killed the witness of a prior crime. For such a 'concealing murder' (*Verdeckungsmord*) the sentence under section 211 StGB is lifetime imprisonment. The BGH said that the reason for this severe sanction was that the killing of a human being with the aim to conceal another crime was extremely 'reprehensible, unscrupulous and despicable'. Moreover, the lifetime sanction fulfilled a relevant function as a counterforce for the strong motivation of the perpetrator to kill the witness to avoid being caught and tried. This function would be undermined if such a perpetrator could successfully argue in the murder trial that he panicked because of what he expected from the witness. Therefore there was a high threshold for the courts to assume that a perpetrator who killed a witness while running from the police committed the crime due to panic, fear and terror rather than with the intention to conceal the prior crime.[48] Although this decision does not touch directly upon sections 20 and 21 StGB in this paragraph, the reasoning of the Court shows how normative aspects like the rationale of the law may be relevant in the assessment of 'internal facts' like the ability of a perpetrator to think clearly instead of panicking.[49] Of course, the high threshold applied here is not based on empirical facts, it is

[44] See, eg, BGH, decision of 21 October 1998 – 3 StR 416/98 – juris, Rn 6.

[45] BGH, decision of 23 August 2000 – 3 StR 224/00 – juris, Rn 6.

[46] BGH, decision of 21 January 2004 – 1 StR 346/03 – juris, Rn 34.

[47] BGH, decision of 14 December 2000 – 4 StR 375/00 – juris, Rn 14.

[48] BGH, decision of 23 December 1998 – 3 StR 319/98 – juris, Rn 10.

[49] Of course there might also be cases where the normative decision is (secretly) taken by the forensic expert. Streng has described this in his commentary on StGB, Article 20, 2nd edn 2011, Rn 179, saying that the legal question of whether or not a person was able to control his or her actions was pseudo-empirical and that in fact forensic psychiatrists often answer this question with concealed normative or political (*kriminalpolitisch*) assumptions or valuations.

not a result of the medical forensic experience, that a perpetrator who kills a witness while running from the police *really is* less likely to commit the crime due to panic, fear and terror rather than with the intention to conceal the prior crime. It is a normative threshold, a shift from the empirical, psychological, understanding approach to a normative, forward-looking, standard-setting approach.

iii. Criticism and Alternative Approaches

Many legal scholars and forensic experts have criticised this case law and argued that 'illness' as such and the 'level of illness' are not useful as concepts and criteria to define a disorder (under section 20 StGB): in fact they are too vague and open and allow for too many normative elements to interfere with the first medical assessment.[50]

Psychologists and psychiatrists have suggested that instead the assessment under section 20 StGB should rather be made on the basis of the severity of the mental anomaly and the abnormal behaviour, that is, the intensity (how frequent and how severe is the abnormal behaviour, how much energy is used); chronicity (is the abnormal behaviour just situational or chronic); and the effect on the person (how does the abnormal behaviour effect the person's everyday life)?[51]

C. Alcohol and Drugs as Excusing Circumstances

We have seen that the severity of a crime is sometimes used as a relevant factor in the assessment of a person's ability to act in accordance with the appreciation of the unlawfulness of their actions (in short: 'ability to control oneself'). This is – according to my opinion – even more obvious for cases where the perpetrator's loss of control was caused by alcohol or drugs.

In a quantitative sense alcohol is the most important drug in criminal cases in Germany.[52] The mental state of drunkenness can lead to diminished responsibility under section 21 StGB or in cases of heavy drunkenness even to a lack of guilt or blameworthiness (an excuse) under section 20 StGB.[53] Whilst some

[50] See, eg, A Schiemann, 'Die Variablen der Schuldfähigkeitsfeststellung' (2013) 31 *Recht und Psychiatrie* 80, 82; G Tondorf and B Tondorf, *Psychologische und Psychiatrische Sachverständige* (CH Beck, 2011) II; each with further references to forensic literature.

[51] Tondorf and Tondorf (n 50) II.

[52] H Schöch, 'Section 20' in H-W Laufhütte (ed), *StGB Leipziger Kommentar*, 12th edn (CH Beck, 2007) Rn 95.

[53] The addiction as such is normally not relevant; if at all, it can in severe cases justify the application of StGB, s 21. It may have consequences for the question of probation though and it may of course result in brain damage, a reduced personality and so on that may again give rise to the application of s 21 or even s 20.

categorise drunkenness as a pathological mental disorder, others regard it as a profound consciousness disorder; this dispute has no practical consequences though.[54]

Drunkenness is being invoked as an excuse regularly in German criminal courts. As a starting point judges have to try to establish the level of alcohol in the blood of the accused at the moment of the crime. This can be done either with the help of blood samples taken by the police or – with considerably lower precision – by calculating it on the basis of the (proven) amount of alcohol the accused had consumed. I cannot elaborate on this here; there are countless articles and court decisions on these methods and on how they are to applied.[55]

The BGH has developed guidelines for the lower courts with regard to the indicative effect of the alcohol level for the lack-of-control excuse.[56] If the alcohol level was 2 Promille or higher at the time of the offence, the court has to take into account the possibility of diminished responsibility (possibility of mitigation); if it was 3 Promille or higher the court has to take into account the possibility of a lack of guilt or blameworthiness (acquittal). To take into account means that the judge has to weigh all the arguments and circumstances that speak for and against the ability of the accused to control his or her actions. Such circumstances are, for example, the drinking habits of the accused, tolerance to alcohol, his or her overall condition, the way he or she acted (rational, planned or irrational, spontaneous). In cases where the blood alcohol level was 3 Promille or higher, the court may only convict the accused on the basis of a thorough investigation of all relevant factors. These have to be weighed and the judge or the judges (on the bench) have to be convinced without doubt that the accused was able to control his or her behaviour.[57]

What we see here is a rule for the application of what I above have called the 'presumption of guilt' on the basis of the alcohol level in the perpetrator's blood.

Now, the BGH says that these guideline levels of alcohol are 10 per cent higher in cases of severe crimes, namely crimes against the life of others, that is, 2.2 Promille for section 21 StGB and 3.3 Promille for section 20 StGB, because people generally have a psychological hindrance or barrier to kill other human beings.[58] This 'barrier-theory' (*Hemmschwellentheorie*) is apparently not based on empirical findings. The BGH does not cite any research results or expert opinions for this theory; in fact there seem to be none that would support this theory.[59] It is hard to imagine that any psychiatrist would say that 10 per cent

[54] See Schöch, 'Section 20' (n 52) Rn 96.
[55] For some references, see Schiemann (n 50) 83.
[56] Drunkenness will hardly ever allow the court to assume that the accused lacked the capability to understand the wrongfulness of his actions.
[57] BGH DAR 1993, 395.
[58] See, inter alia, BGHSt 37, 231, 235; BGH NStZ 1991, 126.
[59] Schiemann (n 50) 82.

more alcohol is needed for a loss of control in cases of murder than in cases of bodily harm. Forensic experts have over the years rather questioned the relevance of alcohol levels in the blood as such, saying that due to the quite distinct bodily and mental conditions of human beings and their very different reactions to alcohol, it is not advisable to have such guidelines at all.[60] Moreover, empirical studies show that symptoms indicating a psychological condition increase significantly already at 0.5 and 1.5 Promille.[61]

Despite these facts and this criticism, the BGH said – in a case where the accused had a blood alcohol level of 2.38 Promille when he caused bodily harm to another person – that the question of whether or not the ability of the perpetrator was considerably reduced was a question of law for the judge to decide, taking into account normative reasons, that is, what the legal order asks of a person with this degree of drunkenness. In cases where the accused had to be blamed for his or her drunkenness there would be a strong demand that no reduction in the sentence should be applied.[62] Again we see that the demands of the legal order (or the population?) may be more relevant than the actual lack of control. Ultimately, the accused is being blamed and punished for getting drunk rather than for committing a crime (that he or she committed after having – partially – lost control over his or her actions).[63]

A similar approach is taken with regard to perpetrators acting under the influence of drugs or in the state of detoxification. Both circumstances will hardly ever allow for the application of section 20 StGB, but they can justify the reduction of the sentence on the basis of section 21 StGB. Regarding detoxification the threshold is high: the addiction to drugs will only lead to diminished responsibility for drug-related crimes (mostly theft) if the person has been addicted to 'hard' drugs for many years and if the consumption of these drugs has caused the 'severest changes of personality' or if the person had very heavy bodily effects of detoxification or – in cases of addiction to heroin – acted in fear of such detoxification.[64] In cases where the perpetrator acted under the influence of drugs this will only lead to diminished responsibility if he or she had massive psycho-pathological symptoms such as loss of

[60] For this discussion, see Schiemann (n 50) 82; Schöch, 'Section 20' (n 52) Rn 101.

[61] Schiemann (n 50) 82.

[62] BGH, decision of 29 April 1997 – 1 StR 511/95 – juris, Rn 39.

[63] I have to take a shortcut here, leaving aside some aspects that are relevant in similar cases but not in this one. A punishment can in some cases be based on s 323a StGB, and there also has been a discussion for decades about the legal concept of '*actio libera in causa*', according to which the relevant action constituting the crime is not, eg, the killing as such, but the 'drinking in order to kill'. It would need far too much space to elaborate on this here. S 323a [Committing offences in a senselessly drunken state] para 1 StGB reads: 'Whosoever intentionally or negligently puts himself into a drunken state by consuming alcoholic beverages or other intoxicants shall be liable to imprisonment not exceeding five years or a fine if he commits an unlawful act while in this state and may not be punished because of it because he was insane due to the intoxication or if this cannot be excluded'.

[64] BGH, decision of 19 September 2000 – 1 StR 310/00 – juris, Rn 7.

reality, hallucinations or delusions.[65] Again the BGH said that even if someone acted under the influence of drugs, the court may also assess her ability to control herself on the basis of normative aspects, including the question of what the legal order demands of a drugged person. These demands again being higher the more severe the crime.[66]

If we remind ourselves here that the '*in dubio pro reo*' rule does not apply to normative questions, the result is that judges have a large discretion in assessing the criminal responsibility of the accused.[67] According to my opinion, this discretion does not comply with the general principles of constitutional law on individual responsibility and blameworthiness.

IV. CONCLUSIONS

What I hoped to show in this chapter is that criminal law itself uses a concept of *the criminal law's person* as a free and rational human being with full control over his or her actions, and this concept results in a 'presumption of guilt', whilst the constitutional right of any accused person is to be punished only for crimes culpably committed (*nulla poena sine culpa*). We are therefore not allowed to use the idealistic concept against the actual person being tried in criminal proceedings. In fact, the principle of individual guilt or blameworthiness requires that the capabilities of the offender be examined with scrutiny. The question whether or not a person at the time of the commission of the offence was incapable of appreciating the unlawfulness of his or her actions or of acting in accordance with any such appreciation due to a mental disorder or abnormality, should be assessed on the basis of facts, empirical knowledge and the opinion given by forensic experts and not on the basis of normative reasons. Such 'normative' reasons are in fact in many cases simply reasons of criminal policy.[68]

[65] BGH, decision of 19 September 2000 – 1 StR 310/00 – juris, Rn 13.

[66] BGH, decision of 21 March 2001 – 1 StR 32/01 – juris, Rn 25.

[67] This criticism was expressively raised by the former Supreme Court Justice Theune in his article on other serious mental abnormalities and the principle of individual blameworthiness, see Theune (n 35) 317.

[68] Schiemann (n 50) 86; Theune (n 35) 317; Tondorf and Tondorf (n 50) II.

4

Standard-Setting versus Tracking 'Profound' Blameworthiness: What should be the Role of the Rules for Ascription of Responsibility?

CLAES LERNESTEDT

It is not intended to deny that criminal liability, as well as civil, is founded on blameworthiness. Such a denial would shock the moral sense of any civilized community; or, to put it another way, a law which punished conduct which would not be blameworthy in the average member of the community would be too severe for that community to bear. It is only intended to point out that, when we are dealing with that part of the law which aims more directly than any other at establishing standards of conduct, we should expect there more than elsewhere to find that the tests of liability are external, and independent of the degree of evil in the particular person's motives or intentions. The conclusion follows directly from the nature of the standards to which conformity is required. These are not only external ... but they are of general application. They do not merely require that every man should get as near as he can to the best conduct possible for him. They require him at his own peril to come up to a certain height. They take no account of incapacities, unless the weakness is so marked as to fall into well-known exceptions, such as infancy or madness. They assume that every man is as able as every other to behave as they command. If they fall on any one class harder than on another, it is on the weakest. For it is precisely to those who are most likely to err by temperament, ignorance, or folly, that the threats of the law are the most dangerous.[1]

[1] OW Holmes, *The Common Law*, 46th edn (Little, Brown and Company, 1923) 47 f.

I. INTRODUCTION

THE LARGER OBJECT of this volume is 'the criminal law's person'. This person, made material in the construction and application of the criminal law's rules, may differ – and often differs to a considerable degree – from how the person, the human being, is pictured in other spheres of life, society, science and (indeed) law. One prominent reason for such variations in description is that these various persons are constructed for different *purposes*, because the constructors have different *objectives*.[2]

Turning specifically to the *criminal law's* person, the hub of its construction will largely be found in the rules for ascription of responsibility, as well as in their underpinnings brought in from various sources (not least, as things stand today, from philosophy). This cluster of rules is often referred to as the criminal law's *general* part. Undoubtedly one also finds much interesting information on how criminal law sees, or produces, its person in the rules of the criminal law's *special* part (regarding particular kinds of crime, for example, rape, forgery and theft),[3] but (or so I argue) if one wants to get to the core of the criminal law's person – and the conditions under which this person is produced, the expectations accompanying the production – then one central task must be to examine the general rules, applicable (depending on which rule) to all or many of the crimes in the special part. In what follows I focus on the general part. In section IV I discuss, as an illustration, some of its particular contents, for example, the question of under what circumstances excessive self-defence may be excused.

[2] This said, one might distinguish between propositions regarding the person that are more or less agenda-driven ('agenda-driven' meaning roughly that such a proposition is made with some set of desired consequences in mind). An alternative is disinterested propositions, with no further, ulterior aim or ambition other than trying to describe the object in question as it is, ie, ontologically correctly. For a bit more on the topic see, C Lernestedt, 'The Sounds of Silence. Some Reflections from Elsewhere' in U Kindhäuser et al (eds), *Strafrecht und Gesellschaft: Ein kritischer Kommentar zum Werk von Günther Jakobs*, 1st edn (Mohr Siebeck, 2019) 765 ff. Ideas of personhood include, of course, who counts at all as a person in the relevant area or sense; compare L Farmer, *Making the Modern Criminal Law: Criminalization and Civil Order* (Oxford University Press, 2016) 166: 'In general terms legal institutions establish criteria of who counts as a person for the purposes of the law according to the order which they seek to secure. This can be more or less inclusive: disqualifying those such as slaves, women, or aliens who are seen as lesser classes or categories of person – or not persons at all – or including all humans as relevant persons under the rubric of human rights. And legal systems may have different degrees or categories of personhood for different purposes, distinguishing for example between those who can legally perform certain actions and those who are eligible for the protection of the law but who are not qualified to act. In principle, a legal system can lay down its own criteria of personhood, which may be more or less inclusive; the key point is the identification of the putative properties of the person who is subject to law'. See also, regarding the cover illustration of this volume E Evans, *The Criminal Prosecution and Capital Punishment of Animals*, 1st edn (William Heinemann, 1906).

[3] See, eg, J Gardner and S Shute, 'The Wrongness of Rape' in J Horder (ed), *Oxford Essays in Jurisprudence: Fourth Series* (Oxford University Press, 2000).

Before this, though, other more general issues will be addressed. If we are to discuss the criminal law's responsible and non-responsible person, as this being comes to life in the rules for ascription of responsibility,[4] then a crucial part of the discussion – or perhaps more adequately a necessary precondition for this kind of discussion – is the question why the rules for ascription of responsibility *are there*.[5] What expectations can and should we have of these rules? Which job(s) do they do, and more importantly, which job(s) should they do and be allowed to do? What (kinds of) limitations, if any, should bind or restrict the room for manoeuvre regarding the production of these rules and their application by the courts? What is the *aim* (or for that matter are the aim*s*) of having these rules? With variations in purpose, in aim, follow variations also in construction.

By now someone might object that these are unnecessary questions to raise at all; do we not agree on the answers? No, we do not: interesting differences exist between scholars and, at least historically (but important to emphasise also today), between different criminal law traditions. As we shall touch upon, differences in opinion arise regarding among other things:

(a) Whether (and to what extent) the rules for ascription of responsibility should be seen and used as (partly or fully) *forward-looking* (in the sense that they set and should set standards for future behaviour; compare the Holmes quote at the beginning), or whether they should be seen, and used, as primarily *backward-looking*.
(b) If the latter, how *profoundly* or *shallowly* the criminal law should look upon each individual defendant of flesh and blood.
(c) Relatedly, what, in these matters, should be deemed the relevant *equal treatment* of defendants?

No solid walls exist between (a), (b) and (c); they come, in some senses and versions, intertwined and interdependent. Moreover, when one decides on (b) and (c), various forward-looking concerns might become smuggled in if one is not wary; they are far from easy to leave out. One's opinion of (a), (b) and (c) largely shapes one's wished-for construction and application of the rules for ascription of responsibility and, therefore, also largely shapes the person brought to life and engaged in and by these rules.

[4] Here meaning actus reus, mens rea (absence of) justifying conditions and (absence of) excusing conditions. It should be emphasised here, for the Anglophone reader, that here the justifying conditions are not thought of as primarily part of the "criminalisation' qua special part, but instead of as belonging to the general part. That said, justifying conditions in some senses occupy a kind of middle-ground, for example when the issue is standard-setting for the future; see later below.

[5] They were not always there, one might add; elaborated rules for ascription of responsibility, as we know them today, have existed for only a relatively short period of time. Farmer (n 2) ch 6 is a very interesting read regarding later centuries.

The view I defend is that when making and applying the rules for ascription of responsibility – 'the general part', roughly – the institutions of criminal law should in principle be allowed to look *only backwards*. As will be developed in section III, this should be done in a quest for what might be called 'profound' blameworthiness with respect to each concrete individual. It includes treating defendants equally in a profound manner, meaning, for example, that when yardsticks (standards) for measuring a person's 'blameworthiness' are applied to a concrete defendant, having acted in a concrete situation, these yardsticks should – metaphorically – be placed at the same distance from *this* particular defendant as they would from any other defendant. The yardsticks used must allow for enough profoundness, and thus come close enough to each concrete individual, and they must come equally close to all.

This needs to be the guiding light for the production and application of the rules for ascription of responsibility, if the 'blaming' of concrete individuals is to be a legitimate activity. Returning to the Holmes quote at the beginning, he and I agree that (the word) 'blameworthiness' signifies something crucial regarding liability in the criminal law. We do, though, assign different meanings to the word when the task is to relate it to a person (which is, by the way, exactly what a criminal law court does). Holmes gives it a shallow meaning, advocating standards 'external' and 'general' and emphasising 'conduct' as almost sufficient. I give it instead a more profound, person-sensitive meaning (since the source of Holmes' 'conduct' is an individual). The 'blameworthiness' relevant for the rules of ascription of responsibility should be about how persons *are* (or, more correctly, how they were at the time of the alleged crime), not about how we would *wish them to be* in some future.

My view has, at least, two important consequences. The first is the *goal*: that of backward-looking profoundness when the criminal law deals with a specific person. The second has to do with how to reach this goal. There, the contents of what we might call the 'knowledge base', used by the criminal law when deciding on the characteristics of its person(s), must be discussed. A move in the direction I advocate includes allowing more room than today for psychology, psychiatry, sociology and the like, in assessing each individual. This is in principle a general proposal, but the need for alterations in practice will vary: the need is bigger with respect to some matters in the general part than others. This is because law and philosophy have shaped the criminal law in ways they should not have done in some matters, but not – or only to a lesser degree – in others. As will be discussed in section III, I do not think that a move towards making more room for psychiatry, etc, means that criminal law, as the enterprise we know it, must be abandoned.

The chapter proceeds as follows. Section II initially touches upon some of the criminal law's relevant points of departure, including an ever-present tension between forward-looking and backward-looking considerations, respectively. Then follows a discussion of some of the hows and whys of the rules for ascription of responsibility, including, for example: (a) the question of what kinds of rules actually apply to whom; (b) profoundness and shallowness; and (c) equal treatment. Along the way, the section considers differences between various positions.

Section III briefly discusses a few ways of coping with the potential problems that arise in the search for 'profound' blameworthiness. More specifically, the worry is that if our 'knowledge base' includes more psychology, psychiatry, sociology and the like, then there is a potential end-point where we – *qua* human beings – may be deemed generally incapable of 'profound' blameworthiness in any satisfying sense; or at least that it might be thought that we are incapable of producing adequate answers in matters of 'profound' blameworthiness. I propose a way to handle this that differs a bit, but not very much, from what seems to be today's '*herrschende Meinung*' (or prevailing opinion).

Whereas sections I–III are general and abstract, section IV offers a few specific examples for illustration and discussion, examples where – in my opinion – the construction and/or application of the rules for ascription of responsibility do not sufficiently respect the demand for personal 'blameworthiness'. In addition to excess in self-defence, the section touches on what I have come to think about as a presumption of guilt that is not formally present in the rules but is rather often materially present in crucial matters. I return to the Holmes quote above; ideas in terms of 'well-known exceptions' contribute to forming a presumption that is as strong as a rule where there should not be one (roughly: 'if none of the well-established exceptions is present then the person is liable').[6]

One might think it odd to give a historical writer like Holmes such a prominent position in a discussion of today's criminal law's person – his propositions come from long ago – but the cluster of ideas that he (re)presents are still current, I would argue, and Holmes presents transparently what others deliver more opaquely.

II. CRIMINAL LAW BACKWARDS AND FORWARDS

> I praise my 3-year-old daughter when she does the right thing, not because I believe she is a morally responsible agent who deserves to be praised, but because I want to encourage her to do the right thing again. Perhaps more tellingly, I do not blame her when she behaves badly – she is, after all, only 3 – but I nevertheless express what seems like blame … in order to discourage her from acting in a similar way in the future.[7]

[6] I am not addressing the particular exceptions that Holmes mentions in the quote, but instead the presumption-exception construction.

[7] M Matravers, *Responsibility and Justice* (Polity, 2007) 18.

The criminal law is often described (whether the aims are ontological or agenda-driven) as society's utmost power tool. It should also be described as characterised – always – by a strong tension between

(a) Forward-looking ambitions, among them and foremost the ambition to effectively 'raise' the population for the future, through directing behaviour in wished-for directions.[8]
(b) Various considerations *limiting* goal-fulfilment as in (a), considerations related to what the preconditions of the state being justified in punishing a particular individual for something that he or she *prima facie*, in a shallow sense, has 'done'.[9]

A central part in (b) is occupied by considerations relating to demands for what we tend to call 'blameworthiness'. As noted above, we agree that this concept catches something important. However, we often disagree regarding precisely what it signifies and what demands should flow from respecting it.

I will touch upon the tension between (a) and various aspects of (b) as this tension exists in the relation between criminal law's special and general part, respectively, as well as within some of the rules for ascription of responsibility.[10] My view is that when (a) and (b) are in conflict, (b) – backward-looking demands for blameworthiness – should always defeat (a). Thus, when they conflict, society and the legal order cannot legitimately balance away considerations of kind (b) in order to reach goals of kind (a). When an individual is (convicted and) punished, he or she becomes a tool for society's ambitions of kind (a). Society should not be allowed to take advantage of this if the concrete individual used has not been found blameworthy (enough). Whatever (a) effects might flow from respecting demands of kind (b) are welcome, but their permitted role in the equation is that of side effect.[11]

In what follows I will touch upon a few interconnected themes whilst focusing on the rules for ascription of responsibility. First *ontology*, and the question of to what extent this cluster of rules really *functions* as forward-looking; that is, to what extent and under what conditions they set and transmit standards of behaviour to the population for the future. Then *strategy*, and the question of whether the rules for ascription of responsibility *should* be used in

[8] Perhaps to 'civilise', using the vocabulary of Farmer (n 2).

[9] See, eg, C Roxin, 'Sinn und Grenzen staatlicher Strafe' (1966) 6 *Juristische Schulung* 377; HLA Hart, *Punishment and Responsibility* (Clarendon Press, 1968) esp ch 1.

[10] Such tensions can also be found within some rules for the gauging of penal value; eg, provocation regulations often provide interesting examples. This is clear in such versions of a provocation defence where, even if the defendant was put in a provoked state, there are additional normative demands regarding what reasons for being provoked (physically, emotionally) are 'allowed' for the defence to be applicable. Generally, on provocation, see, eg, J Horder, *Provocation and Responsibility* (Clarendon Press, 1992) (published before the recent UK changes).

[11] Some authors seem to mean that respecting (b) is the most effective way to reach (a); I doubt this is true.

such a forward-looking way. As will become clear, one's opinion of the actual and wished-for functions of these rules will heavily influence one's opinion of how they should be designed (in terms of profundity or shallowness, in terms of the relevant equality between defendants, etc). This means, in turn, that one's opinions on these matters shapes one's preferred construction of the criminal law's person.

Some initial clarifications: criminalisation in the special part, as well as the rules for ascription of responsibility, are brought into existence (eg, by legislation) for later use. In this limited sense both kinds of rules are forward-looking. Furthermore, in a specific case before the court, both kinds of rules are applied *ex post*, to something which has already occurred. In this limited sense, again, both kinds of rules are backward-looking.

I will not focus on such 'technical' issues, but instead on the question of why we think that these two kinds of rules, primarily and ultimately, *exist*: to (generally) direct people's behaviour for the future, or to function as tools for the legal official; for the court's deciding whether this particular defendant in this individual case exhibited the blameworthiness necessary for justified punishment (and thus for society to be justified in using him or her as a tool when trying to reach (for example) the mostly forward-looking goals of the system as a whole).

The aim of *criminalising* a certain type of behaviour would, in a majority of today's jurisdictions (and by a majority of today's scholars), be described as forward-looking; as future-oriented general prevention (of a 'positive' or 'negative' kind). The wish is to prevent – in the best of worlds through the articulated standard of conduct together with a threat of punishment tied to non-compliance – the criminalised behaviour.[12] Of course, other views exist among theorists as to the aim(s) and function(s) of criminalisation.[13] However, for the limited purposes here, and without further discussion, I accept future-oriented general prevention as the main aim of criminalising a certain conduct.

When we turn to *ascription of responsibility*, and the punishment which often follows if the defendant is convicted, the aim of this punishment is often characterised as either prevention (individual or general) or retribution. This is one possible role that retributive ideas can have in the criminal law: as an aim, as a way of obtaining something, in the sense of, for example, a symbolic restoration of the former ('original') respective status of the victim and defendant.[14]

[12] The optimal outcome is, of course, that because of its criminalisation no one commits the act in question.

[13] See, eg, MS Moore, *Placing Blame: A Theory of the Criminal Law* (Oxford University Press, 1997); and RA Duff, *Answering for Crime: Responsibility and Liability in the Criminal Law* (Hart Publishing, 2007).

[14] See, eg, JG Murphy and J Hampton, *Forgiveness and Mercy* (Cambridge University Press, 1988).

But I want to emphasise another possible role or aspect of retribution, relevant to the question of justifying the infliction of punishment on a certain individual: the idea that only *deserved* punishment is justified (whatever otherwise desirable aims there may be).[15] This view is related to ideas of blameworthiness and proportionality: of fitting the punishment to (as I would prefer to put it) the blameworthiness exhibited. In the version of retribution which I focus on here, retributive ideas do no more work than *set limits*: we may punish only if deserved, and only as much as is deserved.[16] Another way of phrasing it is that we may punish only if there was blameworthiness, and not more than what is proportionate to the blameworthiness exhibited.

Let us now, keeping this in mind, turn to the rules for ascription of responsibility and what we might call a factual or ontological question: to what or whom the messages in these rules are *sent*. I see them as only to a small extent addressed at, and sent to, the population. Rather, many such rules seem to be 'transmitted' almost exclusively to legal officials.[17] One reason for this is that I doubt that many of these rules have the capacity, assumed in the ideal account, of setting and sending standards that function to direct behaviour.[18] But other opinions are possible; for example, Anglo-Saxon criminal law theorists seem sometimes to presume that these rules *are* setting standards of behaviour for the future in much the same way as criminalisation.[19]

[15] On retributive ideas see, eg, J Waldron, 'Lex talionis' (1992) 34 *Arizona Law Review* 25; and MH Kramer, *The Ethics of Capital Punishment* (Oxford University Press, 2011) ch 3.

[16] J Braithwaite and P Pettit, *Not Just Deserts: A Republican Theory of Criminal Justice* (Clarendon Press, 1990) 34 ff defines this as negative retributivism. Compare the positive retributivism – again using Braithwaite and Pettit's terminology – found, eg, by Moore (n 13).

[17] eg, M Dan-Cohen, 'Decision Rules and Conduct Rules' in M Dan-Cohen, *Harmful Thoughts: Essays on Law, Self, and Morality* (Princeton University Press, 2002) seems to have a view rather close to mine.

[18] A few remarks. (1) Neither kind of rule is addressed to the people as direct commands ('you shall not do that!' etc). A being completely devoid of the context might read the criminalisations in the special part as some kind of price list. (2) At least justifying conditions, earlier (n 4 above) described as existing in a kind of middle ground, have better capacity here than other rules for ascription of responsibility.

[19] Historically, this view was prominent: see Farmer (n 2) ch 6. Here it is worth mentioning the reluctance – now weaker, earlier stronger – in Anglo-Saxon jurisdictions to the idea of a general part distinct from the special part; they were at least originally seen as one. One partial counter-view is Fletcher, according to whom 'there are a host of issues in the criminal law that cannot properly be stated in these primary norms of prohibition and command. For example, it makes little sense to integrate the issues of insanity, duress, or mistake into a set of directives to the citizenry. The point of recognising insanity and duress as defences is not that the norm is amended to read: "Thou shalt not kill unless thou art insane or under a threat of death". The point of recognising reasonable mistake of fact as a defence in statutory rape cases is not that the norm is correct to read: "Thou shalt not engage in intercourse with a girl under the age of 18 unless thou art reasonably mistaken about her age"'. GP Fletcher, *Rethinking Criminal Law* (Oxford University Press, 2000) 457. See also, eg, 492: 'The question of attribution is resolved under an entirely distinct set of norms, which are directed not to the class of potential violators, but to the judge and jurors charged with the task of assessing whether individuals are liable for their wrongful acts'.

Both these opinions – that the rules for ascription of responsibility do and that they do not guide general behaviours – can be correct at least to some extent: it depends on how the rules are constructed. *If* the rules for ascription of responsibility are to have at least a decent chance of setting and sending standards, *then* these rules (and the standards they contain) must be constructed as *shallow* and *rigid*. Because if they are too flexible, too person-sensitive, then they are not capable of 'sending' anything at all. If they are to be able to send a message, then they need to consist in the main of (in Holmes' terms) 'external' or 'general' standards. Then, in the determination of 'personal blameworthiness' the particular individual would be measured against the one and only yardstick (standard), and if he or she does not pass the test then that is the end to the proceedings. If, by contrast, the rules operate with a more flexible standard, or a 'two-step' one, then far less – or nothing – would be sent.[20]

Let us now – accompanied by some uncertainty regarding the extent to which the rules for ascription of responsibility set and send standards – turn instead to the normative questions of why this cluster of rules *should* be there, and what these rules *should* do. My view is that they should, when produced and applied, function only in a backward-looking way, as a set of tools in the hand of the legal official in the individual case, giving that official (often the court) what is necessary to be able to establish the blameworthiness (or not) of the defendant. Who do we punish? The answer: not the average person, not the reasonable person. What we do is punish *this* concrete person: this concrete Sven, this concrete Ulrika, an individual of flesh and blood with personal characteristics, with a history, within a context, and so on. If punishment is thought of (and meant as) hard treatment, and as something which potentially brings on the offender also other possible bad consequences (stigma, etc), then society is *not* justified in convicting Sven or Ulrika unless both of them have been measured against yardsticks reasonably close to *them*.

Now I wish to develop further the demand for personal blameworthiness as it should show in the rules for ascription of responsibility. One important issue, then, is the *profoundness* of this blameworthiness demand. An interrelated factor is *equality* and the question what the relevant equal treatment of defendants is in this area. Demands for equality may very well – as may practical issues – come into conflict with demands for profound-enough blameworthiness.

[20] 'Two-step' then in the sense that after the concrete individual has been measured against the primary, 'objective' yardstick there is, if necessary, an individual one; 'what could be demanded from *this* particular person?' See further in C Lernestedt, 'Criminal Law and "Culture"' in W Kymlicka, C Lernestedt and M Matravers, *Criminal law and Cultural Diversity* (Oxford University Press, 2014) esp 27.

First something brief on equality between defendants.[21] What options are available? At one end of the spectrum we find the view that, if the use of the epithet 'blameworthy' is to be proper, one needs to consider *everything* regarding each defendant (and the situation in which he or she took part). If 'profound' blameworthiness (together with equal treatment) were to be given a fully decisive role, then it would be easy to construct arguments for this view. We would try to get as close as possible to each person; to know as much as possible. There are, though, reasons against such attempts to go that close. Considering the more practical work of the criminal law system, it is easy to imagine that the more information which is to be gathered regarding the defendant, situation, etc, the higher the risk is for *unequal* treatment.[22] The 'consider everything' option should be dismissed, and with it demands for the most profound versions of personal blameworthiness.

The other extreme would be to consider more or less *nothing* but the outward act, or as little as possible beside it, and thus approach the individual defendant – *qua* construction of the person – more as completely empty of personal characteristics, more as a delimited physical entity (but a human one) in the room, than as a full person. An ideal of strict liability, or of very shallow versions of 'blameworthiness', would be attractive, I guess, if one sees effectively directing behaviour, and/or perhaps equal treatment of a markedly shallow kind, as the proper guiding light of criminal justice. What seems to bring together many such views – even if at least 'strict liability', labelled as such, has a very low ranking in today's criminal law theory[23] – is that *society's* interests are given considerable weight.[24] To pick another illuminating quote from Holmes: when he discusses ignorance of the law as a possible factor reducing blameworthiness, he elegantly describes what society needs

[21] Here it must be borne in mind that when we talk in terms of 'equality' there is almost always the word 'relevant' before it; two objects (or two persons, or how the two persons are treated) can be compared in a number of ways, some of them establishing equality, others not. The question then needs to be 'which equality is most relevant', or 'the best', or 'the most just', etc? As an illustration, think of language rights before the court in a multicultural society: one version of equal treatment is that everyone must use the same language before the court. Another version of equal treatment is that everyone has the right to use his or her own language before the court. Which version one prefers is not a matter (only) of equal treatment (both versions in the example are), but a matter of political choice. The concept of 'equality', in itself, does not bring one to any decisive point. See (in Swedish) C Lernestedt, *Likhet inför lagen: rättsfilosofiska perspektiv* (Norstedts Juridik, 2015).

[22] In a few ways; one risk is that courts etc would differ quite a lot in taking the task seriously (getting the relevant information), another risk (of another kind) is the classical-liberal worry that the more the Lady Justice gets to see, the bigger the risks are that various contextual factors that should not influence (eg, structural factors) do exactly that.

[23] See, eg, for a low ranking, A Simester (ed), *Appraising Strict Liability* (Oxford University Press, 2005).

[24] It is perfectly possible, though, to be of the opinion also that a purely backward-looking search for 'blameworthiness' should stay very shallow; it depends, probably, on one's concerns regarding the risks tied to going more profoundly, see further below.

to (and should) give up, in terms of 'profound' blameworthiness, for society's more important needs to be adequately satisfied:

> The true explanation of the rule is the same as that which accounts for the law's indifference to a man's particular temperament, faculties and so forth. Public policy sacrifices the individual to the general good. It is desirable that the burden of all should be equal, but it is still more desirable to put an end to robbery and murder. It is no doubt true that there are many cases in which the criminal could not have known that he was breaking the law, but to admit the excuse at all would be to encourage ignorance where the law-maker has determined to make men know and obey, and justice to the individual is rightly outweighed by the larger interests on the other side of the scales.[25]

Views such as this one, with the starting point that a very shallow reading of 'blameworthiness' is appropriate, would bring us far away from an ideal of 'profound' blameworthiness with its 'ontological' ambitions. It would, at least potentially, bring us deep into an emphasis on forward-looking functions: setting standards for the future.[26]

Generally, I do not agree with Holmes that justice to the individual should be outweighed by society's interests in the way he suggests.[27] *If* the rules for ascription of responsibility first and foremost should be there – as I argue they should – as tools for deciding whether this particular individual *may* be punished at all (and if so, how much), *then* we (as society) cannot justifiably make the construction of the person too shallow, to approach this particular individual as some kind of 'as if', if we know (or were able to know) that things are otherwise.

Another way to put it is that when it comes to the construction and application of the rules for ascription of responsibility, the criminal law's person should be approached with ontological, not strategic, agenda-driven ambitions.[28] As a consequence, the criminal law should be obliged to produce its normative judgements of blameworthiness *not* as a locked system constant over time and place, but as contingent; as changing in light of what those outside the criminal law know about how human beings function. There are good reasons for not trying to go too far towards 'profound' blameworthiness (see above), but the ideal of profound blameworthiness should nevertheless guide us. To summarise thus far, for rules of ascription of responsibility where normative yardsticks are to be (constructed and) used:

1. Forward-looking aspirations (future prevention, setting of standards, etc) should be given no intrinsic weight (what might follow as mere *consequences*

[25] Holmes (n 1) 46.

[26] See, eg, Farmer (n 2) ch 6.

[27] Even if, as should be conceded, ignorance of law is a tricky area in this sense.

[28] C Taylor, Cross-Purposes: The Liberal–Communitarian Debate' in N Rosenblum (ed), *Liberalism and the Moral Life* (Harvard University Press, 1989).

of respecting justified demands is another issue). The rules for ascription of responsibility should be about evaluating, without future agendas, what is and has been.

2. Respect for a demand for 'profound' blameworthiness necessitates that criminal law's investigation gets close enough to *this* defendant (in *this* particular situation, etc). Equal treatment (and this in its most narrow, demanding sense) necessitates that such yardsticks in the concrete case are placed at equal distance to each and every defendant: not closer to anyone than to anyone else.[29] Thus, the yardsticks must be equipped with a certain degree of sensitivity and flexibility.

So, going profoundly (and equally profoundly) is one part of my proposal. The other part is, *qua* necessary tool, a partially new and more flexible *knowledge base*. The image of the person, as operationalised in the rules for ascription of responsibility, is in some senses close to antiquated. If a search for 'profound' blameworthiness is the guiding light, then the criminal law is not justified in *not* taking into account, as part of the knowledge base, relevant issues in psychology, psychiatry, sociology and the like.

In relation to such sciences, though, criminal law – and not least criminal law scholars – often emphasise that (a) what the criminal law does and needs to do is deliver normative judgements, in terms of blame and non-blame, etc, *and* (b) this somehow makes it necessary that criminal law is kept as a rather closed or locked normative system; one which does not let in too much from (what gets defined as) the 'outside'.

At stake here seem to be smaller and bigger issues. One such seems to be the idea that giving psychiatry and other natural and social sciences more influence would weaken the possibility of adequate normative judgement (here especially judgements of blame, etc). Another issue seems to be the idea that such influence would collapse the whole system of criminal law, *qua* system of blaming, because the result would be a belief that the kind of freedom that would legitimate blame and punishment 'really' does not exist (it would, thus, make criminal justice depend on resolving the 'big' free will – determinism issue). Finally, there also seems to be a naked component of who gets to be in charge.

I consider these issues in the next section. I think of them as partly conflating questions of different kinds (and perhaps also 'bubbles' of different kinds) that can, and should, be kept logically separated: allowing more of psychiatry, psychology and the like, into the knowledge base of the bubble named 'blaming is a moral practice' does not mean that the bigger bubble, the one that keeps the general determinism versus free-will problem on the outside, will collapse.

[29] This is important to emphasise, eg, in the light of criticism from various structural perspectives; see Lernestedt, 'Criminal Law and "Culture"' (n 20).

III. WHAT IF? A FLEXIBLE WITHIN

> Die Juristen reden heute gern von Wertung, wenn sie keine Rechenschaft darüber ablegen können, was sie tun.[30]

> The very notion of being a person is closely tied to that of being obligable: genuinely to see another being – or oneself – as a person is to see that being as the bearer of responsibility ... if to understand all were to forgive all, then, even more obviously, to forgive all would be to forgive nothing.[31]

In the previous section I recommended, among other things: (1) that the rules for ascription of responsibility should be exclusively backward-looking; (2) that they should track in a profound way blameworthiness (or its absence) in the defendant; and also (3) that this necessitates more openness to psychiatry, psychology and the like; not in order to find alternatives or substitutes to (and thus challenge) criminal law's normative evaluation of acts and persons, but instead in order to improve (including to 'update') the base on which such evaluations are made.

But what if such encounters with other sciences would inevitably lead us (lawyers, society) on to 'bigger' questions including, ultimately, the conclusion that we humans (as everything else) are determined in a way which should make us refrain from thinking in terms of persons and their acts as potentially 'blameworthy'? *Or*, perhaps, we would reach the conclusion that we, at least with respect to individual cases, have become so unsure that we cannot know what we need to know to keep the system as it is, something which would make distinctions we draw – between blameworthy and not blameworthy, blameable and not blameable – insufficiently grounded for us to have confidence in them? There are various ways of dealing with such worries.[32] I will mention a few, and at the end suggest which of them I deem the most reasonable.

One *first* approach would be to suggest that since we cannot prove the existence of a justifying basis for the system of punishment (built on hard treatment) we need to abandon this system. In addition, perhaps, arguing that other kinds of conditioning are available for the governing of people, for example, the use of rewards to make them do the right thing instead of negative sanctions (like (threats of) punishment) to stop them from doing the wrong thing. Or, for that matter, constructing the person's environment in a way that does not give opportunities to behave in unwished-for ways (I'll return to this one shortly below). This would mean completely giving up the idea of criminal law.

[30] I Puppe, 'Juristische Methodenlehre für die Strafrechtshausarbeit. Ein Trockenkurs für Vorgerückte' [1989] *JA* 345, 364, fn 51. A rough translation (mine) would be: 'Nowadays, jurists are inclined to talk in terms of normative evaluation, when they cannot give any account of what they are doing'.

[31] R Richman, *God, Free Will, and Morality* (Springer, 1983) 136.

[32] Or perhaps for 'getting over them', as a participant at this project's York workshop suggested to me.

A *second* approach, partly related, might in an Anglophone setting be represented by Wootton (almost as historical as Holmes, and like him a very clear writer). Significant parts of what we think of as 'blameworthiness' are related to what goes on inside the (head of the) person. Wootton argued (as many others in her time in related ways, not least in Sweden, which embraced social engineering *par excellence*) that – since we cannot answer such questions in a satisfactory way – what went on in the individual's head should not be of importance for conviction.[33] According to Wootton, inner facts should be of interest only at a later stage: when the question is which measures are needed to make the person abstain from future crime. Wootton did not assign to the criminal law the high degree of particularity that many criminal law scholars do: her opinion was that when choosing between using criminal law measures and social law measures, the choice should be guided exclusively by forward-looking considerations, relating to which of the sets of rules would best 'evoke the desired response' in the particular individual at hand.[34] This approach would, like the first, mean giving up the criminal law at least as a distinct mode of control resting on ideas of guilt, blame etc, *either* as difficult to handle in individual cases and (partly) thus unnecessary, *or* as *tout court* unnecessary. If the latter, we could, with Skinner for example, try instead to create a world of 'automatic goodness':

> [I]t should be possible to design a world in which behaviour likely to be punished seldom or never occurs. We try to design such a world for those who cannot solve the problem of punishment for themselves, such as babies, retardates, or psychotics, and if it could be done for everyone, much time and energy would be saved.[35]

Let us turn to a *third* and *fourth* approach. They are closely related to each other in at least one important sense: the ambition to look upon human interaction (also by and through the system of criminal law) as existing inside a bubble where 'ultimate' issues, like the free will versus determinism one, are not (allowed) to interfere with the evaluation of human action and interaction. Understandably, one does not want to have to answer the 'ultimate' questions since, among other issues, there will probably not be an 'answer' to them able either to support or to challenge the instinctive conviction that persons, *generally*, possess the characteristics needed to be held responsible; to be (rightly) praised, to be (rightly)

[33] See B Wootton, *Crime and the Criminal Law: Reflections of a Magistrate and Social Scientist*, 1st edn (Stevens and Sons, 1963). At least slightly related kinds of arguments – and with similar kinds of consequences – seem to be put forward in parts of the more recent literature relating to neuroscience and criminal law. Here might be mentioned that in 1965 Sweden abandoned imputability as a demand for criminal conviction, arguing that this was a more or less practical, otherwise unproblematic, matter. See C Lernestedt, 'Insanity and the "Gap" in the Law: Swedish Criminal Law Rides Again (2009) 54 *Scandinavian Studies in Law* 79.

[34] I do not recall Wootton emphasising the idea of criminal law as setting behaviour standards for the future; instead, the aims seem to have been mostly directed at individual prevention.

[35] BF Skinner, *Beyond Freedom and Dignity* (Knopf, 1971) 66.

blamed, etc. In light of the critique (which, in my opinion, is devastating) against the idea of freedom of the will on a metaphysical level it is not surprising that many efforts from philosophers tackling the topic of freedom, responsibility, etc, on *that* level revolve around whether no more than something like freedom of *action* is, or should be deemed (which might be a slightly different question), all that is needed to justify society in using its harsh criminal law sanctions on an individual.

A more common strand of thought, though, seems to have to do with 'bubbles'. The ambition is to leave completely the level of the 'ultimate' and metaphysical, and instead take as points of departure that, for example, blaming is a social practice, existing within (and thus within the particular context of) smaller or larger groups of human beings, *and* that views on blameworthiness (and its absence) cannot exist at all except within such a context. There is, as it might be put, no relevant 'outside' to be taken into consideration. Strawson, who will be returned to below, has been hugely influential in the formation of such an approach. Here, though, I choose a quote from Honoré to try to capture the general spirit of it (containing, as it seems, also forward-looking ambitions of various kinds):

> The question is not which view is exclusively correct but which is preferable when we assess people's behaviour in everyday life and the law. The answer must be that in general we do well, indeed we are impelled … to treat ourselves and others as responsible agents. But the argument for welcoming this conclusion is not that our behaviour is uncaused – something that we cannot know and which, if true, would be a surprise – but that to treat people as responsible promotes individual and social well-being. It does this in two ways. It helps to preserve social order by encouraging good and discouraging bad behaviour. At the same time, it makes possible a sense of personal character and identity that is valuable for its own sake … The worry remains that, though it may make sense to treat people as responsible for their conduct, if human actions are caused by circumstances, people are not *really* responsible for what they do … [But] how far back it is rational to go in tracing causes must depend on the purpose for which we want to get at the cause of something that has gone wrong. This must apply also to the causes of human conduct. It is rational to treat people as the authors of their actions in the context of a system of responsibility that we regard as valuable both for individuals and for society as a whole. To treat human actions as a stopping point beyond which causal inquiries are not ordinarily pursued is sensible and indeed indispensable. Perhaps we can dimly imagine an alternative world in which people were regarded as mere automata. In that world, to treat people as the authors of their actions would be a bad way of explaining events. As things are, what (if anything) determines peoples' decisions includes their make-up, preferences, and ideals, so that the hypothesis that their decisions are determined hardly makes them victims of circumstance.[36]

[36] T Honoré, *Responsibility and Fault* (Hart Publishing, 1999) 125, 136–37. The part quoted does not regard criminal law specifically, but it is of importance also there.

But – and this is one of the crucial questions raised by the quote – how are we to move from the general, as described by Honoré, to the more specific? What bearing do these kinds of 'bigger' perspectives and points of departure on human beings and human interaction within the bubble actually have on the construction and application of the specific rules in criminal law's general part; specific rules forming the demands needed to be met for ascription of responsibility – with all its possible (negative) connotations – that need to be proper and justified? We must now distinguish a third approach from a fourth.

The *third* approach reacts to the situation by attempting to lock the criminal law's normative cosmology as a kind of closed system, built on (and built *by* representatives of) philosophy and criminal law, and with (1) an intense interest in how persons in everyday life actually go about blaming, praising, etc, each other, and (2) a marked scepticism towards what, for example, psychology might have to offer, as if that would be something completely *different*.[37] The risk is then obvious that not only the overarching points of departure, but also the interpretation of particular rules (and, in the end, particular cases), to a large extent will be 'locked' over time. If the base does not change with time, then the criminal law's person might at least partially become successively more distant from the everyday person existing outside the criminal law and in everyday life. This is not to say that the two should always be the same – they should not (see below). It *is* to say, though, that (consciously or unconsciously) letting them become too distant (a) does not respect a profound-enough meaning of 'blameworthiness', and (b) could easily be used for (attempted or successful, conscious or unconscious) incorporation of forward-looking ambitions in terms of standard-setting.[38]

A *fourth* approach, which I think is the correct one, closely resembles the third, but lacks the scepticism (hostility) towards psychology, psychiatry and

[37] I find the following quote from Duff illuminating in this context: '[T]he question of responsibility, of the criteria by which it should be determined, is not a psychiatric question, or one on which psychiatrists or psychologists can claim expertise. It is a question about the criteria that should structure the various practices in which responsibility is attributed, argued, accepted, or rejected (practices that include but are not limited to our moral interactions and the criminal law); it is therefore an ethical question, whose answer depends upon an understanding of those practices, of the principles by which they are structured, and of the conditions that make it appropriate or inappropriate to include someone within them (or to exclude someone from them). Once we have a clear conception of what it is to be or not to be, a responsible agent who can participate in these practices, we can look to psychiatry and to other scientific disciplines for expert advice in diagnosis and (if we are lucky) treatment; but the question of what it is that requires diagnosis, explanation and treatment – which is the questions that concerns me here – is an ethical rather than a scientific question'; A Duff, 'Psychopathy and Answerability' in L Malatesti and J McMillan (eds), *Responsibility and Psychopathy: Interfacing Law, Psychiatry and Philosophy* (Oxford University Press, 2009) 199.

[38] It could also be the case that criminal law, being the kind of enterprise it is (here I'm particularly thinking about the harmful tools it is equipped with and recall that some jurisdictions operate with the death penalty as a possible sanction) not only should be careful not to be left behind but also try to be in the front line; see further below.

the like. Strawson's influential argument in *Freedom and Resentment* seems sometimes to get used as a kind of defence of the third approach. This is in my opinion correct when the issue is whether the 'ultimate' questions may be set aside or not (I agree they may), but it is not correct regarding the two-fold argument that, roughly: (1) *since* blaming is a moral practice within a (larger or smaller) group; (2) no, or only a little input, from psychology, etc, should be allowed in.[39]

Such an argument seems to rest on the assumption – perhaps built on historical reasons, perhaps guided by more profane thoughts about who is to be master – that *if* one unlocks *this* smaller bubble to let in psychiatry, psychology and the like, *then* this will inevitably lead on also to attempts to collapse the bigger bubble; the bigger 'as if', as well. I think that this is wrong. In the best of worlds the two bubbles can – and *should* – be distinguished from each other.[40] This means also that the fourth approach *can* be distinguished from the first and second approaches, even if representatives of criminal law and philosophy might want to argue that it cannot.

The section, sketchy as it has been, ends with the recommendation that we should – and are allowed to – continue blaming, but that we should do it only if it is proper to do so taking into account a more flexible, richer knowledge base. When we decide matters regarding blameworthiness in the general part – in the making of the rules as well as in their application – the backward-looking ambitions that should rule must open up more than they do today towards psychiatry, psychology, etc. If this were to be orchestrated in a correct way, then the (construction of) the criminal law's person would be brought closer to where it should be.[41] Such a thing does not come for free, though: it would require a higher level of understanding between experts. From my point of view (which in this sense no doubt is a view from *somewhere*)[42] this is far from impossible.

[39] One problem here might be the idea that of interest seems to be 'what it is actually like to be involved in ordinary interpersonal relationships' (PF Strawson, *Freedom and Resentment and Other Essays* (Routledge, 1974) 7. In 'ordinary interpersonal relationships' there is no mandate to punish, to send people to prison (or to death, for that matter). The criminal law needs, exactly because of its particularity, to search for blameworthiness in more careful ways than the layperson does in everyday life.

[40] Compare Strawson (n 39) 25 on the possibility of change within the bubble: 'Inside the general structure or web of human attitudes and feelings of which I have been speaking, there is endless room for modification, redirection, criticism, and justification. But questions of justification are internal to the structure or relate to modifications internal to it. The existence of the general framework of attitudes itself is something we are given with the fact of human society. As a whole, it neither calls for, nor permits, an external "rational" justification'.

[41] The criminal law system as a whole, though, does not seem to have a generally 'closed' or 'locked' attitude: see the rather fast travels made by, eg, concepts like 'frozen fright' and 'battered women syndrome'. It seems easier, though, to travel fast if the suggestion is not for the good of the defendant.

[42] Sweden in this case, where, eg, forensic psychiatry is a distinct branch of its own, and is, in important senses, distinguished from general psychiatry.

Moreover, *if* we – through such an increase in contact and understanding between the professions, through admitting more influence from psychiatry, psychology, or (for that matter) for some other reason – *would* eventually reach a situation where the 'ultimate' outside and the inside of the bubble meet or clash in a way which radically also changes the inside (we would experience a change of paradigm and substitute one profound instinctive belief with another), so that we honestly and profoundly would come to think that human beings (including individual versions – the Sven, the Ulrika) are determined in such a way that punishment (at least when it comes vested in a vocabulary of blame, guilt etc) is not legitimate, *then* we will have far bigger existential issues to confront than the one concerning the legitimate use of the criminal law.

IV. A FEW EXAMPLES

In what might almost seem an appendix, this section considers a few concrete examples (one from the US, the rest from Sweden) to illustrate some of what has been discussed more abstractly above: rules and situations – and ways of thinking – where the construction of the criminal law's person (or the construction of the rules said to deal with it) takes the evaluation of the concrete person too far away from respecting a search for 'profound' blameworthiness (or, as in the first example, does not evaluate the concrete person at all).

(i) In a US murder case, a person who refused to testify claimed something like necessity – in order to escape responsibility for this refusal – in that her reason was fear for her and her children's lives were she to testify. The court seemed to have aggregate future harms in mind if this witness were to stay unpunished when not giving testimony. The idea most likely was that the message for the future sent by such a decision would not have been received only by this particular witness but also (and with huge interest) by massive numbers of possible *future* witnesses. As a result, the court found it out of the question that this case (but read: this *type* of case, ever) could be one where the defendant is excused on grounds of necessity: '[Fear] is not a valid reason for not testifying. If it is a valid reason then we might as well close the doors'.[43]

In light of all the arguments above, a jurisdiction cannot be justified in fully ruling out the possibility of witnesses being in such peril, etc, were they to give testimony, that we could not reasonably demand of them (qua *concrete* persons, in *concrete* situations) that they do so. And, it should be emphasised, this must be the case even if respect for this kind of backward-looking demand in an individual case would have significant negative effects for ambitions to reach

[43] *People v Carradine*, 114 Ill App 3d 82, as referred to in Dan-Cohen (n 17) 50.

important forward-looking goals (here: the goal that witnesses do testify, thus rendering threats against them ineffective).[44]

(ii) Let us now turn to Swedish criminal law (but I take it that what will be discussed has bearing also outside Sweden). First, what I have come to think of as a (too strong) 'presumption of guilt' in court practice, in relation to the criminal law's demand for an 'act', for this act to be a 'conscious' one, etc. One might perhaps call it a presumption of responsible agency, not too distant from the *formal* presumptions that at times in the past could be found written in the law.[45] Even though such formal presumptions today belong to history, their *material* contents have, to some extent, remained. Again (see section III above), we seem to be moving between the 'inside' and the 'outside' of a bubble. When describing (and discussing) such manoeuvres, what must be distinguished quite clearly is, on the one hand, more general views of the person, the human being (including the presumption, on a very general level, that the human being has the capacity to be 'blameworthy'), and on the other, matters which – on a lower level in the cosmology and demanding much more concretisation – concern particular (specific) rules. On a very *general* level, we take as our point of departure that human beings are – in principle – capable of responsible agency in a way which – again, in principle – enables blameworthiness, etc (see the third and fourth approach described in the last section).

But such a belief or conviction regarding the 'grand' question does not help much (or, one might say, *should* not be allowed to help much) for the work that must be done by the criminal law. The general conviction needs to be operationalised, and when we leave the general level and turn to the rules for ascription of responsibility, one thing that seems to happen is that the general conviction or belief gets split and used in different specific rules for ascription of responsibility, and yet seems to stay the same in this process, partly in ways that it should not. With respect to some particular demands, the presumption rather easily seems to mutate into a *rule*: (1) it starts with a presumption (not in the law, but in the head of the judge, who is also a person) that the specific demands (that there was an act, that it was intentional, etc) are met; (2) some exceptions are established (so that, eg, spasms and sleep are seen as capable of ruling out the possibility of what was done being 'an act' (or, with sleep, a 'conscious act')).

And the problem is that these exceptions do not confirm an otherwise existing *presumption*: they confirm – stabilise, cement – what in practice becomes a *rule*. The consequence is that if the defendant in a concrete case does not match any of the exceptions, there is only little (in practice nothing) that this defendant can do: the presumption is more or less impossible to challenge.

[44] I'd like to clarify here that the characteristics (the experienced threat, etc) in this particular case are not of interest. What is of interest is the formulation of the court.

[45] See Farmer (n 2) ch 6.

Particularly problematic in this sense are cases where what happened, what the defendant in some sense 'did', carried the *outwards signs* of (what normally is) a conscious act. One need not communicate long with representatives of psychiatry to learn that there is quite a wide space with a number of conditions *between*, on the one hand, the defined exceptions, and on the other, conscious acts in a relevant sense, and in this wide space the question should be much more open than it is today as to whether the defendant actually met the (proper) requirements of the criminal law. This is of course not least in cases involving various kinds of mental disorder, where mantras like 'the inside is visible from the outside' are too readily accepted (at least in Sweden).

This is not to suggest that such presumptions should be abandoned, and there are many cases where it really is quite unproblematic to go from the visible outside to the inside, but rather to suggest that the rigidity – the dichotomous black-or-white, on-or-off mode of structuring things – in this area are tools not worthy of a criminal law claiming to base its convictions (and the punishments that follow them) on 'blameworthiness'.

(iii) Last, if someone in a situation of self-defence, or necessity, did more than what would have been justified (eg, used excessive violence in the defence) there remains a possibility for the person to be excused, if the court deems that it could not be demanded (more or less, that it would not be fair of the legal order to demand) that he or she maintained sufficient self-control to stay within the limits of what was justified. Regarding this possibility, in various Swedish preparatory works, it has been clearly stated that such judgments regarding the issue of excusing or not should take the concrete defendant *as he or she was*, not replace him or her with some kind of average (or 'reasonable') person and ask what such a fictive being could have managed or not in the situation.[46] The idea of taking the defendant as he or she was means that personal characteristics – of a temporary (eg, fear, surprise) or a more permanent (eg, relevant mental disorder) kind – must be taken into account. Thus, the message is that from *some* should be demanded more than from *others*. We might say, returning to Holmes, that the standards used should be 'internal' and 'specific', not 'external' and 'general'. I deem this an adequate way of assessing personal blameworthiness.[47]

Turning to court practice, though, the 'external' and 'general' get much more (and far too much) room, for reasons – I think – of standard-setting and (probably) simplifying the courts' task.[48] I'd like to touch upon three

[46] Preparatory works are generally of great importance in Swedish law.

[47] A clarification: in one sense (in relation to fixed, 'objective' standards) more should be demanded from some than from others (in terms of actually meeting the standard), but in another sense (in relation to the persons themselves, with their varying capacities) equally much is demanded from all.

[48] Other and 'objective' factors (related to the situation) are also to be taken into account, and according to the preparatory works to be given relatively more weight than the personal ones, but this alone cannot explain the small weight given to the personal characteristics.

problems, of various kinds, regarding the criminal law's person and excess in self-defence.

The first has to do with defendants with various kinds of *mental disorders*. Regarding some of them – depending on what kind of disorder was at play at the time of the alleged crime, of course – it seems clear that their weak (or almost non-existing) ability to cope with a stressful situation such as an assault should excuse them for their excessive self-defence (or excessive putative self-defence). It simply would be unreasonable to ask from them, *qua* persons, that they stay within the limits of what is justified. In cases where this kind of problem is actualised, though, the courts only seldom (and far too seldom) take the disorder into account as decisive (as something which actually excuses the person). This, at least to some degree, has to do with various forward-looking ambitions.[49]

The second issue has to do with the courts' views on how quickly a person can reasonably be expected to calm down – to get her or himself together – when under attack. To exaggerate a bit – but only a bit – Swedish criminal law's stand on the matter: if you are attacked the criminal law gives you (very) limited time, a limited number of seconds, during which you are allowed not to be in full control of yourself (in the sense that you are excused for not being in such control). But after the first surprise has disappeared, you are expected to be calm (enough) again, meaning that you should (be able to) control yourself and stay within the limits of what is justified. The problem here is that research on how arousal levels work with respect to persons in traumatic situations points distinctly in the other direction: persons stay on the high arousal level for much longer than does the criminal law's person as constructed by the criminal law system. We tend to accept the longer arousal period in many areas of expertise (and also in some areas of everyday life, I would argue), but we do not accept it in the context of the criminal law. There, instead, the standards tend to become general, external, distant from the defendant of flesh and blood, and (on various grounds) forward-looking.

A third and related problem is the criminal law's view that if I for some reason expect or know beforehand that when I reach a certain place something might happen to me – I might (or perhaps even with some greater certainty will) be attacked when I get there – then the court will not allow me to be excused, even if I happened to lose control completely of myself in the situation. The argument behind this is that, because I was mentally prepared for the risk that something might happen, it is expected of me that I should remain calm(er). By contrast, outside the criminal law such a situation might be

[49] In this kind of case, a forward-looking ambition parallel to that of standard-setting is to get the person 'into the system', something which would not be possible (or not as easy) were the person to be acquitted. And, it could be added, even if standard-setting for the future was not the goal, this way of approaching things moves the evaluation too far away from this concrete defendant and his or her blameworthiness.

looked upon in a potentially different way, working in the opposite direction. The tenseness, and stress levels, brought about by the anticipation that something can happen might make me prone to 'explode' when something – not necessarily the attack – occurs. This does not happen, though, to the criminal law's person. And the reasons for this are of a moral, forward-looking kind: the criminal law's person is not allowed to look for trouble. If he or she does and loses control in a way which would normally count, it will nevertheless *not* count. The criminal law's person is only seldom allowed to be in (or even less search for) situations where decent people would not be, and the system definitely wants to discourage such ambitions.

V. CLOSING COMMENTS: THE CRIMINAL LAW AND EVERYDAY PEOPLE

> Sometimes I'm right and I can be wrong
> My own beliefs are in my song
> The butcher, the banker, the drummer and then
> Makes no difference what group I'm in
> I am everyday people, yeah yeah
> There is a blue one who can't accept the green one
> For living with a fat one trying to be a skinny one
> And different strokes for different folks
> And so on and so on and scooby dooby doo
> Oh sha sha we got to live together
> I am no better and neither are you
> We are the same whatever we do
> You love me you hate me you know me and then
> You can't figure out the bag I'm in
> I am everyday people, yeah yeah.[50]

The chapter has come to touch upon rather 'grand' matters. Summing up, I'd like to say a few things. Which person your criminal law will construct, when it comes to the production and application of the rules for ascription of responsibility, will depend on for what you want this person, and how you wish the criminal law to engage with him or her. To the extent, that is, that your account of the criminal law operates with 'him' or 'her' and not just 'it': it matters whether you want your criminal law to look upon this person mostly as an entity to (try to) steer for the future, or to use (through general prevention)

[50] *Sly and the Family Stone*, 'Everyday People', Epic Records 5-10407 (1968).

him or her for doing the same to others, *or* whether you want the criminal law to see and engage with this person, in the person's double-role of model and addressee, as a concrete individual of flesh and blood, an agent with whom society, through the criminal law, engages in some kind of meaningful two-way moral communication.[51] Should you wish (only) for the former, the recommendation is that you adopt shallow interpretations of 'blameworthiness', 'equality' and so on.

Should you instead wish for the latter – which is what I have advocated – the recommendation is that the aim should be defined as a search for (something like) 'profound' blameworthiness in the concrete person – the concrete Sven or Ulrika – regardless of if they happen to be the perfect role-model inhabitants of the jurisdiction or the complete opposite. This approach necessitates, among other things, closer contact and more porousness between, on the one hand, the criminal law, and on the other, psychiatry, psychology and the like, but endorses nevertheless that the proceedings, the practices, could (and should) be orchestrated *within* the bubble of blaming as a social practice (at least as things stand today, I do not think that we need to enter into the free will versus determinism issue to accomplish this). This means that there is room for blameworthiness, there is room for the practice of blaming (and for that matter praising, if someone were to be interested in that in a criminal law context). The blaming only ('only') needs to be built upon the most proper ground possible.

This said and having spoken in terms of 'proper ground', there is of course a lot more that could be discussed. With limited space offered I will restrict myself to one issue relating to the actors (and opinions) revolving around – being involved in – the construction of the criminal law's person. It also relates to the adequate roles of what we might think of as three different 'kinds' of philosophy when it comes to how to use the criminal law: moral philosophy, political philosophy and criminal law philosophy. For our purposes here, the first could be defined as dealing with horizontal relations and issues (how should I be, towards myself and others), the second as dealing with a vertical relation (what can, may, should, etc, society do in relation, *qua* society, to those under its jurisdiction), and the third– which I cannot think about as anything else than a particular branch and ultimate extension of the second, manifesting the vertical relation *par excellence* – as dealing with when society can, may, should, etc, use not just any of the tools in the toolbox but the tool called *the criminal law*.

The issue that I would like to address a bit further is the frequent use of references, from the side of criminal law and philosophy, to the practices of

[51] Today, such a 'communicative' idea seems to be the ideal for many. However, if that is the ideal, it seems that at the stage of trial and conviction, the criminal law needs to come close to the concrete person on trial. After all, what would there be for society to 'communicate' about with someone who is not in fact able to meet society's objective, rigid yardsticks?

blaming (etc) *in* everyday life, *by* everyday (or 'normal', or 'ordinary') people who are not professionals (or the deciding body in criminal law matters great and small),[52] and of an argument which seems to be more or less that 'this is how "we" (*qua* human beings) basically do things, and – thus – this is how we (*qua* system of criminal law) also *should* do things'.

I am not fully comfortable with this move from the 'is' to the 'ought', involving a move from an ontological claim in *one* setting to a strategic one in what I take should be *another*: the system of criminal law. *If* the criminal law is to be looked upon and treated as the serious business that scholars from criminal law and philosophy of criminal law regularly tell us that it is, and if it might do tremendously harsh things to a person found 'blameworthy' (including, in some places, the death penalty),[53] *then* it is not correct to cherish as a more or less (sufficient) knowledge base for issues relating to, for example, the ascription of responsibility, what ordinary people think and do; how they go about interacting with one another in their everyday life situations (or, for that matter, in relation to issues that are dealt with by the criminal law).

Because given the criminal law's claimed particularity, it is *not* your everyday part of the law, and it is *not* (as perhaps Wootton – at least to some extent – would have claimed) an everyday tool for society's use. Equally important: neither is the criminal law a private person – or a group of private persons – but it is something else, another body, that needs to establish its own standards of behaviour for itself *qua* system of criminal law. And that, as noted above, is ultimately a matter of political, not moral, philosophy: it is about how the criminal law, as an authoritative, specialised tool in the hands of the state can, should, may (etc) be used against the individuals in its jurisdiction.

This particularity makes it troublesome when – as very often occurs – discussions of, and recommendations regarding, how the criminal law should be designed in certain areas tend to leap from moral philosophy directly to criminal law philosophy (and thus miss the importance of 'general' political philosophy). This makes it easier to forget that the system of criminal law, *qua* part of the state and in the hands of society, is something qualitatively other than persons or groups of persons on an individual level.[54] But an interpersonal conflict is far from the same as a 'conflict' between a person and the criminal law. It might be that the criminal law needs its own catalogue of sentiments; for example,

[52] Except, that is, for lay judges.

[53] For an interesting discussion regarding the possible legitimacy of capital punishment, see Kramer (n 15). I reviewed Kramer's book in C Lernestedt, 'The Ethics of Capital Punishment: A Philosophical Investigation of Evil and its Consequences, by Matthew H Kramer' (2015) 124 *Mind* 361.

[54] Compare R Duff, 'In Response' in R Cruft, MH Kramer and MR Rieff (eds), Crime, *Punishment, and Responsibility: The Jurisprudence of Antony Duff* (Oxford University Press, 2011), discussing Andreas von Hirsch's contribution in the same volume: 'Criminalizing Failure to Rescue: A Matter of "Solidarity" or Altruism?'

the 'forgiveness' offered by the criminal law *qua* entity is not – and should not be – of the same kind as the forgiveness which could be offered (or not) by a person in an interpersonal relationship.[55] And, it should be emphasised, even the kind of more 'impersonal' judgements and sentiments by persons discussed, for example, by Strawson do not transcend the person-based context enough to transform into something qualitatively else and equal to (what) the system of criminal law (should be and do).

This means that good reasons exist for suggesting that the criminal law should ensure that its construction of the criminal law's person does not get left *behind* too much; too distant (in a way that disadvantages the defendant) from the parallel person outside the criminal law (see section IV above). More than that, the criminal law should also perhaps aim to go *before*, to be in the forefront when it comes to taking into account (bringing into the 'knowledge base') what is of interest in other sciences.

Now the time has come to mention something that might seem self-evident and thus too trivial, but that I think is not: when it comes to the assumptions and points of departure that we live and cope with regarding the criminal law's person, *what we already use today* rests on – another way to put it is that it is a product and consequence of – various kinds of assumptions of (what today would be labelled as of) a psychiatric, psychological, etc, kind regarding how human beings function. It is just that these assumptions and their origins are not made explicit (they were perhaps once, but if so that is now forgotten). Contingent as they were (or at least some of them) they are now seen to be carved in stone.

This might be why, I think, scholars on the side of philosophy, on the side of criminal law, bravely claim that what might come from psychiatry, psychology and the like is of no direct interest for the normative questions that the criminal law has to handle: because these scholars already have had *their* person constructed, based on knowledge partly from psychology, psychiatry and sociology of what is now a (partly!) antiquated kind. To the extent that this is true, what is at stake here is in part not a battle of branches of science, but instead a battle between different ages within the same branch: older ones (as now represented by scholars in philosophy and criminal law) and younger ones. If this is accepted as correct or partly correct, and one *still* wishes to stay with the old, the shallow and the 'everyday' people, then I suspect that forward-looking agendas are in practice more important, and backward-looking ideas of 'blameworthiness' less important, than one claims them to be.

My conclusions, in relation particularly to the issues dealt with in this last section, will be two. A first conclusion is that the references to ordinary people in their everyday lives fits very badly with a criminal law based

[55] Compare the related discussions in PE Digeser, *Political Forgiveness* (Cornell University Press, 2001) with, eg, Murphy and Hampton's (brilliant) *Forgiveness and Mercy* (n 14).

on an idea of 'profound' blameworthiness (and indeed with any criminal law stating that 'personal blameworthiness' is important). The suspicion is that such arguments, based on what ordinary people do and think and feel, are not much more than varieties on a by now well-known theme: the overarching idea is that the criminal law, including its rules for ascription of responsibility, are there to set standards for the future. If one wants to steer the population, one must speak to the population in a manner that they can hear.

A second conclusion – and a worry – is that the ambitions that today seem to be present – ambitions to banish psychology, psychiatry and the like, from the knowledge base used in the construction of the criminal law's person, are ambitions that rightly should be packaged in terms of power; not because one thinks that one necessarily is better than the other when it comes to measuring blameworthiness (or delivering the knowledge base necessary for such an activity), but because one wants to be in charge of it. From a Swedish perspective and considering the power struggles earlier in history, for example, between the criminal law and forensic psychiatry, it is understandable that representatives of the criminal law want to have a firm grip on the *formal* power to decide. This needs to be questioned in a few areas relating to ascription of responsibility. But *even if* one were to be of such an opinion regarding all aspects of the formal powers, this does not, of course, necessarily mean that the use of that power should stay materially uninfluenced by psychology, psychiatry, etc, still *within* the bubble, *within* the practice of blaming (as a moral practice).

5

Attributability and Accountability in the Criminal Law

ROBIN ZHENG*

ACCOUNTS OF RESPONSIBILITY abound in theories of criminal law because the criminal law represents the severest, most powerful and hence most potentially problematic means available to us of morally responding to individuals. Because the immediate hard treatment of criminal punishment places tremendous burdens on individuals, and the long-term negative repercussions of a criminal record greatly worsen their life prospects, criminal law and the criminal justice system stand in need of heavy-duty social and moral justification. Such justification can be found (at least in part) in theories of criminal law that provide accounts of criminal responsibility. The primary question to be answered is this: who can (or should), and under what conditions, be tried and punished by the criminal law? This is typically undergirded by a further question: what is the relationship between criminal responsibility and moral responsibility? By defining highly circumscribed conditions under which people can be held criminally responsible, and by grounding these conditions in deeper moral principles, theories of criminal responsibility thus serve (among other things) to justify the entire enterprise of criminal law as a whole. In this chapter, I examine several prominent theories of criminal responsibility, drawing on an extant distinction from the moral responsibility literature to divide them into what I call 'attributability-first' and 'accountability-first' theories of criminal responsibility. On that basis, I distinguish two different conceptions of the person in the criminal law.

I. TWO CONCEPTS OF RESPONSIBILITY

The distinction between responsibility as attributability and responsibility as accountability is by now a long-standing and well-established distinction in

* I am grateful to participants of the Criminal Law's Person workshops for their helpful feedback on earlier versions of this chapter.

the philosophical literature on responsibility. Unfortunately, it is also a rather changeable and variegated distinction, used for different ends by different people under different names. The situation is further complicated by the many taxonomies of different types of responsibility that also populate the literature.[1] Following TM Scanlon, my view of the attributability–accountability distinction takes as its starting point the idea that questions about responsibility arise from two separate and distinct sources of philosophical concern.[2] This is reflected in the distinction's having influence in two distinct areas of philosophy: moral psychology on the one hand, within which Gary Watson's 'Two Faces of Responsibility' represents the canonical presentation,[3] and political philosophy on the other, as represented by Scanlon's discussion in *What We Owe Each Other*. On Watson's view of the distinction, attributability is a necessary condition for accountability. Attributing an action to an agent amounts to forming an aretaic appraisal of her virtuous or vicious qualities on the basis of that action, whereas holding an agent accountable for some action amounts to further subjecting her to negative sanctions for it. Only the latter question raises issues of fairness – it is not unfair to judge a person vicious if she really is, but it might be unfair to subject her to hard treatment for it if she had no opportunity to avoid becoming so (and it would be even more unfair to subject her to hard treatment for an action that is not attributable to her as an exercise of her agency).

By contrast, on Scanlon's view of the distinction (between what he calls 'responsibility as attributability' and 'substantive responsibility'), one can possess attributability without substantive responsibility and vice versa, because they have 'different moral roots'.[4] For an agent to have responsibility as attributability for an action is just for that action to be a legitimate basis for praising or blaming her, whereas to have substantive responsibility for an action is for her to be legitimately assigned burdens or obligations as a consequence of it. One can have substantive responsibility without responsibility as attributability, Scanlon claims, in cases such as strict liability, for example, a milk vendor whose conduct is absolutely faultless – and hence provides no grounds for blame – but unluckily sells some contaminated milk. Even without responsibility as attributability, however, the vendor is still substantively responsible in this case, that is, subject

[1] HLA Hart, *Punishment and Responsibility: Essays in the Philosophy of Law* (Oxford University Press, 2008); JM Fischer and NA Tognazzini, 'The Physiognomy of Responsibility' (2011) 82 *Philosophy and Phenomenological Research* 381; D Shoemaker, *Responsibility From the Margins* (Oxford University Press, 2015).

[2] T Scanlon, *What We Owe to Each Other* (Harvard University Press, 1998); R Zheng, 'Attributability, Accountability, and Implicit Bias' in J Saul and M Brownstein (eds), *Implicit Bias and Philosophy, Volume 2: Moral Responsibility, Structural Injustice, and Ethics* (Oxford University Press, 2016).

[3] G Watson, 'Two Faces of Responsibility' in G Watson, *Agency and Answerability: Selected Essays* (Oxford University Press, 2004).

[4] Scanlon (n 2) 290.

to penalty (or requirement to compensate sick victims, etc) because entering the milk business represents entering an 'affected area' within which one simply must uphold certain obligations and has no right to complain about being penalised for not upholding them. Notably, Scanlon's discussion of substantive responsibility leads him to justify criminal punishment without relying on the retributivist idea that punishment is deserved. Instead, his justification relies only on the fact that the law marks out an 'affected area' of illegal actions such that persons have no right to complain against being penalised if they perform them. Scanlon is careful to note that this is 'only a partial account of the conditions under which punishment is justified – an account dealing only with the "penalty" aspect of punishment' and not the condemnation that is additionally expressed by criminal punishment, which would require responsibility as attributability.[5]

On my view of the attributability–accountability distinction, however, we can arrive at a full justification of criminal punishment, because the two 'routes to responsibility', as I call them, can ultimately converge.[6] With respect to attributability, the specific concern – a metaphysical and action-theoretical one – that motivates questions about responsibility is the problem of what features of an action render it attributable to an agent as a genuine exercise of her agency. When an action has whatever feature is constitutive of (moral) agency, then directly on the basis of that action the agent deserves some (moral) appraisal *qua* agent, because that action is reflective of her agency. Paradigmatic forms of such appraisal include praise, blame and punishment. Attributability is thus the concept of moral responsibility as it is traditionally understood, the one that most occupies the moral responsibility literature.

Figure 1 Attributability and Accountability Routes to Criminal Responsibility

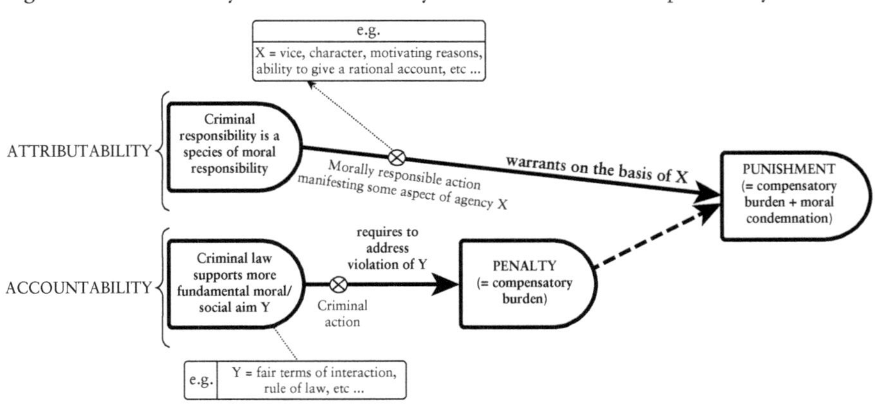

[5] ibid 267.
[6] Zheng (n 2).

By contrast, the fundamental concern along the accountability route – a moral and political one – is the problem of 'what we owe each other', as Scanlon puts it, or (more technically) how to distribute duties and burdens across a moral community in a fair and just way. When a person fails to carry out her 'responsibilities' in this sense, the purpose of a concept of accountability is in the first instance ensuring that the moral community takes up the costs of restitution for victims who have been harmed, damage that has been done, etc. It is not yet to ask whether she has acted badly or well, or what kind of agent she is. I have argued in previous work that this further question does not necessarily need answering on the accountability route, so long as the primary purpose of dividing up burdens has been fulfilled;[7] there are cases in which we can simply distribute 'penalties,' that is, burdens imposed on an agent without any accompanying moral appraisal, as remedy.[8] Whether we should investigate further into the agent's moral quality depends on larger moral and social aims of the community, and it is this further question which takes us back to the question of attributability and explains why the two concepts are so often conflated. From two different starting points and two different sets of questions, we can (but need not) arrive at the same questions of blame, punishment and the reactive attitudes.

The important point for this chapter, however, is that the further question of attributability *can* be asked, even along the accountability route, and there are cases in which answering the question is properly understood as a part of redressing harm. Indeed, the criminal law is the quintessential example of a practice of assessing attributability for the purpose of fully holding someone accountable.[9] In the case of criminal violations, it is typically (or at least paradigmatically) the case that failures of responsibility are so egregious that further investigation into the quality of the agent's conduct (ie, fault) is necessary,[10]

[7] ibid.

[8] I follow Feinberg (J Feinberg, *Doing & Deserving: Essays in the Theory of Responsibility*) (Princeton University Press, 1970)) in drawing this kind of distinction between mere 'penalty' and 'punishment'. However, I do not take a stand on whether the moral condemnation in punishment must take the form of hard treatment, eg, incarceration, that is distinct from the compensatory burdens of penalty. I am grateful to Matt Matravers for discussion on this point.

[9] But see N Lacey and H Pickard, 'From the Consulting Room to the Court Room? Taking the Clinical Model of Responsibility Without Blame into the Legal Realm' (2013) 33 *Oxford Journal of Legal Studies* 1; N Lacey and H Pickard, 'To Blame or to Forgive? Reconciling Punishment and Forgiveness in Criminal Justice' (2015) 35 *Oxford Journal of Legal Studies* 665 for a proposal according to which punishment ought to be conceived as a form of forgiveness and holding responsible *without* the affective and condemnatory aspects of blame and resentment. They make clear that such a clinical model of punishment does not aim at morally evaluating, but instead caring for and rehabilitating those who violate the criminal law. Such a view represents one way in which an accountability-first theory even of criminal responsibility might stop short of asking further questions about attributability.

[10] RA Duff, *Answering for Crime: Responsibility and Liability in the Criminal Law* (Hart Publishing, 2007) 88.

because some kind of punishment is required for fully rectifying the harm done or for deterrence. Punishment consists of moral condemnation on top of the burdens of penalty, and such condemnation is only justified if it can be established that the agent genuinely acted badly (ie, lacks an excuse, and so on). In the next section I turn to examples of theories of criminal law that take these two different routes to responsibility.

II. TWO ROUTES TO CRIMINAL RESPONSIBILITY: THE ATTRIBUTABILITY ROUTE

Let me begin with a few important clarifications. First, the attributability–accountability distinction distinguishes two different *concepts* of responsibility, but does not itself provide any substantive first-order conceptions of responsibility,[11] either as attributability or accountability. As shown in Figure 1 above, different conceptions of attributability – that is, proposals concerning which feature(s) of agency are required for criminal/moral responsibility – include such things as motivating reasons,[12] the ability to give a rational account of one's actions,[13] free will or choice, etc.[14] Similarly, different conceptions of responsibility as accountability – that is, proposals concerning the more fundamental social aims underwritten by the criminal law – include the fair terms of interaction between citizens,[15] the rule of law,[16] consequentialist aims, etc. (I will say much more about all of this shortly.) This means that two theories of criminal responsibility might agree on a particular conception of responsibility, while still addressing two different concepts of responsibility. In other words, they might agree substantively on the first question I posed – who and under what conditions criminal sanctions are justified – while disagreeing on the second question – the relationship between criminal responsibility and moral responsibility. I distinguish theories of criminal responsibility according to their answers to this second question: attributability-first theories that treat criminal law as just another practice of moral appraisal, and accountability-first theories that treat the moral appraisal inherent in criminal law as serving part of a larger project of the social and moral division of duties and burdens.

[11] See Rawls for further discussion of a 'concept,' the general specification of some notion, and a 'conception', one particular proposal as to what substantively realises or instantiates that concept: J Rawls, *A Theory of Justice* (Belknap Press, 1971; 2009).

[12] V Tadros, *Criminal Responsibility* (Oxford University Press, 2005).

[13] Duff, *Answering for Crime* (n 10).

[14] J Gardner, *Offences and Defences: Selected Essays in the Philosophy of Criminal Law* (Oxford University Press, 2007).

[15] A Ripstein, *Equality, Responsibility, and the Law* (Cambridge University Press, 2001).

[16] A Ripstein, *Force and Freedom: Kant's Legal and Political Philosophy* (Harvard University Press, 2010); Thorburn, ch 6 in this volume.

Victor Tadros' theory of criminal responsibility is an attributability-first theory *par excellence*.[17] According to Tadros: 'The practice of holding an agent criminally responsible for breaching the law is a specific instance of the more general practice of holding agents responsible for what they do'.[18] His answer to the question of what makes criminal responsibility a distinctive practice of responsibility, which derives from his view of the communicative function of the criminal justice system, is as follows:

> Central to the idea of criminal conviction is that the agent is morally criticized in a public forum for performing the act in question. That fact has implications for the nature of criminal responsibility. For it is only those who are deserving of such criticism, those who have displayed a moral vice through their conduct, who deserve to be convicted of a criminal offence. And if that is the case, a theory of criminal responsibility will involve distinguishing those who have manifested the appropriate kind of vice from those who have not, as well as distinguishing those who are responsible for the appropriate kind of action from those who are not.[19]

From this it is clear that Tadros conceives of moral responsibility in terms of attributability, where the primary purpose is moral criticism of an agent: in particular, moral criticism that is only deserved when agents display a moral vice through their conduct. And the distinct function of the criminal law as a practice of responsibility is to broadcast this moral criticism to the wider community.

On this attributability route to criminal responsibility, then, we must determine what feature of actions and agents render an action properly attributable to her as a manifestation of vice. Indeed, this is the third of Tadros' four elements of criminal responsibility: 'it is necessary to show that the action was appropriately related to the agent qua agent'.[20] If we can determine that an agent is appropriately linked to her action in this way – in other words, that it is an exercise of her agency – then she counts as responsible (in the attributability sense) for her action. Directly on the basis of the action, then, the agent deserves the public moral criticism and hard treatment of the criminal justice system. Responsibility as attributability is thus the only concept of responsibility with which Tadros' theory is concerned. As he puts it, 'In holding an agent responsible for an action, we imply that the action reflects on the agent in some way … Such imposition [of criminal responsibility] says something personal about the agent qua agent'.[21]

The particular conception of attributability that Tadros adopts, which he calls 'attribution-responsibility', is a kind of reasons-responsiveness theory. For Tadros, attributability is grounded in the 'motivating reasons' behind an

[17] Tadros (n 12).
[18] ibid 71.
[19] ibid.
[20] ibid 101.
[21] ibid 39.

agent's psychology, that is, the reasons in light of which an agent's actions and attitudes seem in some sense worthwhile or warranted by her own lights. This is because these psychological states of agents – their actions, beliefs, desires and emotions – are what Tadros calls the 'constituents of agency', such that 'insofar as an action is performed under the guidance of a motivating reason of the agent … that action is performed under the guidance of the agent'.[22] Furthermore, however, the motivating reasons must be ones from which the agent is not alienated. Tadros proposes that they must be coherently related to the agent's entire system of values; for even if an agent is alienated from one value, she cannot be alienated from her entire system of values because the system itself constitutes the agent.[23] This picture forms the basis of Tadros' defence against the spectre of the free will problem, which he takes to be 'central to any account of criminal responsibility'.[24] If all that is required for attributability is that an action be under the guidance of motivating reasons that are compatible with an agent's system of values – and not that she needed to be able to choose or do otherwise – then determinism no longer represents a threat to criminal responsibility.

Other conceptions of attributability might be adopted, however, and Tadros' theory is not the only attributability-first theory on hand. Character theories of criminal responsibility, more generally, are all examples of the attributability-first approach, because the core idea is that the criminal law exists to condemn or otherwise negatively pronounce judgement on an agent. In order to justifiably condemn or negatively judge an agent, however, it must be established that the agent genuinely possesses the vices or flaws under condemnation. This amounts, again, to determining that the criminal act is properly attributable to the agent as a manifestation of her agency: character theorists use the notion of 'character', rather than motivating reasons, to capture this idea. Theories of legal moralism (and retributive theories of punishment), according to which it is intrinsically valuable to punish individuals for moral wrongdoing, are another species of criminal law theory that takes the attributability route, because the notion of deserving punishment for some act is only intelligible when we understand that act to be one that truly reflects on the agent; people do not deserve punishment for actions that did not flow from their own agency.

On the attributability route to criminal responsibility, then, the foundational question of the criminal law is how to go about determining when some criminal act is properly attributable to an agent as an exercise of her agency. And this is because the criminal justice system is conceived of as just a particular instance of our more general practice of holding one another (attributively) responsible.

[22] ibid 31.
[23] ibid 40–41.
[24] ibid 69.

III. TWO ROUTES TO CRIMINAL RESPONSIBILITY: THE ACCOUNTABILITY ROUTE

On the accountability route to criminal responsibility, by contrast, the story is a bit more complicated. While the task of the criminal justice system is still to determine when people are at fault for their harmful actions, and hence subject to morally condemnatory appraisal, this aim is not (necessarily) intrinsically valuable in and of itself. Rather, it is grounded in a more fundamental aim of appropriately distributing the burdens required to redress harms. Hence the relationship of criminal responsibility to moral responsibility traditionally understood (ie, attributability) is importantly different: the entire enterprise of criminal law is subordinate to and derivative of larger moral and social aims of the moral community. In other words, there exists no independent moral standard for governing the practice of assigning criminal responsibility and imposing criminal sanctions, if this is conceived of as somehow external to a society's aims.

Perhaps the clearest exponent of an accountability-first theory of criminal is Arthur Ripstein's account in *Equality, Responsibility, and the Law*.[25] According to Ripstein:

> [L]egal responsibility is related to moral responsibility, but distinct from it. The role of law and of a conception of fairness are, as Kant put it, to make freedom possible, rather than to make morality actual. Their primary concern is not with the quality of a person's will or character, but with the external aspects of action.[26]

He continues:

> The strategy is to make responsibility a question that is – to borrow another phrase from Rawls – political, not metaphysical. To say that it is political is not to say that it is always best decided by democratic assemblies, nor that it is inevitably the result of partisan struggles for power. It is to say instead that the account is specific to political morality, rather than dependent on a more comprehensive moral or metaphysical account.[27]

For Ripstein, then, the entire practice of criminal responsibility serves to undergird the more fundamental aim of maintaining fair terms of interaction between the members of a society. The central problem here is one of distributing 'losses' and burdens in a fair and just way in the aftermath of harm and wrongdoing; according to Ripstein, 'questions about responsibility become pressing for political philosophy in those cases in which things do not work out quite as planned'.[28] When things go wrong in these ways, there is in the first

[25] Ripstein, *Equality, Responsibility, and the Law* (n 15).
[26] ibid 4.
[27] ibid 12.
[28] ibid 3.

instance a problem of dividing up the costs, that is, of determining when 'losses appropriately lie where they fall' and when they should instead be transferred to someone else in ways that maintain relations of equality and fairness between the parties involved.[29] It is clear, then, that this is a concept of responsibility as accountability rather than as attributability. The question at hand is not a metaphysical or action-theoretical one of determining which actions can be attributable to agents, as suitable bases of appraisal in order to 'make morality actual'; it is rather a question of political philosophy, of finding, as Ripstein puts it, 'some principled way of determining whose problem it is'.[30]

Against this backdrop, the purpose of the criminal law is to redistribute the costs of particular kinds of wrongdoing in ways that maintain fair terms of interaction between individuals. Ripstein understands the latter in terms of a balance between liberty and security: since fair terms of interaction 'must allow people freedom to do as they please, but also make sure that they are secure from the activities of others',[31] their function is to 'set limits within which people must moderate their behaviour in light of the claims of others [but within which] people are free to do as they choose'.[32] On this accountability route to criminal responsibility, then, ascribing responsibility and imposing sanctions serves the more fundamental aim of fairly distributing duties and burdens across the moral community in a fair and just way. 'Corrective justice, criminal law, and tort law together', Ripstein writes, 'set out the conditions of the responsibility, the conditions under which agents appropriately bear the costs of their choices'.[33]

Ripstein's particular conception of accountability is one according to which there is some background distribution of unavoidable risks that people impose on one another in the ordinary course of being members of a cooperative society, that is, risks which are simply inherent to the actions involved in living together with others. Some actions, however, impose unreasonable risks on others because they do not give appropriate weight to others' interests, and when such a risk 'ripens into an injury', the agent who performed the action is required to 'own' the risk and make up that loss to the victim in order to restore the background distribution of risks and hence equality between agent and victim.[34] While both tort law and criminal law serve this same function, criminal law is reserved for cases in which a person 'seeks to substitute private rationality for public standards of reasonableness', that is, when a person deems the pursuit of their own ends to outweigh the interests and rights of others. Here, the mental element of *mens rea* is crucial because 'a person must be aware that the rights of others

[29] ibid.
[30] ibid.
[31] ibid 6.
[32] ibid 9.
[33] ibid 3.
[34] ibid 53.

are in jeopardy if his action is to count as such a substitution'.[35] After all, if an agent only unintentionally harms an agent, then it does not represent an attempt by that agent to privilege her private ends over the rights of others; the harm to the victim can in these cases be rectified merely by paying damages under tort law.

This account of how tort and criminal law occupy distinct domains but perform a single unified function allows Ripstein to mount a justification of criminal punishment according to which – unlike in Scanlon's theory of substantive responsibility – hard treatment is truly essential to punishment, but also according to which – unlike in attributability theories – hard treatment is not (necessarily) something that is deserved by the agent as a form of moral appraisal. Instead, for Ripstein, the hard treatment inherent to punishment vindicates the system of rights that was violated by the perpetrator of the crime, and thus restores fair terms of interaction. He writes:

> Punitive damages serve both to denounce such behaviour as unreasonable and to ensure that it is irrational, by shifting the cost–benefit analysis so that the apparent advantage disappears. They denounce by denying the claim that other people's rights are merely prices.[36]

In these cases of morally egregious harm – murder, theft and so on – merely requiring that the perpetrator repay damages suffered by the victim would not do justice to the fact that the victim's rights were violated, and that the harm that befell the victim was not merely some cosmic misfortune or accident. It is for this reason that – even along the accountability route – we reach questions about punishment, which necessarily depend on at least some minimal investigation of an agent's intentions and other mental states. Notably, Ripstein does not deny that 'some other standard of responsibility, external to settled legal practice' could be ultimately be used to determine criminal responsibility.[37] In other words, once it has been established that criminal sanctions might be relevant, we could return to a specific conception of attributability to determine if they really are justifiable in the particular case at hand, that is, whether the criminal act really is attributable to the agent in such a way as to deserve punishment. But Ripstein seeks to show that a conception of responsibility as attributability need not necessarily be involved, and that even if we do make use of one, it does not represent the ultimate aim or function of the criminal justice system as a whole. Instead, the criminal justice system as a whole is justified by its role in ensuring the proper distribution of duties and burdens that constitute fair terms of interaction – that is, as a practice of responsibility as accountability.

[35] ibid 134.
[36] ibid 153.
[37] ibid 135.

In his later *Force and Freedom: Kant's Legal and Political Philosophy*,[38] Ripstein defends a different view of the fundamental aim underwriting criminal punishment, which is to provide the transcendental social conditions necessary for the possibility of individual freedom. By promising *ex ante* that it will punish transgressions, and then following through with the punishment, the criminal law ensures the supreme authority of the state against offenders who seek to exempt themselves from it. This account, along with other rule-of-law accounts such as Malcolm Thorburn's,[39] are also accountability-first theories because their primary aim is not to morally appraise agents, but to ensure the rule of law (which in turn makes possible individual freedom, equal rights of all persons, etc). Another prominent theory taking the accountability route is HLA Hart's,[40] who explicitly rejects both the moralist's retributive justification of punishment as well as the expressive theory of punishment. Hart argues that the role of the 'principle of responsibility' – the constraint against punishing someone who lacked the capacity and fair opportunity to do otherwise – is not justified because criminal law is a practice of moral responsibility, but rather because such a requirement serves the greater aims of justice and fairness, and the value of ensuring individual choice to 'predict and plan the future course of our lives within the coercive framework of the law'.[41] Thus, Hart is not concerned with moral appraisal and attributability, but rather with accountability and an overall (broadly consequentialist) system of fairly distributing burdens.

Before I conclude this section, let me briefly compare and contrast two other prominent theories of criminal responsibility using the attributability–accountability distinction. Both John Gardner and Antony Duff adopt the same specific conception of attributability: a conception on which the core notion is that of an agent giving a rational account of her actions.[42] Agents that are capable of doing so – that is, those with the capacity to respond to reasons – are

[38] Ripstein, *Force and Freedom* (n 16).

[39] M Thorburn, 'Constitutionalism and the Limits of the Criminal Law' in RA Duff et al (eds), *The Structures of Criminal Law* (Oxford University Press, 2011); M Thorburn, 'Criminal Law as Public Law' in RA Duff and G Stuart (eds), *Philosophical Foundations of Criminal Law* (Oxford University Press, 2011); Thorburn, ch 6 in this volume. I am grateful to Malcolm Thorburn for discussion of these issues. In my view, the attributability–accountability distinction does not quite line up with the utilitarian–moralist distinction that Thorburn (in this volume) draws, because accountability concerns about the fair distribution of burdens – as in Ripstein, Duff and Hart's accounts – can still lead down the road to 'moralised' investigation into whether an agent was acting badly when she violated the law.

[40] Hart (n 1).

[41] ibid 182.

[42] It is worth noting that Shoemaker (n 1) has argued that this notion of appropriately being expected to give an account of oneself, 'answerability', represents a distinct concept of responsibility; he thus adopts a tripartite theory of responsibility as attributability, answerability and accountability. As my discussion of Gardner and Duff indicates, however, I suspect that answerability may ultimately be subsumed under either attributability or accountability.

responsible, and agents that cannot do so are not.[43] For Gardner, however, the criminal law serves to delineate the conditions under which actions 'show people in a bad light';[44] an excuse, for example, is 'something that blocks the path from an adverse judgment about an action to a correspondingly adverse judgment about the person whose action it is'.[45] It is clear from this that Gardner's theory takes criminal responsibility to be a special kind of responsibility as attributability. Thus, he argues that the value of the law should be thought of as 'first and foremost intrinsic rather than instrumental', where that intrinsic value consists of providing individuals with a forum for giving rational explanations for their actions.[46] He writes: 'The fundamental point [of criminal law] is to have structured explanatory dialogues in public ... This point is not a point relative to which the procedure is instrumental; rather the point is in the procedure'.[47]

For Duff, by contrast, responsibility as attributability – which, again, he like Gardner conceives of in terms of being appropriately subject to the demand for a rational account of one's actions – is ultimately grounded in 'prospective responsibilities', that is, in duties to perform certain actions and treat people in certain ways, which are themselves grounded in specific role relationships that pick out what types of actions are owed and which people have a right to claim these types of treatment. One is (attributively) responsible for some action 'only if and because' one had a prospective responsibility to someone, which required the performance or omission of it.[48] Thus prospective responsibilities are the actual source of the reasons to which people are capable of responding to or not, and for which they must answer when they fail to properly respond. This picture of prospective responsibilities, then, is another substantive conception of accountability (comparable to Ripstein's conception of a background distribution of risks). On this accountability route to responsibility,[49] questions of

[43] Elsewhere, Duff writes that the 'element of truth' in character theories is that 'the actions for which a person is convicted and punished must be "hers": they must be suitably related to attitudes or motives which are aspects of her continuing identity as a person' – RA Duff, *Criminal Attempts* (Oxford University Press, 1996).

[44] Gardner, *Offences and Defences* (n 14) 127.

[45] ibid 122.

[46] ibid 188.

[47] ibid 189.

[48] Duff, *Answering for Crime* (n 10) 29.

[49] Duff's accountability-first theory of criminal law is completed with an explanation of why we must sometimes take up the *further* question of criminal sanctions, as opposed to merely recompensing victims for harm. He writes: 'Sometimes, even when a wrong has been done, it is indeed more important to seek to repair harm, and unhelpful to focus on the wrong: but sometimes it matters that we recognize and respond to wrongs as wrongs ... [because] we owe this to their victims, to their perpetrators (if we are to treat them as responsible agents), and to ourselves as citizens of the policy' (ibid 88). In the first place, then, what matters is holding people accountable for failing to live up to their duties to act and treat others in certain ways, but particularly egregious breaches of such responsibilities are not fully redressed until the perpetrators are called to give accounts of their actions. Compare, again, Ripstein's explanation that criminal law is invoked particularly in cases where victims have not just been harmed but have had their rights violated.

whether an agent can properly be called on to give a rational account of her actions derive from the more fundamental aim of ensuring that people uphold their prospective responsibilities. There is no concern here with whether some action reflects badly or well on an agent, but only on whether that action was owed to someone as part of a distribution of duties and burdens across the community. Duff's discussion of control, for instance, is not grounded in the thought that uncontrolled actions do not reflect an agent's character, but rather in the thought that one cannot have duties to bring about things over which one has no control.[50] The different origins of Gardner's attributability theory and Duff's accountability theory of criminal responsibility explain their disagreement over whether responsibility is essentially relational, that is, whether an agent's rational account of her actions must be directed towards a specific interlocutor.[51] On an attributability-first theory which functions primarily to determine what sorts of moral appraisal and sanction an agent deserves on the basis of her action, responsibility is not essentially relational because appraisal does not depend on any specific interlocutor. But on an accountability-first theory, responsibility *is* essentially relational because it arises from a distribution of duties and burdens among the members of a community.

IV. TWO PERSONS OF CRIMINAL RESPONSIBILITY

Thus far I have argued that theories of criminal responsibility can be divided into attributability-first theories, which take criminal responsibility to be a species of moral responsibility (as attributability) with the primary purpose of appraising agents on the basis of their actions, and accountability-first theories, which view the appraisal inherent in ascribing criminal responsibility as subordinate to more fundamental social and political aims of enforcing a certain distribution of moral duties and burdens across a community. In this section I draw out the two different persons assumed by these different concepts of responsibility in criminal law.

I begin with the responsible person in the attributability sense, as it is perhaps the more familiar one. The defining characteristic of the attributively responsible person is she expresses herself in action. For it is only when actions are expressive of her agency that they can serve as the basis for moral appraisal, including the public condemnation of criminal punishment. What is presupposed by the notion of an agent expressing herself in action? First, there must be a self. It is no surprise, then, that the term 'responsibility' is a relatively recent one, first appearing as noun only in the latter part of the eighteenth century,[52] after the

[50] Duff, *Answering for Crime* (n 10) 58.

[51] ibid 25; Gardner, *Offences and Defences* (n 14) 187.

[52] R McKeon, 'The Development and the Significance of the Concept of Responsibility' (1957) 11 *Revue Internationale de Philosophie* 3.

Enlightenment and the emergence of the modern self – or more specifically, we might say, the post-Kantian[53] self. The post-Kantian self is 'an individualized, unified self – organized around the will',[54] or the 'free individual, enjoying autonomy and control as a responsible, choosing being',[55] who is born from the oppositional relationship of 'the I to the Not-self [which] is crucial in all the post-Kantian systems'.[56] This self emerges from what Richard McKeon in his essay on the historical development of the concept of responsibility calls the 'problem of imputation', that is, the 'question whether or not the causality of human actions is essentially the same as the causality of physical motions'.[57] For Kant, of course, the answer is no. The post-Kantian self is thus set apart from nature, subject to (moral) laws which are distinct from the physical laws of nature that drive everything else; there are thus actions that may be attributed to the self and actions that are external to it, the latter of which are mere parts of the Not-self. Notably, this self is inextricable from the free-will problem, because it is conceptually dependent on the dichotomy between moral and physical causality.

In much of criminal law theory, then, the person is conceived of in terms of the post-Kantian self.[58] This is why attributability-first theories of criminal responsibility take the latter to be merely an instance of the former. Alan Norrie writes:

> 'As with morality, so with law' – this is the motto of modern criminal justice thinking. Both criminal law theory and the philosophy of punishment possess the same Kantian, retributive emphasis on individual responsibility as the proper basis for legitimate punishment. There is a homology between the forms of legal practice and those of moral philosophy, and the common core, in a variety of hues, is a Kantian, retributive philosophy of punishment.[59]

So what is crucial for the criminal law's person on the attributability route is maintaining the self, that is, maintaining the dichotomy between the self and what is outside the self. Character, choice and capacity theories all serve this purpose, albeit in slightly different ways.[60] According to choice theories of

[53] By 'post-Kantian' I simply mean to refer to views from Kant onwards, since the specific differences between Kant and those who followed in his footsteps are less important for my purposes than what they have in common.

[54] LJ Daston and P Galison, *Objectivity* (Zone Books, 2010) 33.

[55] AW Norrie, *Punishment, Responsibility, and Justice: A Relational Critique* (Oxford University Press, 2000) 94.

[56] L Hurtrez, 'Nature and Subjectivity; Coleridge and Fichteanism' (2001) 18 *Coleridge Bulletin* 1, 6.

[57] McKeon (n 52) 10.

[58] Norrie (n 55).

[59] ibid 3.

[60] See MS Moore, *Placing Blame: A Theory of the Criminal Law* (Oxford University Press, 2010); and Tadros (n 12) for a slightly different taxonomy of these categories; I have formulated mine so as to preserve elements of both. The theory of choice (understood as composed of capacity and opportunity) described here belongs to Hart (n 1).

criminal responsibility, the criminally responsible person – the appropriate subject of criminal law and sanctions – is one who freely chooses her actions. A large part of free choice is cashed out in terms of capacity: thus, on capacity theories of criminal responsibility, the criminally responsible person has the psychological capacity to do otherwise than she actually does. (The remaining part of free choice is cashed out in terms of opportunity: even if an agent is fully psychologically capable, the alternative options to her action may have been so costly, especially as compared with others' options, that it would be unreasonable to expect her to have acted otherwise. In such cases, she suffers from diminished opportunity rather than capacity.) In short, the thrust behind choice and capacity theories is the notion of an agent being able to do otherwise than she actually did – a concern that is ultimately grounded[61] in the post-Kantian injunctive to distinguish action caused by the self, rather than the physical laws of causality governing what is outside the self.

Character theories typically do not try to draw such a strong division between Self and Not-self; they argue that the absence or strength of a given capacity may itself reflect an agent's self.[62] Yet character theories still require that there is a self. Recall that Tadros mounts a defence against the problem of free will on the grounds that any theory of criminal responsibility must be able to give a principled answer as to why some actions are properly attributable to an agent while others are not. He writes: 'But such a distinction can only be articulated by showing the way in which the idea of agency is capable of being distinguished from other kinds of causes of action'.[63] Again, what matters here is the post-Kantian notion that the self must be driven by something other than the causal laws that drive everything outside of the self. Tadros' defence consists of an account of the self, according to which it is constituted by a system of values. For Tadros, the system of values can itself be determined by causal laws, but what the system of values affords is a normative perspective on the world – an agent's sense of the reasons why something ought to be the case over and above what it is the case – which still manages to achieve the required separation between Self and Not-self.

This picture of the attributively responsible person is further exemplified in the criminal law's treatment of insanity, which Michael Moore has argued is the site where 'the law's presuppositions about persons are closest to the surface'.[64] According to Moore, there are four main proposals as to why

[61] Compatibilist choice and capacity theorists might balk at the latter clause ruling out physical causal laws. But insofar as their task is to advocate an understanding of free choice that retains the spirit of being able to do otherwise while eschewing deeper metaphysical claims, ie, insofar as they are defined against incompatibilists, it is still this post-Kantian concern that motivates the project.

[62] J Gardner, 'The Mark of Responsibility' (2003) 23 *Oxford Journal of Legal Studies* 157; Tadros (n 12).

[63] Tadros (n 12) 69.

[64] Moore (n 60) 595.

individuals with mental illness are not criminally responsible persons, namely: that the actions of such individuals are (1) caused by illness rather than free choice; (2) not intentional; (3a) performed out of ignorance of fact; (3b) due to irresistible compulsion; or – Moore's preferred explanation – because such individuals are (4) irrational.[65] These proposals may all be read as explanations of how mentally ill individuals lack the proper post-Kantian self. In (1), (2) and (3b) there is no self with its own principles of causality (eg, intention) to be distinguished from other physical causes (eg, illness, compulsion). In (3a) and (4), even insofar as a self is distinguishable from the Not-self, it is not properly 'hooked up' to the world in a way that makes it recognisably similar enough to ourselves to enable appraisal. (Though I shall return to reconsider (4) in a later section.) I will not elaborate any further here on the more detailed psychological attributes involved in the view. What matters is that for attributability-first theories of criminal responsibility, the crucial feature of the person who expresses herself in action is that of a post-Kantian self, separate and distinct from everything and everyone else. Such a person can be morally appraised on the basis of her actions. And because her actions can be attributed to her as reflecting badly or well upon herself, she deserves to be judged blameworthy, and to receive the hard treatment and condemnation of the criminal law.

I now turn to the criminal law's person as conceived of by accountability-first theories, which is perhaps somewhat less familiar. The defining characteristic of the accountable person is that she takes up her part of the moral duties and burdens shared by the community. Such a person, unlike the attributively responsible person, is thus essentially defined in relation to others; the accountable person could not exist in isolation from a community of others. Certainly, the accountable person will need some of the same psychological attributes that the attributively responsible person does: one cannot fulfil one's share of moral duties without being able to perform goal-oriented actions, to think and act in response to reasons, to connect up belief and desire to form an intention, and so on. But these basic psychological attributes of agency are the minimal preconditions of being a member of a moral community, rather than the criterial conditions on which membership turns. One simply cannot be a member of a moral community if one does not communicate with others through language, for example, or if one is an entity that lacks mental states; my claim is that the ability to make free choices is on a par with these. What matters for accountability – the subset of relevant psychological attributes, which are emphasised – are instead relational attributes.

Ripstein, for instance, writes: 'The only features of human action that are of interest to the law are the uncontroversial ones … Most philosophical discussions of action are driven by issues that legal theory need not resolve'.[66] To illustrate,

[65] ibid 598.
[66] Ripstein, *Equality, Responsibility, and the Law* (n 15) 14.

he cites the classic problem of the 'accordion effect', that is, that actions can be represented under different descriptions incorporating different consequences and mental states, for example, moving a finger, turning on a light, alerting a burglar and concludes with the following:

> But all competing accounts start from the shared belief that it makes perfectly good sense to say that someone did all of them … In the context of legal and political morality, the appropriate description of what someone has done will always depend in part on *its relation to the protected interests of others*.[67]

Such different descriptions matter for ascribing the criminal responsibility to the attributively responsible person, since a description of an act on which a person did not perform it intentionally (eg, alerting the burglar) would mean that it cannot be attributed to her for the purpose of criminal sanction understood as moral appraisal. But they do not matter for ascribing criminal responsibility to the accountable person, for this requires only that she did something that falls under the purview of certain relationships to others in which she stands. As Ripstein puts it, criminal responsibility (as accountability) requires only that ordinary fact that persons, with the exception of children and the mentally ill, are 'capable of moderating their behaviour in light of the interests of others'.[68]

Similarly, Duff begins his answer to the question of 'Who can be responsible?' by stating that we possess responsibilities 'in virtue of satisfying any of a wide range of normatively significant descriptions – in virtue of our participation in that wide range of social practices within which such descriptions have their normative significance'.[69] These normatively significant descriptions – parent, neighbour, shopkeeper, employer – are in effect social roles that define sets of relationships (parent–child, neighbour–neighbour, shopkeeper–shopper, employer–employee) across which specific duties and burdens get divided (eg, that employers fairly compensate and maintain decent working conditions for their employees, that employees perform the work for which they are compensated). While Duff goes on to say that having responsibilities presupposes that one is a rational (ie, reasons-responsive) agent, the reasons to which agents respond – those relevant for responsibility – are specifically those grounded in social roles and participation in social practice. He writes: 'The connection between responsibility and reason-responsiveness should now be clear. Our prospective responsibilities generate reasons – for action, thought, or feeling – to which we should attend'.[70] Like Ripstein, and unlike Tadros, Duff then deflects the problem of free will by suggesting that it will either dissolve or lose force 'once we are clear about the criteria and conditions of responsibility

[67] ibid (emphasis mine).
[68] ibid.
[69] RA Duff, 'Answering for Crime' (2006) 106 *Proceedings of the Aristotelian Society* 87.
[70] Duff, *Answering for Crime* (n 10) 40.

that obtain within our responsibility-ascribing practices, and realise that we can – because we do – participate successfully in such practices'.[71]

On an accountability-first theory, then, insanity would exempt an individual from criminal responsibility primarily because the illness prevents her from being a full member of the moral community. In other words, it would prevent certain relationships from being possible insofar as individuals with mental illness are unfit to occupy certain social roles. While I do not know of any account in the literature (Ripstein only mentions mental illness in passing) that explicitly espouses such a view, it is straightforward enough to see how an accountability theory could generate exemptions for mental illness just as easily as attributability theories. While an attributability theory would hold that mentally ill individuals are not fit for certain kinds of moral appraisal, an accountability theory would hold, again, that mentally ill individuals are not fit for certain kinds of relationships. (Such an account could, of course, hold that an individual's mental illness might render her unfit for some relationships while still allowing for others.) It is possible, for instance, that Moore's proposal that mental illness exempts persons from criminal responsibility because they are irrational is actually grounded in concerns with accountability rather than attributability. When he writes that we can only ascribe responsibility to a person when we 'understand her in the same fundamental way that we understand ourselves and others in everyday life', this might be understood as the claim that we cannot view such a person as member of our moral community, as much as a claim that we cannot judge such a person blameworthy.[72]

On accountability-first theories, then, the criminally responsible person is – to use a Rawlsian turn of phrase – an essentially political rather than metaphysical being: what is most relevant is not the features that serve as the conditions that make the person into a moral agent, which are mere preconditions for accountability, but instead the features that make the person into a member of a moral community. To put it another (and again Rawlsian) way, what matters is not so much that the person is rational in the sense of being responsive to reasons, but that the person is reasonable in the sense of being responsive to reasons stemming from the interests of others. And to further mine this Rawlsian and Kantian line of thought, this is because the law is not an instrument of cosmic justice or actualiser of morality but is rather subordinate to the more fundamental social and political aims of a cooperative society.

V. ATTRIBUTABILITY VERSUS ACCOUNTABILITY

So far, I have not argued for the superiority of the attributability approach over the accountability approach. In this concluding section, I briefly present

[71] ibid 42.
[72] Moore (n 60) 608.

some preliminary considerations that seem to favour accountability-first over attributability-first theories.

In the first place, I should note that when it comes to the criminal law, considerations of both responsibility as attributability and responsibility as accountability seem unavoidable.[73] Even the most thoroughgoing attributability-first theorist surely must concede that there is an important distinction between moral wrongdoings that warrant the particularly harsh form of moral appraisal of the criminal law, and other wrongs which do not – and however this distinction is cashed out, it will typically refer to broader social and moral aims that ground responsibility as accountability. And accountability-theorists are typically constrained by at least some considerations of fairness that refer to the same features of agents that make acts attributable to them as agents. This means, perhaps, that there are not two wholly distinct persons of the criminal law according to the two kinds of theories. As I stated in the previous section, the psychological features required for minimal agency presupposed by accountability-first theories are in some sense 'thinner' than the social and relational attributes they emphasise, but they are in another sense quite 'thick' if we view them from the perspective of attributability-first theories. I am happy to concede, then, that it is more a difference in emphasis than a difference in kind.[74] But such a difference is important, and not only because the relational attributes crucial for accountability are much less often highlighted in discussions of the criminal law's person.

For one thing, attributability-first theories are by their nature essentially backward-looking, and hence may find it more difficult to accommodate other recognisable aims of the criminal law, for example, deterrence, reformation, rehabilitation, that are forward-looking. And whether or not a person deserves some negative appraisal is a separate matter from whether that appraisal should be expressed; the moral responsibility literature, for instance, distinguishes sharply between judging that someone is blameworthy and actually blaming them (which is often thought to add some extra ingredient such as reactive attitudes, emotions, or modifications of a relationship).[75] By contrast, accountability-first theories naturally incorporate forward-looking considerations by beginning with the more fundamental moral and social aims to which the criminal law is subservient, and backward-looking concerns about attributability arise only later. Another concern for attributability-first theories is that it is somewhat unclear why moral wrongdoing per se should be any business of the modern liberal state, whereas accountability-first theories easily avoid this worry by subsuming any moral appraisal incurred under the social aims they serve (where those social aims do involve some, more minimal moral considerations).

[73] I am grateful to Matt Matravers and Alan Norrie for pushing me to clarify this point.
[74] I am grateful to Susanna Blumenthal for discussion of this point.
[75] DJ Coates and NA Tognazzini, *Blame: Its Nature and Norms* (Oxford University Press, 2013).

Finally, one other difference is discernible in two recent kinds of challenges to the legitimacy of the criminal justice system, which can be viewed as challenges corresponding to the attributively responsible person, on the one hand, and the accountable person, on the other. The first, which comes from the increasingly powerful investigatory and predictive tools made possible by neuroscience and behavioural genetics, is really just the old challenge of the free-will problem in modern guise. The purported challenge is that if a person exhibits brain abnormalities or normal underdevelopment (eg, in adolescence) detectable through neuroscientific methods or possesses genes that have been demonstrated to predict certain behaviours and traits (eg, aggressive behaviours, alcoholism), then that person lacks moral blameworthiness and hence moral responsibility (as attributability) for her actions because they were caused by features of her brain or by her genes rather than herself. This particular challenge has, in my view, been handily met by criminal law theorists who have clarified the actual use of neuroscientific and genetic evidence in the law (which occurs mainly in sentencing rather than conviction), and who have made clear that insofar as there is no simple or linear causal path from neuroscientific or genetic factors to behaviour, such evidence has very limited bearing on particular cases in the criminal law.[76] Moreover, such a challenge does not affect theories that take the accountability route to criminal responsibility.

A different challenge, however, which comes from social psychology rather than neuroscience or genetics, does concern accountability-first theories of criminal responsibility. Consider the growing body of evidence of racial disparities in policing,[77] capital sentencing[78] and the decision-making of juries and judges,[79] along with experimental evidence suggesting some of the cognitive mechanisms, for example, implicit biases, that may underwrite such disparities.[80] While such results might be taken to indicate only technical issues in the implementation of criminal law, they present more serious challenges for accountability theories of criminal law that rest on background assumptions

[76] DW Denno, The Place for Neuroscience in Criminal Law in D Patterson and MS Pardo (eds), *Philosophical Foundations of Law and Neuroscience* (Oxford University Press, 2016); NA Farahany and JE Coleman, *Genetics, Neuroscience, and Criminal Responsibility: The Impact of Behavioral Sciences on Criminal Law* (Oxford University Press, 2009) 183–240; OD Jones, 'Behavioral Genetics and Crime, in Context' (2006) 69 *Law & Contemporary Problems* 81.

[77] A Gelman, J Fagan and A Kiss, 'An Analysis of the New York City Police Department's "stop-and-frisk" Policy in the Context of Claims of Racial Bias' (2007) 102 *Journal of the American Statistical Association* 813.

[78] A Alesina and E La Ferrara, 'A Test of Racial Bias in Capital Sentencing' (2014) 104 *American Economic Review* 3397.

[79] D Abrams, M Bertrand and S Mullainathan, 'Do Judges Vary in Their Treatment of Race?' (2012) 41 *Journal of Legal Studies* 347; S Anwar, P Bayer and R Hjalmarsson, 'The Impact of Jury Race in Criminal Trials' (2012) 127 *Quarterly Journal of Economics* 1017.

[80] J Correll et al, 'Across the Thin Blue Line: Police Officers and Racial Bias in the Decision to Shoot' (2007) 92 *Journal of Personality and Social Psychology* 1006; EA Plant and BM Peruche, 'The Consequences of Race for Police Officers' Responses to Criminal Suspects' (2005) 16 *Psychological Science* 180.

about fair terms of interaction (eg, Ripstein)[81] or that the duties and burdens imposed on citizens of the law are reciprocated by the law's living up to its own duties toward its citizens (eg, Duff).[82] In connection with this question, Duff considers the example of a Black defendant brought to trial in apartheid South Africa. Where such a person has been rendered – not through personal unfitness, but through the systematic prejudice of society – not a full member of the moral community, that person could justifiably claim that 'he is not responsible for his conduct before this court, or to this polity'.[83] In other words, such persons could claim that they are not responsible to the law. Critical theorists might argue even more strongly that such evidence establishes that the criminal law exists precisely as instrument for maintaining racial hierarchies.[84] The essentially relational nature of responsibility as accountability, grounded in relationships specifying fair and just distributions of duties and burdens, means that addressing such challenges is indeed relevant for the justification of today's criminal justice system. Insofar as accountability-first theories emphasise or draw attention to this second type of challenge rather than the free-will problem, then, that also seems to be a point in their favour.

There is much more to be said on all of these matters. But I hope to have established in this chapter that theories of criminal responsibility can usefully be divided into two types, and that these two types give rise to two different conceptions of the person in the criminal law: one metaphysical and defined primarily through psychological attributes; the other political and defined primarily through relational attributes. By distinguishing between attributability-first and accountability-first theories of criminal responsibility, I hope we may be better able to understand the philosophical foundations and justifications of the criminal law.

[81] Ripstein, *Equality, Responsibility, and the Law* (n 15).

[82] Duff, *Criminal Attempts* (n 43).

[83] Duff, *Answering for Crime* (n 10) 191.

[84] IB Capers, 'Critical Race Theory and Criminal Justice' (2014) 12 *Ohio State Journal of Criminal Law* 1.

6

In Search of Criminal Law's Person

MALCOLM THORBURN*

I. INTRODUCTION

THE CRIMINAL PROCESS can go wrong in many different ways. Sometimes, as was the case in the infamous 'show trials' of the late 1930s in Stalin's Russia, the problem is one of procedural fairness: the presumption of innocence has been violated, false evidence has been submitted, witnesses have been coerced, etc.[1] At other times, as was the case in much early common law criminal law, it is a matter of getting the rules of criminal responsibility wrong: the tests for fault,[2] for duress,[3] necessity, provocation,[4] or entrapment do not capture our intuitions of criminal responsibility.[5] But sometimes, the problem lies even deeper: it is a category mistake about the sort of entity who is on trial. This is the case when we treat what ought to be legal persons as mere things without rights; and it is also the case when we treat persons who lack the basic requirements of responsible agency as responsible agents. This last set of problems – category mistakes about who should be the object of criminal law – concern what I shall call 'criminal law's person'.

Consider the case of Pope Formosus. In Rome, in the year 897, Pope Stephen VI had the cadaver of his predecessor, Pope Formosus, exhumed, dressed in papal

* I am greatly indebted to Matt Matravers and Claes Lernestedt for putting together three wonderful workshops where we could work through these issues together. I owe special thanks to Michael Law-Smith for thoughtful comments and suggestions and for his excellent editorial work.

[1] R Conquest, *The Great Terror: A Reassessment* (Oxford University Press, 2007).

[2] The 'reasonable person' is at work in fault standards, duress and necessity claims, among other places in criminal law. See M Moran, *Rethinking the Reasonable Person: An Egalitarian Reconstruction of the Objective Standard* (Oxford University Press, 2003).

[3] Model Penal Code definition of duress §2.09 (American Law Institute, 1985) 37.

[4] Criminal Code of Canada s 232(2) defines provocation (in part) as follows: 'Conduct of the victim … that is of such a nature as to be sufficient to deprive an *ordinary person* of the power of self-control is provocation' (emphasis added).

[5] Much of the voluminous literature on 'criminal responsibility' concerns these various tests. But this is not our topic here. See: N Lacey, *In Search of Criminal Responsibility: Ideas, Interests, and Institutions* (Oxford University Press, 2016); V Tadros, *Criminal Responsibility* (Oxford University Press, 2005); AM Duff, *Answering for Crime: Responsibility and Liability in the Criminal Law* (Hart Publishing, 2007); MS Moore, *Placing Blame: A Theory of the Criminal Law* (Oxford University Press, 1997) etc.

robes, and put on trial for perjury and for illegally acceding to the papal throne. He was convicted and punished by having the three fingers used in a papal blessing cut off and the rest of his body thrown into the Tiber river.[6] This infamous trial – the so-called 'cadaver synod' – is troubling for many reasons, but perhaps the deepest problem with it is the fact that it was a dead person who was put on trial. No matter the fairness of the procedures, the reliability of the evidence, and the appropriateness of the standards of criminal responsibility at work, the trial is grotesque because it takes the wrong sort of object: a dead person.[7]

Now consider the case of the murderous pig of Falaise. In the year 1386 in the French city of Falaise, in Normandy, a sow was tried, convicted and executed for the murder of a child.[8] Whether or not the evidence was good, the jury impartial and the tests of criminal responsibility the right ones, it was a travesty of justice for the simple reason that it is the trial of the wrong sort of object: an animal, rather than a human being.

In this chapter, I shall discuss two aspects of the idea of 'criminal law's person'. The first aspect ties it to the broader idea of legal personality more generally. One reason why it makes no sense to put animals and dead people on trial for criminal wrongdoing is that, as legal non-persons, they are not capable of being subject to legal duties. To commit a criminal wrong is (among other things) to breach a legal duty. But since only legal persons are capable of legal relations such as holding legal duties (or legal rights, powers, etc), they are not capable of committing criminal wrongs. This simple proposition becomes complicated, however, once we notice that there is considerable disagreement as to who or what, precisely, should fall within the category of legal persons. Some, like Michael Moore, insist that only responsible moral agents are legal persons; Roman law and the civilian legal tradition make clear that all living human beings are in the category of legal persons; virtually all legal systems recognise some forms of corporate legal persons (like states, cities and business corporations); and, in recent years, there has been increasing discussion of the possibility of recognising the legal personality of some animals and even natural phenomena such as rivers.

There is also a second, more criminal law-specific, aspect of 'criminal law's person' that merits our attention. Whether or not we find them to be legal persons, we still insist that animals and dead people are not the sorts of things that are capable of committing criminal wrongs. Large classes of what are usually agreed to be legal persons – infant children, for instance, and those with severe intellectual impairments (and, on some accounts, those suffering mental

[6] The 'cadaver synod of 897' is described in P Llewellyn, *Rome in the Dark Ages* (Constable & Robinson, 1996) 292 ff.

[7] Of course, dead people were once living. So if the trial in question concerned acts committed while alive and competent, the problem is a different one. It is a problem of fitness to stand trial and to be punished, rather than the capacity to commit criminal acts.

[8] HL Carson, 'The Trial of Animals and Insects. A Little Known Chapter of Mediæval Jurisprudence' (1917) 56(5) *Proceedings of the American Philosophical Society* 410.

disorders) – are generally excluded from the possibility of criminal trial and punishment on the grounds that they are *doli incapax*: they are, simply in virtue of their status as infants, insane, etc, incapable of criminal wrongdoing. Here, too, there is considerable controversy about the proper scope of the category and the grounds for its recognition. Utilitarians and distributive justice theorists (both of whom think of criminal justice as a mechanism for the distribution of deterrent sanctions) usually argue that as a matter of status, even infants and the insane might be subject to criminal punishment – it is just that there are good utilitarian or fairness reasons not to do so. Those who think of criminal law as a mechanism for the recognition of moral wrongdoing,[9] by contrast, insist that it would be a category mistake to treat infants and the insane as proper objects of criminal responsibility: the capacity to provide an intelligible account of oneself is a necessary precondition to criminal responsibility, and they lack that capacity.

In this chapter, I examine these two debates surrounding 'criminal law's person' – concerning legal personality and criminal responsibility – in criminal law theory today. In both cases, I argue, there are good reasons to resist instrumentalist arguments on one side and moralist arguments on the other. Instead, I argue that the best way to understand both legal personality and criminal responsibility is to see them as legal categories that reflect deep commitments in a rule of law legal system. According to that way of thinking, the category of legal persons includes living human beings, all of whom have the moral right to independence, and those corporate entities that such human beings may form. And the category of criminal responsibility includes all those who are capable of challenging the state's exclusive claim to law-making power.

II. LEGAL PERSONALITY

The most basic conception of 'criminal law's person' is the broader idea of the legal person – a category that operates across the legal system. In any area of law, it is a prerequisite to being held responsible, to holding rights, to exercising powers and much else that makes one fall within the category of legal persons. At least since Roman times, the legal person has been a central organising idea in legal thought. The *Institutes of Gaius*, dating from the second century CE, state that '[a]ll the law which we use concerns either persons or things or actions'.[10] And from that time to this,[11] persons have been defined as all and only those

[9] In what follows, I shall observe the usual custom among criminal law theorists and refer to theorists who take this view of criminal law (and only to them) as 'moralists'. Although utilitarianism is itself a moral theory, it is usually excluded from this set of theories about criminal law.

[10] *Institutes of Roman Law by Gaius* (trans Edward Poste), 4th edn (Clarendon Press, 1904) 1, 8 Dig 1, 5, 1.

[11] I do not mean to suggest that the distinction between persons and things has always been scrupulously observed throughout the intervening millennia. But the conception of law's business set

entities that have 'the capacity for legal relations'.[12] In most civilian jurisdictions, the law of persons is the first and, in many ways, the central element of the civil code.[13] The reason for this is not hard to see, for if we are concerned with what rights (say, in property) each of us has against others, what duties we owe (say, in criminal law or tort), what powers we may exercise (say, in contract) and so on, it makes good sense to first establish what sorts of entities are candidates to bear all of these legal relations. Persons (and only persons) can own property or have a right to bodily integrity or owe a duty of care to their neighbours or exercise the legal power to make a contract or a will; mere things cannot do any of these things.[14]

The formal importance of the category of legal persons is clear; what is less clear is precisely who or what belongs within the category. In recent years, many legal systems have recognised non-human agents such as business corporations as legal persons; in a recent treaty, New Zealand has recognised a river as having legal personality;[15] and throughout much of human history, systems of slavery have denied the legal personality of slaves.[16] As Ngaire Naffine reminds us, 'Perhaps the greatest political act of law is the making of a legal person … and in the same move, the making of legal non-persons'.[17] How, then, should we define the category of legal persons?

Three accounts of who ought to be recognised as a legal person dominate the modern debate. Each is guided by a particular understanding of what best justifies the existence and operation of a legal system more generally.[18] Legal realists deny the conceptual integrity of the category of legal persons; legal moralists such as Michael Moore insist that for the category of legal persons to be meaningful, it must match the moral category of responsible agency; and finally rule of law accounts see legal personality as the starting point of legal order and something that must extend, at least, to all living human beings.

out in the Institutes and the distinction between persons and things that flow from it have a long and distinguished history in Western legal thought.

[12] Sir John Salmond, *Jurisprudence*, 5th edn (Stevens and Hayes, 1916) 272.

[13] Code Civil du Québec art 1: 'Every human being possesses juridical personality and has the full enjoyment of civil rights'; German Bürgerliches Gesetzbuch (2002) art 1: 'The legal capacity of a human being begins on the completion of birth'.

[14] Legal personality is just as much a precondition to having legal rights or being subject to legal duties in public law as it is in private law, of course.

[15] Treaty granting legal personality to the Whanganui river in New Zealand. See: www.theguardian.com/world/2017/mar/16/new-zealand-river-granted-same-legal-rights-as-human-being.

[16] The Roman law on manumission was highly developed, since the significance of a human being's transition from one fundamental category (property) to the other (person) changed almost everything about how the law would deal with him. See B Nicholas, *An Introduction to Roman Law* (Oxford University Press, 1993) 71 ff.

[17] N Naffine, 'Who are Law's Persons? From Cheshire Cats to Responsible Subjects' (2003) 66 *Modern Law Review* 346, 347.

[18] Naffine, ibid, draws a similar distinction between these three accounts of the person. But this is where the similarity with her article ends. Hers is a deeply instrumental account of the role of persons in the law – deeply at odds with the anti-instrumentalism for which I argue here.

A. Instrumentalism about Law

The first account of legal personality is part of a larger instrumentalism about law according to which traditional legal categories are mere tools to be used in whatever way best serves our policy objectives of the moment. On this way of thinking, a sophisticated legal theorist ought to look past the language the law uses and consider only the effects that the system imposes upon us.[19] As FH Lawson puts the legal realist point, 'Legal personality and legal persons are, as it were, mathematical equations devised for the purpose of simplifying legal calculations'.[20] And, like mathematical equations, legal personality has no deeper moral significance. On this account, there is no necessary connection between the category of legal person and any particular set of objects in the world; legal personality exists 'only in contemplation of law'.[21] That is, we may call something a 'person' if it serves our policy purposes to do so and deny it that status if it does not.

Some argue that this reductionist way of thinking about legal persons is reflected in the tendency of many legal systems over centuries to treat some human beings (viz, slaves) as things for many legal purposes rather than persons and in the contemporary practice of recognising the legal personality of non-human agents such as business corporations.[22] As I shall argue below, however, neither of these examples show that the category of legal personality lacks a meaningful conceptual structure. Indeed, the conceptual confusions wrought by trying to treat some human beings as things (as in the Roman law of status slavery)[23] supports the proposition that legal personality has a necessary conceptual structure, which the practice of slavery violates. Further, the recognition of corporate persons, too, can be shown to be something more than just an ad hoc addendum to the idea of legal persons. But we will come to those arguments a little later in this chapter.

In criminal law, this instrumentalist account of persons is, not surprisingly, most closely associated with theorists such as Jeremy Bentham or Barbara Wootton who disregard any deep conceptual distinctions between persons and things and try to use the criminal law as nothing more than a tool for bringing

[19] This is expressed most strikingly by OW Holmes in his early essay, 'The Path of the Law' (1897) 10 *Harvard Law Review* 457, 461, as follows: 'Take … the notion of legal duty, to which already I have referred. We fill the word with all the content which we draw from morals. But what does it mean to a bad man? Mainly, and in the first place, a prophecy that if he does certain things he will be subjected to disagreeable consequences by way of imprisonment or compulsory payment of money'.

[20] FH Lawson, 'The Creative Use of Legal Concepts' (1957) 32 *NYU Law Review* 907, 915 (quoted in Naffine (n 17).

[21] Lawson, ibid, 914.

[22] Naffine (n 17) I argue against this understanding of corporate personality below, in section II.C.

[23] JE Penner, *The Idea of Property in Law* (Oxford University Press, 1997) 125: 'So although a slave-owner owns a slave, he cannot own another "person", for slavery reduces the slave below the status of person … [T]he legal model of status slavery is incompatible with the reality of the situation: it treats the slave both as a person and not as a person at the same time'.

about desirable results in the world. It is no surprise to see this link between reductionism about legal concepts and instrumentalism about criminal law. The central idea behind much of American legal realism is that we must overcome the limitations imposed by long-standing legal categories in order to make proper use of the law to achieve our desired policy ends. Hanoch Dagan, citing the eminent American Legal Realist Karl Llewellyn, summarised the instrumentalist project in just these terms: 'our classifications can be excused only in so far as [they are] necessary to the accomplishing of a purpose'. And because our purposes may change, we should periodically re-examine 'the available tradition of categories'.[24] This is precisely the project of criminal law embraced by strict utilitarians such as Bentham and Wootton: to transcend the old conceptual categories of legal personality, criminal responsibility, etc in order to make the most effective use of the state's coercive criminal law powers in pursuit of valuable policy ends. We also see echoes of this view in contemporary criminal law thinking focused on harm-reduction without concern for the distinction between persons and things.[25]

The merits of this way of thinking turn crucially on the power of the arguments in defence of the conceptual structures at work in the law. If there are no good arguments in their defence, then there is little reason to resist the instrumentalist lure of using criminal justice institutions (and the rest of the legal system, too) to pursue valuable policy ends. Let us turn, then, to the arguments in defence of the concept of legal personality to see if it can be redeemed in the face of the instrumentalist challenge.

B. Legal Moralism about Legal Personality

A second conception of legal personality is at the heart of at least one branch of legal moralism in criminal law theory. On moralist accounts, legal rules and institutions are not mere tools for bringing about desirable consequences. They are (or at least ought to be) reflections of our best understanding of the truth about how we relate morally to one another. The language and the categories of law are filled with moral significance and this ought to be taken seriously: we should call wrong that which is truly wrong; we should recognise legal duties only where there is a genuine moral duty, and so on.

Many legal moralists generally ignore the category of legal personality, but Michael Moore puts it at the centre of his account. According to Moore,

[24] H Dagan, 'The Realist Conception of Law' (2007) 57 *University of Toronto Law Journal* 607, 648, citing KN Llewellyn, 'A Realistic Jurisprudence: The Next Step' in *Karl N Llewellyn, Jurisprudence: Realism in Theory and in Practice* (University of Chicago Press, 1962) 3, 27.

[25] This is part of the movement that Markus Dubber traces in the rise of 'police science' (which is concerned with the management of things) and the decline of criminal law (which is concerned with jurisdiction over persons). See M Dubber, *The Police Power: Patriarchy and the Foundations of American Government* (Columbia University Press, 2005).

we should ascribe legal personality only to morally responsible agents. In short, Moore openly and explicitly conflates the categories of legal personality and responsible agency. He writes:

> [T]he law's metaphysical views about what sort of being can hold legal rights is the same as its views about the sorts of beings who can be held responsible. In each case, rights and responsibilities are ascribed only to those practically reasoning agents we call persons.[26]

Since we shall consider the category of responsible agency in greater detail later in this chapter,[27] I will only touch on it here. It is made up of all those who have what John Gardner calls 'basic responsibility':[28] they can provide an intelligible moral account of their actions. This means that those whose account of themselves is unintelligible because (as with psychotics) it is based on fundamental delusions, or (as with small children) on a systematic failure to appreciate the importance of moral categories, or (as with the severely intellectually disabled) because their moral reasoning is so consistently illogical, should be excluded from the category of legal persons. To ascribe legal personality – the capacity for rights and duties, powers and liabilities – to small children or the mentally disordered, on Moore's account, would simply be a category mistake. No plausible moral practice could hold them responsible for the breach of a legal duty; and although they might engage in conduct that looks like the exercise of a power, it would be a mistake to take it to be an intelligible choice that is deserving of recognition as such by the law.

Now, there is no reason why one must identify the category of legal personality with the category of those who are capable of intelligible moral reasoning. One could – indeed, the law in most jurisdictions does – recognise that there are a great many rights that can be held by one party and yet the decisions about how they may be exercised will consistently be made by another party. This is, of course, true of small children and adults who are incapable of making decisions for themselves. But it is equally true of shareholders of a corporation: shareholders have ownership rights in the corporation, but it is the board of directors and the officers of the corporation who make the day-to-day decisions on the corporation's behalf.

Moore is driven to this vision of legal personality, it seems, because of his particular understanding of the point of legal rights. For Moore, the point of legal rights is to give us the power to affect the world around us in ways that reflect the outcome of our choices. In order for it to make sense for us to have a legal right, then, we must have the capacity to exercise legal powers over the object of that right. '[B]uilt into the concept of the right', he argues, 'is an image

[26] MS Moore, *Law and Psychiatry: Rethinking the Relationship* (Cambridge University Press, 1984) 91.

[27] See section II.

[28] J Gardner, 'The Mark of Responsibility' in J Gardner, *Offences and Defences Selected Essays in the Philosophy of Criminal Law* (Oxford University Press, 2007) 182.

of its holder as one who chooses. [H]aving rights presupposes the capacity for rational choice … Only beings that can make rational choices about these matters have such rights'.[29] He very clearly puts incompetent humans and non-human things in the same category of non-persons, as follows: 'Plants, dogs, earthworms, stones, corpses, very young infants, and very crazy adults all either hold no rights, or suffer very serious disabilities because they lack the capacities of intelligent choice that is presupposed by the ascription of rights'.[30]

Notwithstanding his numerous appeals to the present state of the law, Moore's project is a decidedly revisionist one. For the fact is that the law in most jurisdictions does recognise the legal personality and, indeed, the rights of individuals who are incompetent to make rational decisions with respect to their own rights. But the doctrinal point need not detain us; Moore's most basic challenge is normative: why should we recognise legal personality in those who lack basic responsibility? For someone who has no present ability to make rational choices, there is no obvious purpose served by recognising that she has legal personality and is therefore a proper object of legal relations. What rationale might there be, then, for recognising the legal personality of all human beings, even those without the present ability to make legally valid decisions concerning their rights? This question finds an answer in the third account of legal personality, based on a conception of the rule of law.

C. Legal Personality and the Rule of Law

We can find a more plausible rationale for the category of legal personality in a certain understanding of the point of legal order and the rule of law. On this account, legal categories and reasoning are not mere tools for generating desirable consequences (as legal realists would suggest), but neither are they mere reflections of a freestanding metaphysical truth about moral reality (as Moore would maintain). Instead, legal categories such as the category of legal persons are best understood as the terms according to which we justify the coercive apparatus of law and state to each and every person who is subject to its power. Seen in this light, certain legal categories are of deep normative significance, but not as straightforward reflections of some independent moral reality. They are important, instead, as structural features of a legitimate, coercive legal order.

On a rule of law understanding of the importance of legal order, the concept of the legal person plays a central role. Whether this is set out in the language of Roman law, according to which all legal persons were understood to be their

[29] Moore, *Law and Psychiatry* (n 26) 92–93. (He adds: 'The young, the retarded, and the insane are disabled from the rights to make wills, deeds, contracts, to manage their own property, to refuse certain treatments, to marry or divorce, to be granted custody of children, or to have abortions on demand'.)

[30] ibid 93.

own masters (or *sui juris*),[31] or whether it is understood in the early modern language of social contract theorists according to which '[t]he natural liberty of man is to be free from any superior power on earth, and not to be under the will or legislative authority of man',[32] the point is broadly the same. It is that all human beings, simply in virtue of being human, have the right not to be subject to the arbitrary power of any other person.[33] It is this right to independence that leads social contract theorists to insist that our coercive state institutions must ensure the independence of all human beings who are subject to them. It is that same right to independence that led Roman lawyers in ancient times and that leads private lawyers today to recognise that all human beings must have legal personality, for only then can they be capable of claiming rights against interference by others and of enforcing those claims through the courts.[34]

So far, it is not yet obvious how the rule of law account differs from Moore's choice-based view of legal personality. Moore readily recognises the special importance of human beings in virtue of their capacity for choice. But this recognition leads him to the view that only those who can actually exercise intelligible choice should be recognised as legal persons. Why should the rule of law account, which also focuses on our special status in virtue of our ability to choose, lead to a different conclusion? The answer lies in how we conceive of choice as significant for law. If, with Moore, we take it to be law's task to promote our valuable purposes, then we will insist that institutions are morally valuable insofar as they allow us to make such choices. In the rule of law account, by contrast, we do not take it be law's task to promote our ends. Instead, the law's business is to articulate each individual's enduring status as a free person, subject only to those choices that one has made for oneself – the right to be 'free from any superior power on earth', as John Locke puts the point. And this is a right that can be enjoyed by anyone who, as a matter of status, might at some time be capable of choice. Small children will become adults who will be capable of meaningful choices, and the elderly who have lost the ability to make intelligible choices are the continuation of adults who were once capable of making

[31] Gaius (n 10) I.8: 'The chief division in the rights of persons is this: that all men are either free or slaves. Some persons are legally independent (*sui juris*), while some are subject to the power of others. Slaves are subject to the power of a master'.

[32] John Locke, 'Second Treatise of Government' in *Two Treatises of Government*, 2nd edn (P Laslett (ed), Cambridge University Press, 1967) 283.

[33] The same point is made in the American Declaration of Independence: 'all men are … endowed by their Creator with certain unalienable Rights, that among these are Life, Liberty and the pursuit of Happiness. – That to secure these rights, Governments are instituted among Men, deriving their just powers from the consent of the governed, – That whenever any Form of Government becomes destructive of these ends, it is the Right of the People to alter or to abolish it, and to institute new Government'.

[34] On the connection between legal personality and the right to enforce a claim, see Sir Hersh Lauterpacht, *The Development of International Law by the International Court* (Cambridge University Press, 1982) 178: 'It would appear that, apart from physical or similar incapacity, the right to bring a claim is of the essence of juridical personality'. (I am grateful to Arthur Ripstein for bringing this passage to my attention.)

such choices. As such, they have the right throughout their lives to be free from arbitrary interference by others at all points during their lives.[35] Although our present ability to make intelligible choices might come and go – as we grow out of infancy or into senility, as we move in and out of mental disorder, or (more quotidianly) as we fall into and rise from sleep – our enduring status as creatures that have a right to independence in virtue of our capacity to set and pursue ends for ourselves and to structure our lives through those choices, continues from the beginning of our lives to its natural end.

In most legal systems, the class of legal persons, further, extends beyond the class of living human individuals. It generally also includes a variety of public and private collectivities such as business corporations, states, cities and charitable foundations. Why should the law grant such entities, which are not moral persons – they have 'no soul to be damned, and no body to be kicked'[36] – the status of legal persons? There are, of course, instrumentalist arguments that recognising their legal personality might serve some valuable end such as deterrence. But can we explain how the legal personality of corporate entities of this sort could be rendered consistent with a rule of law conception of legal personality? Although we must leave a full working out of this idea to another day, the beginnings of such an account are visible from the fact that all such corporate entities are ways in which individual legal persons may organise and operate together as a unity. That is, the creation of corporate personality is a mechanism through which those already possessed of legal personality may gain recognition as genuinely collective entities who operate as a unity, rather than as a plurality of diverse persons.

III. RESPONSIBLE AGENCY IN CRIMINAL LAW

As important as the broad concept of legal personality is to a great deal of criminal law thinking, we should also consider another idea of 'criminal law's person' that is specific to the criminal law. This is the class of entities that are candidates for being held criminally responsible for their actions. Although legal personality is a necessary condition for being criminally responsible, it is not a sufficient condition. For legal personality is a matter of our enduring status, but criminal responsibility is a function of our present abilities, which may come and go. How, then, should we define the sub-class of legal persons who may be held criminally responsible for their actions?

[35] As John Rawls glosses the point, 'we say that a person is someone who can be a citizen, that is, a fully cooperating member of society over a complete life. We add the phrase "over a complete life" because a society is viewed as a more or less complete and self-sufficient scheme of cooperation, making room within itself for all the necessities and activities of life, from birth until death'. ('Justice as Fairness: Political not Metaphysical' (1985) 14 *Philosophy and Public Affairs* 223, 233.)

[36] Edward, First Baron Thurlow, quoted in HL Mencken, *A New Dictionary of Quotations on Historical Principles from Ancient and Modern Sources* (1942) 223.

When examining this question, we quickly learn that our answer to it is always a function of our conception of what criminal justice is all about. And, just as we found with the category of legal personality, we find that there are three broad camps on the question. Much of mid-twentieth century criminal law theory was based on the instrumentalist assumption that criminal justice is, first and foremost, a mechanism for distributing hard treatment as a means to deterring undesirable conduct. On this account, legal concepts such as criminal responsibility are seen as tools for ensuring that hard treatment is distributed according to some favoured criterion. Strict utilitarians like Jeremy Bentham and Barbara Wootton insist that punishment should be distributed according to a principle of maximum efficiency in the pursuit of deterrence. Within the camp of instrumentalists about punishment, a second group of theorists insist that effective deterrence is not the sole criterion of distribution; fairness must play an important role, as well. Theorists such as HLA Hart[37] and TM Scanlon[38] refer to this criterion as a principle of 'fair opportunity'. This way of thinking about criminal justice dominated the scene for much of the twentieth century and it is threatening to make a comeback in the twenty-first.[39] The conception of the person at work in this understanding of criminal justice was the person as the object of distribution: since all living human beings are the proper objects of utilitarian distribution or of distributive justice, they are also, according to these criminal law theorists, the proper objects of criminal justice.

Late twentieth century theorists such as Antony Duff, Michael Moore and John Gardner, turned towards various forms of legal moralism as ways of making sense of the operations of criminal justice, insisting that the central function of criminal justice is to identify (and, for Moore, at least, to condemn and punish) moral wrongdoing. The conception of the person at work in moralist accounts follows that rationale precisely: it is the responsible moral agent – or the 'person of basic responsibility', in Gardner's formulation.[40] Whereas small children, the insane or the seriously intellectually disabled might be the proper objects of efficiency and fairness reasoning about the distribution of sanctions, they are not the proper objects of our judgements of moral wrongdoing. Since criminal justice is, in the moralists' view, a mechanism for making judgements of moral wrongdoing, only responsible moral agents who can provide an intelligible moral account of themselves and their actions are of interest to the criminal law.

[37] HLA Hart, *Punishment and Responsibility*, 2nd edn (Oxford University Press, 2008).

[38] TM Scanlon, *What We Owe to Each Other* (Harvard University Press, 1998) 267 suggests that punishment has two aspects, one of which concerns blame for wrongdoing, but another aspect concerns the fair distribution of penalties. This 'value of choice' principle for the distribution of penalties closely mirrors Hart's principles of fair choice.

[39] The 'political turn' in criminal law theory: Vincent Chiao, Erin Kelly and others. See footnotes below for references to these works.

[40] Gardner (n 28) 182.

As with legal personality, there is a rule of law account of what criminal justice is all about that gives rise to a conception of the criminally responsible agent. Here, too, this is the account that I shall defend. To see the strength of this account, however, it is essential first to work through the shortcomings of its main rivals. Let us turn now to them.

A. Instrumentalism about Punishment

i. Orthodox Utilitarians

The orthodox utilitarian account of criminal law and justice put forward by Jeremy Bentham is an attempt to reform our institutions of criminal law and punishment. For Bentham, the guiding principle in all human practices is the principle of utility according to which we must seek to maximise happiness and (most importantly when thinking about criminal law) minimise harm. This gives rise to the apparent paradox of criminal law: how could we possibly justify an institution the central operation of which is the infliction of harm by way of criminal punishment? On this account, criminal punishment is 'in itself evil'[41] and must be redeemed by its ability to deter substantial harm as a counterweight to the harm it so clearly inflicts. It is this aim of harm prevention that provides the unifying idea behind Bentham's account of almost all criminal law doctrines, including rule of law requirements (such as the need for clear, precise, public, ex ante prohibitions), fault requirements (where the offender was unaware of the harm he was about to cause), and excuses (where the act was committed under duress or in circumstances of necessity).[42] Insofar as there are any legal categories at work in criminal law, Bentham insists, they must be nothing more than heuristics guiding us to utility-maximisation.

We can see this concept scepticism and instrumentalism at work throughout Bentham's account of criminal justice. Most controversially, he insists that it is for utilitarian reasons of deterrence that we do not punish the innocent. Since the point of punishment is to deter harmful conduct, there is no useful purpose served by punishing when the underlying conduct was not harmful (either because it caused no harm, because the harm was consented to, or because the harm was outweighed by the harm it prevented).[43] Further, he insists that what we normally consider to be denials of responsible agency, such as infancy or mental disorder, are also best understood as of merely instrumental value. What are normally thought of as denials of responsible agency, Bentham categorises

[41] J Bentham, 'An Introduction to the Principles of Morals and Legislation' in J Bentham, *A Fragment of Government with An Introduction to the Principles of Morals and Legislation* (Blackwell, 1948) 281: 'all punishment in itself is evil. Upon the principle of utility, if it ought at all to be admitted, it ought only to be admitted in as far as it promises to exclude some greater evil'.

[42] ibid 281 ff.

[43] ibid 282.

as cases '[w]here the penal provision, though it were conveyed to a man's notice, could produce no effect on him from engaging in any act of the sort in question. Such is the case in extreme infancy … in insanity … [and] in intoxication'.[44] Bentham's instrumentalist rationale does not seem to justify the categorical exclusion of infants and the mentally disordered from criminal responsibility, however. As Bentham himself later acknowledges,[45] children and the mentally disordered can often be affected by incentives. So if we categorically exclude children and the insane from criminal responsibility, it must be for other reasons.

Wootton, another orthodox utilitarian, proposes a different instrumentalist explanation for the different treatment of children and the insane. It is not that they are unreachable by the law's incentives; their status as children, mentally disordered or intellectually disabled is 'relevant, not to the question of determining the measure of his culpability, but to the choice of the treatment most likely to be effective in discouraging him from offending again'.[46] Instead of ordinary criminal punishment, we should choose education for children, psychiatric care for the mentally disordered, etc, simply because these will be more effective in bringing about long-term harm-reduction. It is along similar lines of thought that the Swedish Criminal Code of 1962 insisted that mental disorder ought not to be treated as a ground for excluding someone from criminal responsibility but should instead be considered as a sentencing factor.[47] For if we are interested in criminal law as nothing more than a set of techniques for reducing the incidence of aggregate harm in the community, then our focus should be on the appropriateness of various forms of intervention rather than on whether individuals are capable of providing an intelligible moral account of themselves and of their conduct.

In the background of all three utilitarian accounts, lies a tacit assumption that all living human beings – even infants and the insane – are, in principle, objects of the criminal law. This is why some instrumentalist argument is required to show why we have good reasons of policy not to inflict criminal sanctions, say, on infants or the deeply mentally disordered. It is not obvious, however, that this assumption reflects any moral theory of the responsible person in criminal law. As HLA Hart explains, in the Benthamite account of criminal law and punishment, we conceive of persons just as 'alterable, predictable, curable or manipulable things'.[48] So talking of a utilitarian conception of responsible agency in criminal law is perhaps a misnomer; but we can say with

[44] ibid 284.

[45] ibid 284, fn 1: 'notwithstanding what is said here, the cases of infancy and intoxication … cannot be looked upon in practice as affording sufficient grounds for absolute impunity'.

[46] B Wootton, *Crime and the Criminal Law: Reflections of a Magistrate and Social Scientist* (Stevens and Sons, 1963) 77.

[47] See C Lernestedt, 'Insanity and the "Gap" in the Law: Swedish Criminal Law Rides Again' (2009) 54 *Scandinavian Studies in Law* 79, 80.

[48] HLA Hart describes the Benthamite position in these terms in 'Punishment and the Elimination of Responsibility' in HLA Hart, *Punishment and Responsibility* (n 37) 183.

confidence that utilitarian criminal law theorists are in principle open to holding any living human being liable to punishment.

ii. Hart, Distributive Justice and the 'Political Turn'

Hart's project in several of the essays in *Punishment and Responsibility* is to show that a legitimate system of criminal law should not only impose coercion for utilitarian reasons (what Hart called punishment's 'general justifying aim'), it should also allocate that coercion among members of the community fairly. Hart famously insists that criminal punishment must be distributed according to a principle of 'fair opportunity': fault standards, excuses such as duress, and even denials of responsibility like infancy and mental disorder are all best justified according to a distributive justice rationale.[49] It is on the basis of the fair opportunity principle that Hart insists that objective fault standards in criminal law are acceptable. Similarly, it is on the basis of fairness considerations that Hart insists that those who lacked a meaningful choice – because they were under threat in duress cases, or because they lacked the requisite mental abilities in infancy or mental disorder cases – should not be subject to criminal punishment even if they did, in fact, carry out a prohibited criminal act.

Hart's focus on distributive justice in his analysis of general doctrines of fault, excuse and criminal responsibility is sometimes obscured by the language he uses to describe his project, which emphasises choice, rather than fairness. But at crucial moments, he makes clear that fair choice is only a way of satisfying the demands of justice – by which he means distributive justice. 'In this way', Hart writes, 'the criminal law … distributes its coercive sanctions in a way that reflects this respect for the individual. This surely is very central in the notion of justice'.[50] The point here is that the reason why choice is the appropriate criterion for the distribution of punishment is that it is a principle of fair distribution. Not all consequences of our choices should be visited on us, Hart insists, but only where choice can be understood as a principle of fair distribution. If we had a fair opportunity to avoid criminal wrongdoing but still chose to undertake it, we cannot complain that it is unfair for the burden of deterrence to fall on us.

It is important to emphasise that Hart's choice principle is only one candidate among many to fill the role of 'fair principle of distribution for punishment'. In recent years, many political theorists have started to take a serious interest in punishment theory and many criminal law theorists have taken a more serious interest in political theory. Many of these political punishment theorists

[49] Hart, *Punishment and Responsibility* (n 37) 46: 'If … we turn back to criminal law and its excusing conditions, we can regard their function as a mechanism for similarly maximizing within a framework of coercive law the efficacy of the individual's informed and considered choice in determining the future and also his power to predict the future'.

[50] ibid 49.

have assumed, like Hart, that the central question of punishment theory is the determination of the appropriate principles for the distribution of punishment. Thus, writers such as Erin Kelly[51] and Vincent Chiao[52] have put forward other principles of distribution for punishment that they take to be more in line with their conceptions of distributive fairness. Whatever the merits of their favoured understanding of fairness, however, their accounts are of interest to us only if we accept their starting premise that the allocation of punishment is not already determined by other principles.

In short, Hart's *Punishment and Responsibility*, like many other works in the recent 'political turn' in criminal law theory, is at one with Bentham on the deep point about criminal justice even as it criticises him on how to apply it. That is, whereas Hart rejects the efficient pursuit of utility in favour of a principle of 'fair choice' as the distributive principle for criminal punishment, he accepts the basic utilitarian premise that criminal justice is fundamentally about the distribution of hard treatment in pursuit of some shared societal end that can be understood independently of the legal system. The conception of the responsible person at the heart of Hart's account of criminal justice, then, is the same as Bentham's: it is the person as the object of distribution. Unlike the strict utilitarians, however, Hart takes seriously the idea of the person as the object of distribution. For utilitarians, there is no reason in principle why we couldn't make any creature (such as dogs) that can experience pleasure and pain and respond to incentives, objects of utility-maximising deterrent sanctions; it is just for contingent reasons that we restrict the scope of our enquiry to human beings. For Hart, however, there are important reasons of principle for why it is human beings (and not any other creature that might feel pleasure and pain) that are the only proper objects of distribution. Hart's thinking on this question is nicely captured by (the early) John Rawls: 'equal justice is owed to those who have the capacity to take part in and to act in accordance with the public understanding of the initial situation'.[53] Importantly, Rawls points out that it is not in virtue of who we are in all of our empirical specificity that we deserve to be accorded equal justice; rather, 'moral personality refers to a capacity and not to the realization of it. A being that has the capacity, whether or not it is yet developed, is to receive the full protection of the principles of justice'.[54] In short, since criminal justice is an exercise in distributing harsh treatment fairly across a population, it takes as its proper object the same class of persons as the practice of distributive justice more generally. And that is the class of all living human beings, whatever their present abilities.

[51] E Kelly, *The Limits of Blame: Rethinking Punishment and Responsibility* (Harvard University Press, 2018).

[52] V Chiao, *Criminal Law in the Age of the Administrative State* (Oxford University Press, 2018) applies Elizabeth Anderson's conception of equality to the distribution of punishment.

[53] Hart, *Punishment and Responsibility* (n 37) 442.

[54] ibid 445–46.

B. Legal Moralism and Basic Responsibility

Legal moralism about criminal law is based on the claim that criminal justice cannot be fully understood merely as a tool for carrying out our policy objectives, even when disciplined by considerations of distributive justice. Instead, criminal law doctrine must be a function of basic moral categories that reflect the underlying moral structure of wrongdoing, blame and culpability. Fault standards in criminal law, on the moralist view, are important because they distinguish morally culpable acts from the mere causing of harm. Justification and excuse defences are important because they represent morally significant answers to the call to explain one's moral wrongdoing. Underlying this whole structure, on the moralist account, is the demand that the accused be the sort of person who is capable of providing an intelligible account of himself and his actions. As Duff has taken great pains to point out, the criminal process is not merely a forensic enterprise, designed merely to determine as efficiently as possible whether the conditions for punishment are present in the particular case. It is, instead, a dialogical process in which the accused's meaningful participation is essential.[55] The accused is not treated as a mere thing to be investigated at trial; he is taken to be an interlocutor who is accused of wrongdoing, against whom allegations are substantiated, and who is called to account for his alleged wrongdoing.

An essential precondition for that sort of moral dialogue with the accused is what Gardner calls 'basic responsibility'.[56] As Gardner puts it:

> [R]esponsibility in this basic sense is none other than an ability to offer justifications and excuses. In the idioms we more often use, it is the ability to explain oneself, to give an intelligible account of oneself, to answer for oneself, as a rational being.[57]

If someone (say, a small child, or a severely mentally disordered person) does not have basic responsibility, we will not hold her criminally liable for her actions, but this is not because she has lived up to our standards of acceptable conduct. It is, rather, because she is simply not capable of entering into the sort of moral dialogue that is part and parcel of the criminal process. Small children, the mentally disordered and the severely intellectually disabled are legal persons and they might do terrible things, but they cannot offer an intelligible moral account by way of reply when called upon to explain themselves. On the moralist account, then, criminal law's responsible person is the same as morality's responsible person. Since criminal justice is thought to be just an institutionalisation of moral practices of calling to account, answering or blaming for

[55] RA Duff, *Trials and Punishments* (Cambridge University Press, 1986); RA Duff, *Answering for Crime: Responsibility and Liability in the Criminal Law* (Hart Publishing, 2007).

[56] Antony Duff has a very similar understanding of the candidate for being held criminally responsible. He calls it the responsable person. See *Answering for Crime*, ibid, 39.

[57] Gardner (n 28) 182.

wrongdoing, it stands to reason, then, that the proper object of one should be the proper object for the other.

C. The Rule of Law Account on Criminal Responsibility

The rule of law account we encountered above in the discussion of the legal person also gives rise to a distinctive account of the responsible agent in criminal law. The account of the responsible agent is similar to the moralist account in many of its practical details (although, as I shall outline below, there are some notable differences), but it has a very different normative basis. This difference in normative foundations is especially important today when the foundations of the legal moralist account of criminal law is coming under sustained attack.

The best way to make sense of the workings of criminal justice on the rule of law model, is to see it as essentially an auxiliary, supportive institution – the 'sanction of all other laws', as Jean-Jacques Rousseau describes it[58] – whose justifying purpose is fundamentally derivative of the legal institutions it supports. The justification of criminal justice institutions must proceed not by showing that they provide any straightforward payoff (such as deterring undesirable conduct or identifying moral wrongdoers), but rather by showing that they make it possible for a state to establish and maintain its exclusive authority to make laws in a jurisdiction – a feature that is necessary for it to maintain the rule of law. Criminal wrongs, on this account, are wrongs against the state's exclusive authority; by condemning and punishing wrongdoers, criminal justice maintains the state's exclusive authority which is, in turn, necessary for it to carry out its basic justificatory purpose, which is to establish and preserve the independence of each person living under it.

What conception of the criminally responsible subject is appropriate to the rule of law vision I espouse? It is, like the account of criminal justice of which it is a part, rather more complex than either of the major alternatives. Since the major justificatory purpose of criminal justice is to ensure the exclusive authority of the state to make laws in the jurisdiction, we must take account of the conception of persons at work in the structure of laws more generally. And here, the appropriate conception of the person is, at its core, the living human being from birth until death. The rule of law conception is concerned with a form of wrongdoing, but a different form of wrongdoing from the one that concerns the legal moralist account. Only those who are capable of genuine wrongdoing are candidates for being held criminally responsible for their actions. But because the rule of law account is concerned with a very particular sort of wrongdoing – the usurping of the state's exclusive right to make the

[58] J-J Rousseau, *On the Social Contract and Other Later Political Writings*, 2nd edn (Cambridge University Press, 2019) 83: '[C]riminal laws … at bottom, are not so much a specific kind of law as they are the sanction for all the others'.

law around here – it is concerned with a particularly high standard of criminal responsibility. It includes only those who are capable of understanding the special nature of criminal wrongdoing and its relation to the state's exclusive authority to legislate.

What is the difference between this conception of criminal responsibility and a more run-of-the-mill conception of moral responsibility? A German court recently tried to explain the special requirement for criminal responsibility (beyond ordinary moral responsibility) as follows:

> The ability to understand [that is necessary for criminal responsibility] … requires a state of development which enables the young person to recognise that his act is not compatible with the orderly and peaceful coexistence of people and therefore cannot be tolerated by the legal order.[59]

That is, it is not enough simply to engage in intelligible moral reasoning about one's conduct; one must, further, understand the significance of one's conduct for the stability of the social order within one's jurisdiction. What the court does not mention here, but should, is that there is one way in which all criminal conduct is incompatible with orderly and peaceful coexistence. Whatever the substantive merits of one's conduct, it is, simply in virtue of its status as criminally prohibited, inconsistent with the state's claim of exclusive jurisdiction to determine what conduct is and is not permissible within the jurisdiction. If that is at the heart of criminal wrongdoing, as the rule of law account insists that it is, then an agent must be capable of understanding this claim before he can be held criminally responsible for his actions.

IV. CONCLUSION

Before we ask any questions about how the criminal justice system ought to operate – which evidence is appropriate to present at trial, how to structure the trial, which tests of criminal responsibility we ought to apply, etc – we must first determine who (or what) are the appropriate objects of the criminal law's concern. This is the question of 'criminal law's person'. Or, as we have seen, it is more accurate to say that these are the questions of criminal law's person, for there are two distinct questions at stake here: what is the legal person who is capable of bearing rights, duties and powers? And who is the responsible agent who is capable of committing criminal wrongs?

As we have seen, the answers to each of these two questions varies with one's conception of the point of the larger enterprise of which they are a part. Legal realists, who take legal order to be a means to an end, see legal personality as a heuristic for more important ends-driven questions of deterrence and

[59] Landgericht Passau (1996) NStZ 601 (cited in T Crofts, *The Criminal Responsibility of Children and Young Persons: A Comparison of English and German Law* (Ashgate, 2002) 139–40).

rehabilitation and they see criminal responsibility as applicable (in principle, at least) to all living human beings; moralists, who take legal order to be the institutionalisation of ordinary interpersonal morality, see both legal personality and criminal responsibility as stand-ins for moral agency. In this chapter, I have argued that there are good reasons to favour a different conception of criminal law and its place within a larger legal order – one based on the law's special ability to ensure the independence of all moral persons through the state's assumption of the exclusive right to determine our legal rights vis-a-vis one another and the granting of legal personality to all moral persons to enable us all to vindicate our rights should they come under attack. This rule of law conception of the role and place of criminal law gives rise to a distinctive account of legal personality and of criminal responsibility. This account not only fits neatly with settled practice in many jurisdictions, it also provides an understanding of the unique sorts of wrongs that are the stock-in-trade of criminal justice and of the state's reasons to respond to such wrongdoing with coercive criminal punishment.[60]

[60] I develop this conception of criminal law in several places elsewhere. See, eg, M Thorburn, 'Criminal Punishment and the Right to Rule' (2019) 70 *University of Toronto Law Journal* 44.

7

Victims Who Victimise: Guilt in Political Theory and Moral Psychology

ALAN NORRIE

> We have handed many of the responses [to wrongdoing] to a very special formation, the modern state, and we have principles governing what such a state can and should do [so that] our ideas … are … governed by a certain political theory of freedom, not by a moral refinement of the very conception of responsibility.[1]

> The trespasser intended to have to do with another's life, but he has only destroyed his own, for life is not different from life … The injured life appears as a hostile power … and maltreats him as he has maltreated the other.[2]

I. THE PROBLEM OF PERPETRATORS AS VICTIMS WHO VICTIMISE

THIS CHAPTER HAS two focal points, one specific, the other more general. The specific focus is the question of the moral guilt of perpetrators viewed as victims who victimise others in settings of structural social injustice. There is a repeated concern that those taken through the criminal justice systems of Western societies are in the main from the poorest and most socially disadvantaged social groups. Such people are victims of systematic and structural processes of social exclusion who through their crimes victimise others. Those whom they victimise are often themselves living in comparable social circumstances. Such perpetrators are therefore victims of the social system in which they act, who victimise others who are equally victims in that system.

[1] B Williams, *Shame and Necessity* (University of California Press, 1993) 66.

[2] G Hegel, *Early Theological Writings* (University of Pennsylvania Press, 1948) 229–30. While the mature Hegel is a classical proponent of the political theory of punishment, the young Hegel sought a moral psychology of guilt representing in phenomenological terms what it means to feel guilty. In his early writings, a line is drawn between political and legal theory and moral psychology. See also, A Norrie, 'Love in Law's Shadow: Political Theory, Moral Psychology and Young Hegel's Critique of Punishment' (2019) 28 *Social & Legal Studies* 10.

This poses a question for standard theories of punishment, insofar as such theories focus on the justice of punishment. Such theories will in one way or another contemplate the responsibility or the guilt of the accused. Where does guilt lie where perpetrators are themselves victims who victimise others?

The broader focus of the chapter stems from an attempt to think about this question in terms of a deeper analysis of what it means to feel guilty for committing a crime than is provided in standard accounts. My argument here is that mainstream accounts treat the issue of punishment as one element in normative political theory. The central issue for such a theory is the relationship, however conceived, between the guilt of an individual and their justified punishment by a political entity – a state, a polity, a sovereign, the law. This is understandable given that the usual practices under investigation are indeed practices conducted by such entities. There is however a danger of an illicit fusion here of two elements that can and ought to be kept separate. The first element is that just described: understanding the practices of a particular political and institutional form, where the appropriate enquiry is that of normative political theory. That mode of enquiry ought not, however, so to extend its remit that it obscures a second element in our understanding of punishment, an element that I will call the moral psychology of guilt.[3] Yet, I suggest that precisely such an exclusion has significantly affected our discussions of punishment, with the result that we are not able to deal adequately with issues such as the guilt of perpetrators who are themselves victims, described above. This chapter is therefore an attempt to develop some ideas in moral psychology about guilt, and to bring such ideas into the open as an important complement to the normative political theory of punishment.

The chapter has two main sections. The first of these considers the issue of perpetrators as victims who victimise others in settings of structural exclusion, violence and injustice, and how this issue is discussed in normative political theory. It looks at classical formulations of the issue, and then takes up a modern

[3] The idea of a moral psychology stems from Bernard Williams's argument for relating ethical claims to non-ethical elements of human nature, which Jonathan Lear persuasively pushes in the direction of psychoanalysis: see B Williams, 'Replies' in J Altham and R Harrison (eds), *World, Mind, and Ethics* (Cambridge University Press, 1995) 202–05; J Lear, 'Psychoanalysis and the Idea of a Moral Psychology: Memorial to Bernard Williams' Philosophy' (2004) 47 *Inquiry* 515. For Williams, the aim was a less moralised psychology than that offered for example by Aristotle, one which probed the relationship between morals and values and (non-moral) motives and desires in an open fashion. Explaining this, Williams refers favourably among the moderns to Freud, though he pursues the thought himself through Nietzsche. As Lear points out, however, what Nietzsche lacked was precisely an understanding of how human psychology could be dynamically related to moral propositions. That Williams was himself drawn to psychoanalytic understanding can be seen in the way he discusses shame and guilt in the endnote of Williams, *Shame and Necessity* (n 1). This chapter is in the spirit of Williams's and Lear's naturalist understanding of the relation between moral psychology and morality, pursuing a moral psychology of guilt. For further discussion of Williams's account of shame, guilt and moral psychology, see A Norrie, 'Criminal Law and Ethics: Beyond Normative Assertion and Its Critique' (2017) 80 *Modern Law Review* 955.

account in the work of Antony Duff.[4] It shows how these analyses generate an impasse, while in the work of Duff, there is the beginning of moves that could help us reflect on the impasse more deeply, moves which take us in the direction of a moral psychology of guilt. The second section takes up the work of two psychoanalytic thinkers, Melanie Klein and Jessica Benjamin,[5] to put together an analysis of what it means in the terms of a moral psychology to talk about guilt and about more precisely feeling guilty. This is an existential quality that perpetrators might (or might not) feel, even if they are themselves victims who victimise others. In moving from normative political theory to moral psychology, my purpose is not to argue that one approach should be used to the exclusion of another, but rather to suggest that we gain a better understanding of what is at stake in punishment by combining the two approaches. Moving from the analysis of the one to the other helps us see that issues of guilt and justice have deeper foundations in human being than is usually appreciated.

II. NORMATIVE POLITICAL THEORY: THE PROBLEM OF THE IDEAL AND THE ACTUAL

In this section, I rehearse a well-known problem in the modern political theory of punishment, considering both its classical statement and one recent important recapitulation. My aim here is not fully to make the argument for the problem, but to use this section to explore how the problem has been described in normative political theory. This then leads to thinking more deeply about issues of guilt, and the relationship between such theory and an underlying moral psychology.

A. Classical Statement of a Problem

Modern normative political theory in its foundational moments and its more recent forms entails a clash between a vision of why punishment is justified and how crime comes to be committed.[6] With regard to the former, the normative idea is often of a world of individuals, owing obligations to a sovereign, who are responsible for those of their acts which breach the sovereign's laws. This idea may be stated in a variety of ways. Compare, for example, the difference

[4] RA Duff, *Punishment, Communication, and Community* (Oxford University Press, 2001).

[5] M Klein, *Love, Guilt and Reparation* (Vintage, 1998); J Benjamin, *The Bonds of Love* (Pantheon, 1988). I have also found Jonathan Lear's work on Freud most helpful: J Lear, *Love and Its Place in Nature* (Yale University Press, 1990). Lear's work at the crossroads of psychoanalysis and classical philosophy is an untapped resource for legal theory: see J Lear, *Open-Minded* (Harvard University Press, 1998); and J Lear, *Wisdom Won From Illness* (Harvard University Press, 2017).

[6] See A Norrie, *Law, Ideology and Punishment* (Kluwer, 1991); H Carvalho, *The Preventive Turn in Criminal Law* (Oxford University Press, 2017).

between a contractarian approach such as provided by Hobbes or Rawls with a rationalist approach as developed by Kant or Hegel. My aim is not to rehearse the range of options, only to indicate a broad approach subject to a variety of formulations. With regard to the latter, crime is a social phenomenon and has its roots in ideologies, practices and conditions in society as a whole. Again, I do not aim to specify this broad claim in detail, but anyone who has studied criminology will understand that a different set of questions is deployed concerning the nature of criminogenesis than appears in the understanding of normative political theory. This difference in methods matters because it reflects a broad tension in our understanding of crime as either socially caused or conditioned or as a matter of responsibility and political obligation. The effect of the difference is felt within political theory itself, in a tension between what is often called 'the ideal' and 'the actual'.[7]

In brief, the classical philosophers of retribution reflected on this tension as a disjunction between the model of guilt, responsibility or justice they fashioned and the social context of crime. Recognition of a split emerged early between an ideal theory of obligation and an understanding of the actual world in which the theory should be applied. Taking, for example, the case of honour killing – the soldier who kills in a dual, the mother who kills her illegitimate child – Kant wrote that so long as there is conflict between honour and the penal law, the civil constitution will remain 'barbarous and undeveloped' and be 'to blame for the fact that the motives of honour obeyed by the people are subjectively incompatible' with the objective law, 'so that public justice as dispensed by the state is injustice in the eyes of the people'.[8] Hegel similarly wrote of poverty and its impact on crime. The built-in dynamic in modern society was towards impoverishment of those at the bottom of society so that poverty 'immediately takes the form of a wrong done to one class by another'.[9] There is a consequent 'loss of the sense of right and wrong' among the poor, who consequently become a 'penurious rabble'.[10] While he did not pursue the implications of this observation for his theory of punishment, nor did he find a way to reconcile them with his ideal theory.

In Kant, the split between an ideal justice and the justice available in the actually existing world is acknowledged:

> In a world of moral principle governed by God, punishments would be categorically necessary (insofar as transgressions occur). But in a world governed by men, the necessity of punishments is only hypothetical, and that direct union of the concept of transgression with the idea of deserving punishment serves the ruler only as a prescription for what to do.[11]

[7] See Norrie, *Law, Ideology and Punishment* (n 6) chs 2–5.
[8] I Kant, *Political Writings* (Cambridge University Press, 1991) 158.
[9] G Hegel, *Outlines of the Philosophy of Right* (Oxford University Press, 2008) 221.
[10] ibid 222.
[11] A Zweig, *Kant, Philosophical Correspondence 1759–99* (University of Chicago Press, 1967) 199.

And this stems from the antinomialism at the core of his philosophy, where he distinguishes the rational (the ideal) from the actual:

> If I promulgate a penal law against myself as a criminal, it is the pure rightful and legislative reason within me (homo noumenon) which subjects me as a person capable of crime, hence as one person (homo phaenomenon) along with all the others within the civil union, to the penal law.[12]

These problems were not resolved at the beginning of modern thinking about crime and punishment and this remains the case. If poverty becomes 'the form of a wrong done to one class by another' leading to the 'loss of a sense of right and wrong',[13] or if socially accepted motives turn punishment into 'injustice in the eyes of the people',[14] then we have not only a gap between the ideal and the actual, but potentially a radical inversion in which the just becomes unjust, the guilty the innocent, and the perpetrator the victim. Yet, if perpetrators become victims, what has become of their victims? How are we to deal morally with perpetrators as victims who victimise others? If perpetrators as victims are no longer guilty according to the categories of political theory, how are we to think about what they in fact did? Put slightly differently, if the question of guilt has been identified with the issue of political obligation, does the failure of a doctrine of political obligation necessarily entail a fundamental failure of our understanding of guilt? Can we get beyond this impasse in the classical understanding of just punishment?

B. A Modern Restatement

A recent restatement of the problem by Antony Duff offers some ways forward.[15] In its own terms, Duff offers a powerful statement of what a synthetic account of punishment in the modern liberal state should look like. It finds a way of combining backward-looking and forward-looking rationales for punishment that can satisfy both retributivists and consequentialists, achieving this by virtue of an account of punishment as moral dialogue or communication. Punishment aims to communicate to offenders 'the censure they deserve for their crimes, and thus to bring them to repent their crimes, to reform themselves, and to reconcile themselves with those they have wronged'.[16] This is a communicative enterprise between citizens in a liberal community, a form of 'secular penance, which … serves the aims of repentance, reform and reconciliation',[17] where these moral achievements are made possible by the censure that lies in criminal punishment.

[12] Kant (n 8).
[13] Hegel, *Outlines of the Philosophy of Right* (n 9).
[14] Kant (n 8).
[15] Duff (n 4).
[16] ibid 129.
[17] ibid.

Of particular note is Duff's claim that the aims of punishment relate to achieving moral change in a person (repentance, reform, reconciliation), yet these achievements are set in the frame of moral dialogue in a political community. Duff's theory is about how state punishment can be vindicated, and this establishes its problematic. Duff accepts that this setting leaves important matters unresolved, especially around the issue of how theory relates to actual practices of punishment today. Reflecting the distinction between ideal and actual, Duff notes that his account 'depends on an ideal(ised) conception of liberal political community, but we must ask how far our existing political societies come near to actualising such an ideal – and what the implications are if they do not'.[18] As we will see, his identification of the problem is not dissimilar to Kant's and Hegel's two hundred years previously.

Duff lays out in precise terms three related problems, or perhaps three different angles on the same issue. These are: the problem of political obligation for those who reap none of the benefits of political citizenship; the problem of moral standing of those who judge those whose crimes reflect experience of systematic oppression in the liberal polity; and the problem of communication between all parties in a moral community that is structurally and systematically split. Let us consider them.

With regard to political obligation to obey the law, Duff observes that where we move beyond a situation of mere social disadvantage to one of 'serious, persisting, and systematic injustice', those who experience it 'are excluded – politically, materially, normatively – from the community whose law it is',[19] and thus from the obligation to obey the community's law. Such people's actions are not 'wrong qua criminal',[20] since they are not bound by the law in such circumstances. Duff here describes the perpetrator who is himself a victim and is therefore 'not bound to regard the law as a source of authoritative requirements'.[21] The court, representing the community, no longer invokes a political obligation in the offender to obey the law. This then leads to Duff's second point, that the law and its officers in such a setting lack the moral standing to judge the offender,

> since the community in whose name [the court] speaks has so notably failed to treat him in accordance with its declared values, it can hardly claim the right to call him to account for his alleged failure to respect those values as embodied in the criminal law.[22]

Duff's third point concerns the language of law. The criminal law must be what Duff calls a 'common law', that is one that is held in common by a political community. It cannot be viewed as an alien imposition but must be couched in

[18] ibid 130.
[19] ibid 183.
[20] ibid 184.
[21] ibid.
[22] ibid 186.

normative terms that 'the citizens can understand and speak for themselves'.[23] Here Duff begins to push back on the problem of obligation to obey and standing to judge. He views the terms of the criminal law as sufficiently morally thick as to allow citizens to recognise the genuine wrongs that law defines as crimes. He notes that most people 'are not psychopaths to whom the normative language on which the law draws is alien and inaccessible',[24] implying perhaps an obligation to obey based on this deeper moral grounding. Yet at the same time, he accepts that the language of the law will be inflected by the settings in which it is used. With regard to our 'perpetrator-victims':

> Suppose that they are politically, materially, and normatively excluded from many of the community's goods. Suppose too that the accents in which they are addressed … by the law's officials … are the accents not of respect but of contempt, not of authority but of mere power. They cannot then reasonably be expected to hear the language of the law as one that could be theirs … They will rather, and reasonably, hear it as an alien voice that they might have to obey but that they could not make their own.[25]

In this situation, offenders will hear that language,

> not as the voice of a community to which they belong and are treated as belonging, but as the voice of an alien and oppressive power; not as a voice that appeals to values that they share and are treated as sharing, but as a voice that seeks to coerce them into submission.[26]

Duff acknowledges that his 'is not a comfortable position to take' but one that offers at best 'a highly qualified justification of criminal punishment as a necessary but – for the probably extensive time being – morally tainted enterprise about which our consciences should be far from clear'.[27] How then to square the circle of legitimate punishment for the perpetrator-victim? Duff suggests a way forward in these terms:

> In other instances, however, unjustly excluded offenders have still committed genuine wrongs, for which they must be called to account and punished. But their punishment must include some recognition of the wrongs they have suffered and of the morally flawed character of their punishment – which is still tainted by those wrongs.[28]

What though does it mean to commit 'genuine' wrongs, and how does the criminal justice system deal with its own complicity in their commission without appearing hypocritical? The awkwardness of the situation is seen in the role of Duff's sentencer and probation officer. The sentencer should recognise her complicity 'in the regretful or apologetic tones' in which she passes sentence,

[23] ibid 191.
[24] ibid.
[25] ibid 193.
[26] ibid.
[27] ibid 200.
[28] ibid.

while the probation officer's role is to persuade the convicted person to confront and repent their wrongs by persuading them to see 'that their punishment is still justified' while recognising 'the wrongs the offender has suffered at the hands of the community'.[29] But why is it still justified? As Duff has indicated earlier in his argument, 'if the law lacks the standing to call the unjustly excluded to account, it lacks that standing in relation to all crimes, including the most serious mala in se'.[30] So in what sense is it 'still justified'? At this point, we could say that the political theory of punishment has run its course and that it can no longer help us. The gulf between the ideal and the actual means that we lack the ethical wherewithal to think the justice of punishment for crime where the perpetrator is a victim who victimises another. Should we just leave the matter there?

C. A Way Forward

Of note in what has been said is the split that is beginning to open up between guilt as a category in political theory, and guilt as a reflex of something else, a deeper moral instinct, a possible reaction in a perpetrator. In Duff's further account, there are indications of two alternative rationales for thinking through the situation of the perpetrator as victim. While that person is not answerable as a citizen to the political community that has excluded him, this is not to say that 'no one … has the right to call him to account – no one to whom he is answerable'.[31] Normally, he will still 'be answerable to his victim for the moral wrong he has done'[32] and he may be 'answerable to the members of other communities to which he [genuinely] belongs, if he commits a wrong that properly concerns him'.[33] Similarly, his conduct 'can still be judged and criticised by other values and standards than those concerning its conformity to the law'.[34] This is one way forward: to think of deeper moral codes and alternative moral communities that subsist alongside those of the law. Such an argument could also be given deontological foundations, for example by establishing precepts that would allow us to proceed to judge wrong behaviour carried out by persons who have themselves been wronged. It is hard to see that it could bridge the gap between what is morally thick and what is politically obliged. This is a route that in some circumstances we should perhaps pursue,[35] but by itself it may not be

[29] ibid.
[30] ibid 184.
[31] ibid 188.
[32] ibid.
[33] ibid.
[34] ibid 184.
[35] It is one way of understanding the existence of guilt despite large sections of a society appearing to have repudiated it, as in the concept of metaphysical guilt developed to deal with the Nazis in K Jaspers, *The Question of German Guilt* (Fordham University Press, 2000); see also, A Norrie, *Justice and the Slaughterbench* (Routledge, 2017) chs 7 and 10.

sufficient. It still leaves the issue as one of judgement by a group, according to a norm, so that there lacks a sense of why or how the perpetrator/victim might themselves feel a sense of guilt or a need to repent, reform or reconcile. These are among Duff's aims for punishment and they might be occasioned by judgment or sanction, but at their heart they are self-reflexive, so they point to the moral psychology of the perpetrator, not her relationship to the state or political obligation.

Can we get closer to these moral reflexes? The important point is that not one requires a political body to induce it. The sovereign, the court, the law are all the ancillary expressions of a political settlement which Duff seeks to vindicate, but his argument entails the (non-necessary) fusion of two things: the existence of a political entity (to be justified in the terms of a political normativity) and its alignment with a moral psychology (which exists as an underlying existential quality of human being). We can see this in Duff's account of remorse, which he contrasts with that of shame. Shame is a response that is mediated by the reactions of others rather than coming from one's own 'authentically first-person judgment'. In remorse in contrast, 'I judge and condemn my own conduct for myself'.[36] This, Duff says, is essential to his account because his morally dialogic view addresses the offender as an autonomous moral agent who is 'a member of a normative community'. Membership of that community is possible because we can 'appeal to him to judge his own conduct for himself in the light of values that he has made his own'.[37] Remorse, or what I have described as guilt, as a personal reaction to a wrong done even if one was oneself a victim suggests an alternative way forward for thinking through our problem. It is different from externally induced shame and is the lynchpin for establishing the possibility of self-activated repentance, reform and reconciliation. Herein lies the potential for a moral psychology that exists independently of the aims of a system of state punishment. When we consider our category of perpetrator-victims, can we get a better grasp of their moral position if we explore issues of guilt or remorse at a deeper level than a theory of political normativity permits?

III. THE MORAL PSYCHOLOGY OF GUILT: TOWARDS A MORAL GRAMMAR

What is the moral psychology that underpins our feelings of guilt or remorse, and how does it connect what we do with the subject positions we take or the relationships we form? A good starting point is to be found in the work of Melanie Klein. I use her 1937 essay, 'Love, Guilt and Reparation'[38] as the basis for further exploration of how feelings of guilt (remorse) might be related

[36] Duff (n 4) 117.
[37] ibid 118.
[38] Published in Klein (n 5).

to situations of perpetration by victims. I do this by contrasting developing psychological states based on either equality and recognition or on domination and submission. Crucial here is the interaction in emotional lives between subject positions which know both sets of relations. For this part of the argument, I draw on the work of the feminist psychoanalyst, Jessica Benjamin.[39] My suggestion is that Benjamin's work on identity and its relation to domination, submission, equality and respect can provide the basis for a 'moral grammar' of guilt and its associated terminology that rests on Klein's view that guilt lies at the core of the human psyche. This moral psychology can be understood separately from the normative justification of political practices, though it is not irrelevant to them.

A. Love, Guilt and Reparation: Melanie Klein

Melanie Klein's 'Love, Guilt and Reparation' provides some understanding of the basic rationale for feelings of guilt and the desire to repair (to reconcile) in human life. In Klein's post-Freudian psychoanalytic world, greater emphasis is placed on pre-Oedipal phases in human development, which are seen as central to the development of the child and the subsequent adult. Love, security and wellbeing are felt in the very first interactions between the mother and child, but in this earliest phase, feelings of love jostle with feelings of rage, anger and hate. The child who is not fed experiences extreme anger and 'phantasies' of destruction of the 'bad' mother. Love and hate in these early interactions 'are struggling together in the baby's mind', and this 'struggle to a certain extent persists throughout life' and 'profoundly influence[s] the course and the force of the emotional lives of grown-up children'.[40]

How does this work? At the root of Klein's analysis is a dialectic of love, hate, guilt and reparation. Love and hate are the competing tendencies in the early child. When hate is expressed in phantasy as destruction of the 'bad' mother, this leads to anxiety in the infant (in a primary narcissistic phase) that actual harm has been done to the one that is loved. That anxiety, located in the tension between feelings of love and hate, is the basic form of guilt, which the child seeks to address through further phantasies of reparation, but it can never quite lose the initial feeling-set. Guilt and the need to repair are 'more deeply rooted than is usually supposed',[41] and they become a composite element integrated into the complex emotion of love. This is extremely important to Klein's understanding of certain altruistic instincts in the human being, both as infant and as adult. These instincts are not just 'given' to human nature; rather they stem from the

[39] Benjamin (n 5).
[40] Klein (n 5) 308–09.
[41] ibid 309.

necessary existential development of the love/hate/guilt-reparation complex in the infant:

> Side by side with the destructive impulses in the unconscious mind both of the child and of the adult, there exists a profound urge to make sacrifices, in order to help and to put right loved people who in phantasy have been harmed or destroyed. In the depths of the mind, the urge to make people happy is linked up with a strong feeling of responsibility and concern for them, which manifests itself in genuine sympathy with other people and in the ability to understand them, as they are and as they feel.[42]

Crucial to this view is a sense of consideration or compassion that comes from putting oneself in the place of other people. In identifying with them, we access a capacity 'for identification with another person' which is a 'most important element in human relationships in general, and is also a condition for real and strong feelings of love'.[43] What starts out in the parent–child bond extends ultimately to all our human relations, so that this 'making reparation is ... a fundamental element in love and in all human relationships'.[44] The resulting dynamic is one in which the child is able to transfer love beyond the mother and onto others in friendship and in broader social relationships based on compassion. A good basis for adult life is therefore given in the early emotional drama between parent and child. The love that commences there, mediated by the hate that is controlled by guilt and reparation, sets the dynamic complex in place on which later success or failure in human relations depends.

The important thing to note in this dialectic of love and hate is that these are intertwined so that hate is a part of early emotional life, and care, compassion and reparation are not the product of an 'uncomplicated' love, but rather one in which different proto-emotions conjoin. Feelings of guilt and distress 'enter as a new element into the emotion of love'.[45] They do so because the child and the adult are unconsciously aware of the negative, aggressive emotions of which they are capable. Guilt and the desire to repair are accordingly emotions that are deeply engrained in the human psyche and linked to the early anguish about hating and harming those we love. With regard to our concerns in this chapter, it should be plain that Klein's emphasis on guilt as a fundamental element in the human psyche might be important for our thinking about remorse as a mental instinct in the adult perpetrator. Reparation as a central element in Klein's moral psychology could also be important in terms of understanding repentance, reform and reconciliation. However, the link is so far overly generalised, and we need to understand better the circumstances in which the feeling of guilt might be triggered, and with this, how the situation of the perpetrator-victim can be understood.

[42] ibid 311.
[43] ibid.
[44] ibid 313.
[45] ibid 311.

B. Love, Recognition, Identification: Jessica Benjamin

If Klein provides a foundation, I want to add to this the ideas of Jessica Benjamin, whose work in feminist psychoanalysis follows in the line of Klein and, after her, Donald Winnicott.[46] Winnicott developed Klein's 'object relations' approach to psychoanalysis, which concerns the ways in which early experiences in childhood establish an environment which affirms the child's place in the world. In this approach, psychoanalysis shifts from its Freudian focus on the psyche 'as a force field of drives and defences' to 'an inner drama of ego and objects', meaning by the latter 'the mental representation of others'.[47] How we do that will establish what we feel about our actions and how we act in the world. Key here is the relationship between self and other. Becoming a human being involves entering into loving relations with other human beings, and it is the nature of these relations that indicates the possibility that a differentiated moral grammar will articulate the situations in which we might feel guilt, remorse and sentiments of reparation.

In Benjamin's account, the personality of the child evolves through a process of mutual recognition with others, most importantly in the earliest days, with those parent figures most closely involved in its care. Having an identity depends on being the kind of creature that can develop an identity, but it requires the identification and differentiation that good, loving parenting provides. A child grows in and through relationship to others, coming to see that 'I am the doer who does, I am the author of my own acts'.[48] She does so by being with another person who recognises her acts, feelings, intentions, existence, independence, difference precisely as hers. At the core of recognition is the need for the differentiation of the child, but the paradox of differentiation is that the child's assertion of itself is *only* possible through recognition by another. Autonomy emerges out of an ongoing relation to heteronomy. The sense of autonomy is therefore both real and in tension with a relational state that threatens it. Recognition is reflexive, that is 'includes not only the other's confirming response, but also how we find ourselves in that response',[49] and that response can only be helpful if it is the response of another who is herself independent. If she lacks independence, she cannot give the recognition of independence the child needs to be itself.

[46] On Winnicott and his relevance to political theory, see M Nussbaum, *Political Emotions: Why Love Matters for Justice* (Harvard University Press, 2013). In her recent M Nussbaum, *Anger and Forgiveness* (Oxford University Press, 2016) 129–32, Nussbaum moves away from the psychoanalytic understanding of guilt represented in this chapter, which she previously endorsed, in favour of a more straightforward grounding of justice in love and compassion. This seems to me to short-circuit a true understanding of our moral psychology. For discussion of Nussbaum's argument, see A Norrie, 'Love and Justice: Can we Flourish Without Addressing the Past?' (2018) 17 *Journal of Critical Realism* 17.

[47] Benjamin (n 5) 11–12.

[48] ibid 21.

[49] ibid.

This involves a mutual recognition (from parent to child and thence from child to parent) that can represent a sound basis for development of the child and adult alike, and it can be contrasted with the ways in which mutual recognition may fail and in its place may emerge relations of domination and submission. This is a moral-psychological process in natural human development that can proceed in different ways. Children may dominate parents, and vice versa. A balance is achieved where mutual recognition in a respectful space in which both may thrive is achieved. However it goes, Benjamin's overall emphasis is on the structure of relationships that supervene on and mediate the needs and demands of the child in the child–parent bond. From the point of view of this chapter, the ways in which psychological relations evolve will profoundly affect the nature, and indeed the possibility, of guilt and remorse and their associated moral grammar. If Klein points us towards the underlying relationship between guilt and love, Benjamin takes us into how their interaction might unfold in the dynamics of child development towards separation and self-identity. It is this crucial process of recognition, identification and separation, and the problems caused by different kinds of separation, that I shall suggest constitutes the substratum of the moral grammar of guilt and remorse.

C. Mutual Recognition or Domination?

At the core of mutual recognition and self-identification, as I have said, lies an unresolved tension between self and other that takes the form of exposure to the other. Mutual recognition requires that in asserting myself, I recognise you as different from me, and vice versa. Thus it holds open a space within me that is for you, and you must do the same for me. What is at stake here is not only an understanding of the relationship between parent and child, but something with much broader implications, in terms of the nature of adult and social relations in general.

To explain this, Benjamin relates her exposition to Hegel's account of the relationship between the master and the slave.[50] In this relationship, two self-consciousnesses recognise each other, and they recognise the need for each other. Only a self-consciousness has the capacity to recognise another self-consciousness. But at the same time, on Hegel's account, each self-consciousness sees the other as a threat to its autonomy and so these self-consciousnesses end up in conflict as each seeks to assert its independence against the other. The result is a 'life and death struggle' in which one wins and the other loses. One becomes the master, the other the slave. But as a symmetrical relationship of mutual recognition becomes reshaped into an asymmetrical relationship of dominance and submission, so the value of mutual recognition is lost.

[50] ibid. See G Hegel, *Phenomenology of Spirit* (Oxford University Press, 1977) 111–19.

The master can no longer draw upon the recognition of the other who is now his slave, and the slave can no longer draw on the recognition of the master who has defeated him. Recognition of equals becomes transformed into an unequal relation in which one wins and dominates and the other loses and submits, but both, it may be thought, lose in the long run.[51]

For Hegel, the mutuality in the relation between the two self-consciousnesses breaks down, leading to a relationship of domination. This is plainly an unsatisfactory outcome. How can the struggle for recognition be handled better? Benjamin's account sees sustained mutual recognition as the means of achieving independence in a way that avoids the outcome of Hegel's master–slave dialectic. The experience of the early child–parent relationship provides a similar template to Hegel but a possible different result, one in which mutual recognition persists and breakdown is avoided. This is described in an early phase of infantile development as the 'rapprochement' of the baby to the parent. Prior to rapprochement, the baby has a sense of omnipotence, a sense that its every demand ought to be met. This places it in conflict with the parent, and rapprochement is the struggle that plays this out. The outcome is not predetermined but depends on the relationship between parent and child. There are three possibilities. The first is that the child wins, and the parent continues to accede to its every demand. This looks like a victory for the child, but it is the victory of Hegel's master over the slave because in getting its way, the parent has given in and ceased to be an independent other who can then continue to give the child the recognition it needs. To win is ultimately to lose for the child, and the result is 'negation, emptiness, isolation'.[52] A second possibility is that the parent insists on her own position as against the child and is intolerant of the child's will. This looks like a victory for the parent, but the result is a child that is suppressed and adapts to its suppression, so never gaining real independence, becoming submissive and alienated from the parent.

In the first option, the child becomes the master, the parent the slave, in the second, the roles are reversed. In both, a relationship of dominance and submission takes over from one of mutuality and recognition. The third possibility, then, is that the relationship of recognition remains in place:

> In both [the first and second cases] the sense of omnipotence survives, projected onto the other or assumed by the self; in neither case can we say that the other is recognised, or … that the process of recognition has begun. The ideal 'resolution' of the paradox of recognition is for it to continue as a constant tension, but this is not envisaged by Hegel, nor is it given much place in psychoanalysis … The decisive problem remains recognising the other. Establishing myself … means winning the recognition

[51] In the *Phenomenology*, Hegel portrays the master in consequence of his victory as lacking independence and experiencing uncertainty, while the slave becomes conscious of what he truly is through his work, becoming a self-will, but one still 'enmeshed in servitude' (Hegel, *Phenomenology of Spirit* (n 50) 119).

[52] Benjamin (n 5) 35.

> of the other, and this, in turn, means I must finally acknowledge the other as existing for himself and not just for me.[53]

Putting together Benjamin with Klein, the possibility that things might turn out in these three different ways, two based on domination and submission, the third based on mutual recognition, suggests how and why we might develop a moral grammar of guilt. Let us see how this might work.

D. Two Moral Psychologies: Between Mutuality and Domination

The key to the parent–child relation is two states of being, one based on mutuality or equal recognition, the other based on domination and submission. Benjamin terms the latter a state of 'complementarity'. Mutuality preserves the appropriate tension that is in mutual recognition and which refuses the turn to relations of domination and submission. It involves a sense of 'being with' another which is predicated on an 'evolving awareness of difference, on a sense of intimacy felt as occurring between "the two of us"'.[54] Here, it is the sense that the self and the other are differentiated that 'makes experience of merging have such high emotional impact'.[55] The experience of the other as another makes one feel that 'one is truly being "fed", getting nourishment from the outside, rather than supplying everything for oneself':[56]

> In the [mutual] intersubjective interaction both partners are active … The identification with the other person occurs though the sharing of similar states, rather than through reversal. 'Being with' breaks down the oppositions between powerful and helpless, active and passive; it counteracts the tendency to objectify and deny recognition to those weaker or different – to the other. It forms the basis of compassion, [of] 'co-feeling', the ability to share feelings and intentions without demanding control, to experience sameness without obliterating difference.[57]

Contrast this possibility of mutuality with that represented by a relationship of 'complementarity'. This involves a sense of a fixed inequality between self and other. The result is a 'dual unity' of asymmetrical relations of domination and submission rather than acceptance of a potential equalisation and accommodation of the parts. Who dominates, who submits, can be inverted or reversed, but the underlying structure remains constant. The relationship remains one of 'doer and done-to' rather than, for example, one in which both parties may be 'co-doers'. It is this kind of complementarity that permits relations of powerfulness and helplessness, or of activity and passivity to

[53] ibid 36.
[54] ibid 47.
[55] ibid.
[56] ibid.
[57] ibid 48.

be maintained. For Benjamin, the complementary dual unity 'is the basic structure of domination'[58] and submission. When the tension involved in sustaining and balancing a relationship based on mutual recognition becomes difficult to sustain, the psyche may give it up in favour of polarity and conflict of opposites. As a result, oppositions 'can no longer be integrated [and] one side is devalued'.[59] This is the terrain of domination and submission, resulting from a failure to sustain mutual recognition.

The overall point is that these two ways of being, mutuality and complementarity, are both possibilities, and that human beings can move from one to the other. While the 'complementary dual unity is the basic structure of domination' and is 'certainly one of the structures of the psyche, it is not the only one. To see it as such is to leave no space for equality'.[60] The sense of mutuality is often confronted with 'evidence of the striving for omnipotent control, and the hostility to others'. Nonetheless there are 'aspects of the self ... that can oppose (and help to explain) these tendencies'.[61] From this point of view, the two roads of travel, towards mutuality and equality or towards domination and submission, are both ways of playing out the dynamic of love and hate identified by Klein. With this double moral possibility, we can now think how the feeling of guilt and its associated moral grammar might be activated.

E. The Moral Grammar of Guilt

Recalling Klein's initial identification of a sense of guilt and a desire to repair from the complex of early love and hate emotions, I now link these to Benjamin's account of psychological outcomes in relation to recognition. I suggest these may be integrated so that Klein's feelings of guilt and the desire to repair may be related to Benjamin's two states of being, mutuality and complementarity. Both are possible outcomes of the 'bonds of love', and they represent two poles accessible to human beings as they interact with each other. It would be possible, perhaps, for a person to develop only in terms of mutuality of recognition, or only in terms of domination and submission. We could wish that the former state was true for all of us and the latter for none. In reality, however, the likelihood is that most people operate between and access both states at different times in their lives. Insofar as we experience our relationships as based on complementarity between positions of domination and submission, we are nonetheless also aware of the promise and demands of mutuality. Insofar as we experience relationships in terms of mutuality, we are aware we are capable of dominating or being submissive. It would be in the gap between

[58] ibid.
[59] ibid 50.
[60] ibid 48.
[61] ibid.

the two experienced states that feelings of guilt and thoughts of reparation are triggered. While I act to dominate or am required to submit, I may be aware that there is another way of acting that makes my domination or submission feel wrong. With regard to situations where I have sought to dominate, I may now feel bad about it precisely because I feel the alternative approach based on mutual recognition is available. Similarly, in situations where I was forced to submit, I may have a sense of injustice that I should be treated in this way. To feel either of these things is possible because that part of me, the part grounded in a sense of the need and value of mutual recognition, remains constitutive of my psychological formation – even as I act or am required to act in ways counter to it.

It is true that I may fail to access this side of me, either because I do not see what is going on, or perhaps only come to be aware of it at a later date. It is true also that I may be the sort of person who is so caught up in the need to dominate or submit that I do not grasp the alternative possibilities of mutual recognition. A further possibility is that I may sense that there is something to feel, but block it, and revert to the splitting and other techniques which reinforce my sense of my rightness in 'othering' my victim. The range of subject positions is broad and complex, and I may never revert to the mutuality setting, or ever see that it applies, and then of course I will feel no guilt (or injustice). But insofar as I do, then it is my access to the possibility of understanding and experience of mutuality in practices of recognition, established in early infancy, but of continuing significance in how as an adult I live, that is important. It is the tension caused by acting in relations of domination and submission while being aware of the possibility of mutual recognition that will drive a feeling of guilt and injustice. The potential to view the one from the point of view of the other suggested by Benjamin provides the immediate point for expression of the general sense of guilt of which Klein writes.

From this position, we can link a moral psychology of guilt and reparation to the experience of committing a crime, insofar as that experience involves a sense of violation of another. Criminal acts of a morally serious kind may be viewed as attempts to violate, dominate and force another person to submit. Yet, on the Klein–Benjamin view, the perpetrator who seeks to dominate is at the same time she who may have known mutual recognition as part of their moral experience. Their development as human beings has inculcated in them the sense of mutuality, at the same time as they have acted to dominate in a way that conflicts with it. The conflict between the two directions lies at the core of the perturbation of the self that is the sense of guilt. Once again, it must be said that this is not a necessary experience, but it is a possible one, and its possibility is explained according to the moral psychology outlined above.

Relating this argument to Duff's work, we can appreciate the link from ideas in the moral psychology of guilt and remorse to those of repentance, reform and reconciliation. We have here a basis for making sense of their provenance in human life and to extend our understanding. For example, with regard to reconciliation, the moral psychology of guilt would permit us to think through the related moral concept of forgiveness. The injustice in domination and forced submission that is measured by a moral psychology of recognition is experienced as wrong by the person so affected. She should not have been dominated and forced to submit. Asserting her need for recognition, that person would like the wrong to be addressed, and the position of mutuality restored. Once so restored, for example by apology in word or deed, there would be a basis for responding to the wronging party with recognition that their wrong has been addressed. The return on both sides to a place of mutual recognition could be based upon acceptance of guilt and reparation by a perpetrator and of forgiveness in their light by a victim. The underlying logic of the dialogue is the attempt to shift the moral terms of the relationship away from domination and on to recognition.

Of course, nothing in this simple sketch of the guilt-reparation complex suggests that the practical resolution of problems caused by treating another as an object of domination rather than a subject of recognition is straightforward. All it does is indicate what the logic of moral psychology underpinning the moral grammar of guilt and reparation might be, and how moral feelings that accompany violation might be lodged at the core of human being.

IV. THE GUILT OF PERPETRATORS AS VICTIMS WHO VICTIMISE

It is Klein's dynamic of love and hate, guilt and reconciliation together with Benjamin's space of mutuality or domination that I suggest lies at the core of the moral psychology of guilt or remorse for conduct that violates another. The key point is that the possible space of domination and forced submission may coexist for perpetrators with an alternative understanding of mutual recognition. What Klein gives us is a basic dynamic of love, hate, guilt and reparation, while Benjamin's 'bonds of love' may go awry. Her analysis of recognition, with its different possible directions for good or ill, adds an understanding of how things might play out in different ways, for good or bad. If we start from the complex fusing of love and hate in Klein, leading to reactions of guilt and reparation, but then think of how love is expressed in interpersonal relations in Benjamin, we can understand how guilt and reparation unfold in interpersonal relations too, and with their own moral grammar. Given the link between early childhood and adult experience (Klein) and between personal and political dramas of recognition (Benjamin), we have reason to posit this as the key to guilt and reparation in adult life. What starts as a basic experience of infantile growth remains with us and generates our most basic moral feelings. Insofar as guilt is experienced for wrongdoing, it is informed by our moral understanding of violation as domination and submission, generating the counter-experience of mutual respect and recognition with which it may be contrasted. It is this moral-psychological experience that underlies Duff's repentance, reform and reconciliation. Here, we are not just in the realm of thought. Remorse is a real feeling, something perhaps sickening, experienced in the gut as much as in the head.[62] It is that feeling that we should try to understand, and the moral psychology made possible by psychoanalytic thinking can take us there.

This returns me to the guilt of perpetrators as victims who victimise. Such people may be on the receiving end of social relations of domination. They may be poor, angry, excluded, but insofar as they participate in the domination of their victims, there is still the space for a feeling of guilt in what they have done. I do not say they must feel guilt, only that there is a space for feeling guilt grounded in experiences of mutual recognition they may have had. Most people have had such experiences, through parents, close family and so on. Such feelings exist independently of questions relating to the legitimacy of state punishment. Whether the perpetrator feels under a normative obligation to the state, recognises its authorities as having moral standing, or sees its language of law as common or alien, these all represent different issues from those I have explored here. In practice there will of course be overlap, since it will often be the same violative conduct that is subject to judgment in both the court of the mind and of the state. It would however be possible for the perpetrator as social victim to experience the sense that in one domain they should feel no guilt, while in the other they should. The resulting split and tension reflects the nature of life in a repressive and exploitative social world.

Perpetrators who are victims may not feel guilt in terms of a political obligation to maintain the law, and punishment will then be imposed without a proper moral connection, or society might opt to punish them for non-guilt based reasons such as deterrence. Yet in such a setting, we can say two distinct things: that criminal justice in an unjust society is unjust; and that perpetrators who are victims may feel guilty about what they have done. Both statements may be true, but they cannot easily be conjoined so that, for example, the guilty feelings of the perpetrator who is a victim compensate for the injustice of her punishment. Nor could we say that the injustice of the social system removes or cancels the perpetrator/victim's feelings of guilt. The two claims sit in different registers, one as a matter of normative relations in a polity, the other as an observation about the ethical and affective standpoint of the individual, in a world of social injustice.

There is a theoretical impasse here, but it does not have to be so. It could be resolved in practice by fundamental social change. The answer lies in seeing how just punishment would have to involve two things. The first is a society that genuinely wishes to address issues of social injustice, so that criminal responsibility begins to look less like blaming perpetrators who are also victims. If the past and present victimisation of perpetrators is actively addressed, then any personal guilt they feel can begin to be aligned with the guilt-invoking purposes

[62] H Morris, *On Guilt and Innocence* (University of California Press, 1976) 99.

of the criminal justice system. If this were to happen, it would have a secondary effect. This would become a society in which perpetrators (victims who victimise) would be supported in seeing that what they have done they ought to feel guilty about. It would be a society that in its social commitments was demonstrating that equality and mutual respect, not domination and submission, lie at its core. Such a situation would be one where mutual recognition at the societal level paralleled and reinforced the logic of mutual recognition at the personal level. Guilt as an interpersonal psychological feeling and as a societal practice could then align.

8

Responsibility Beyond Blame: Unfree Agency and the Moral Psychology of Criminal Law's Persons

CRAIG REEVES*

> We need to recast our ethical conceptions ... not in order to escape or adjust ourselves to determinism or naturalistic explanation ... [but] in order to be truthful even to what we know already about our psychology.[1]

> If it is true of any institution that it has inscribed into it a psychology, this is likeliest to be ... the criminal law.[2]

I. INTRODUCTION

IT IS OFTEN claimed that a therapeutic stance towards offenders and respecting them as persons are incompatible: only the retributive or 'just deserts' model, and not the 'treatment' or 'therapy' model, can respect offenders as persons. Treatment or therapy inevitably disrespects offenders, seeing them as less than persons, so criminal justice should be self-consciously oriented to holding responsible, attributing blame and administering punishment according to an abstract and thus impartial set of standards relating to the culpability of conduct. It should self-consciously refrain from a therapeutic stance that takes criminal offending to be a manifestation of some kind of pathology. Therapeutic or rehabilitative interventions are permissible but only as a supplement to retribution, for a departure from retributive reason is bound to entail

* I am very grateful to Alec Hinshelwood, Jaakko Nevasto, Alan Norrie and Matt Sinnicks for their helpful comments on earlier drafts as well as for many excellent conversations on the issues. I am also indebted to Matt Matravers for his insightful comments on and encouragement with the chapter.

[1] B Williams, *Making Sense of Humanity* (Cambridge University Press, 1995) 19.

[2] R Wollheim, *The Mind and Its Depths* (Harvard University Press, 1993) 129.

a denial of the offender's agency and a suppression of their capacity for rights, that is, a denial of the respect owed to them as persons.

In a series of recent papers, Nicola Lacey and Hanna Pickard have challenged this orthodoxy, arguing that, on the contrary, therapy can be reconciled with respect for persons, because we can reconcile therapy with the justice model. They argue that Pickard's 'clinical model' of 'responsibility without blame'[3] based on reflection on therapeutic work with psychopathology shows us how to reconcile the justice model of criminal responsibility and punishment with the reparative and reconciliatory ideal of a therapeutic dialogue animated by a spirit not of blame but of forgiveness.[4]

The retributivist argument that only retributive punishment involving hard treatment in proportion to wrongdoing can respect offenders as persons got considerable mileage out of a stereotype of therapy: that it involves reifying the patient, ceasing to engage with them as a person, and treating them as a mere thing, outside the 'moral community'.[5] Lacey and Pickard insist this stereotype is ignorant of the facts: therapists working with psychopathology of the sorts common among offenders in actual fact do hold patients responsible for their actions and impose consequences, thus deploying the basic norms of the justice model, and they do this as an integral part of their therapeutic practice. But they do this not in a retributive spirit, but from a compassionate stance of therapeutic concern that involves avoiding the blaming emotions.

The clinical case shows that holding responsible for actions and imposing consequences for wrongdoing – 'detached blame' – and the negative moral emotions and the imposition of suffering or hard treatment – 'affective blame' – are separable. The norms of detached blame say essentially that 'responsibility tracks agency', so that people are responsible where their agency was appropriately engaged,[6] but affective blame is distinct from and not entailed by such judgements of detached blame. This distinction is actual in therapy, and if it is actual it is possible, so retributivism is wrong: a criminal process that both holds responsible according to the justice model and thus respects offenders as persons, and approaches punishment in a forgiving and reconciliatory way, is possible.

[3] H Pickard, 'Responsibility Without Blame: Empathy and the Effective Treatment of Personality Disorder' (2011) 18 *Philosophy, Psychiatry and Psychology* 3; H Pickard, 'Responsibility Without Blame: Philosophical Reflections on Clinical Practice' in KWM Fulford et al (eds), *Oxford Handbook of Philosophy and Psychiatry* (Oxford University Press, 2013).

[4] N Lacey and H Pickard, 'From the Consulting Room to the Courtroom? Taking the Clinical Model of Responsibility Without Blame into the Legal Realm' (2013) 33 *Oxford Journal of Legal Studies* 1; N Lacey and H Pickard, 'To Blame or to Forgive? Reconciling Punishment and Forgiveness in Criminal Justice' (2015) 35 *Oxford Journal of Legal Studies* 665.

[5] P Strawson, 'Freedom and Resentment' (1962) 48 *Proceedings of the British Academy* 1, reprinted in J Fischer and D Ravizza (eds), *Perspectives on Moral Responsibility* (Cornell University Press, 1993) 59.

[6] Lacey and Pickard, 'To Blame or to Forgive?' (n 4) 666.

Further, we not only can but ought to institutionalise a model of criminal justice that places forgiving and reconciliatory dialogue, rather than blame and hard treatment, at its core. Although we hold responsible and punish in accordance with the justice model, we need not and should not do so in a spirit of affectively blaming. We can and should aim for criminal practices informed by the reparative forgiveness strategies of communicating the harm done by the offender's behaviour, indicating the potential for repair and maintenance of a valuable relationship (between offender and community) if wrongdoing is avoided in future, and reminding the offender of the importance to them of the valuable things that are at stake in maintaining that relationship.[7] Guided by these, we should eschew punitiveness and put reparative and reconciliatory strategies at the centre of criminal punishment.

This is a richly suggestive account animated by a humane impulse, and it challenges the retributivist revival to take seriously the real psychology of criminal law's persons. Yet to me it seems that Lacey and Pickard's position does not go as far as – according to certain of its own impulses and insights – it ought to in challenging retributivist dogma and our existing criminal practices.

It is unclear, after all, how different their proposals are from those of prominent humane retributivists like Antony Duff. They insist that 'hard treatment' is not essential to criminal punishment, but 'serious consequences', 'no doubt typically negative but occasionally not',[8] are, and it is not clear how deep this distinction goes. It is the stigma, exclusion and condemnation of retributive hard treatment that they oppose, but humane retributivists like Duff are opposed to those as well, construing punishment as about repentance, reparation and reconciliation.[9] They seem to assume that condemnation, stigma and exclusion are primarily a function of 'affective blame', so that if we jettison affective blame while keeping detached blame, this would allow us to remove these painful features of punishment while retaining the basic structure of our practice of holding criminally responsible and punishing. But this is controversial. If it seems unlikely that hard treatment will be able to avoid stigma, exclusion and condemnation, it seems equally unlikely that 'serious negative consequences' imposed in response to criminal conviction within our existing practice will, for in virtue of being so imposed, and thereby of meaning what they mean, they are likely to be painful in the same ways.[10] Stigma and exclusion are to some extent bound to attach to any punishments within our existing criminal justice practices, to any 'serious consequences' imposed for criminal conviction.

[7] ibid 680–81.

[8] Lacey and Pickard, 'From the Consulting Room to the Courtroom?' (n 4) 8.

[9] RA Duff, *Punishment, Communication, and Community* (Oxford University Press, 2001) 106–09.

[10] See J Feinberg, 'The Expressive Function of Punishment' (1965) 49 *The Monist* 397, 397–423.

Perhaps Lacey and Pickard overestimate the importance of 'affective blame' – the blaming emotions – in retributivist theory and practice. While some – notably, expressivist – versions of retributivism do explicitly see punishment as properly expressing blaming emotions like anger, resentment, indignation or hatred,[11] most do not make affective blame central to punishment at all. For Duff, for example, punishment's point is not to express negative emotions but to communicate moral criticism in a rational dialogue, and through that dialogue to encourage reparation and reconciliation. Even for retributivists who, like Michael Moore, give the blaming emotions a central place in the justification of retributivism,[12] punishment is not itself about expressing those blaming emotions; its point is to give effect to the moral demands that our moral emotions reveal. And in actual practice as well it is unclear that affective blame plays much of a role in retributive punishment.

This might explain why, when we jettison affective blame and keep detached blame, we are still left with something in the ilk of humane retributivism. Lacey and Pickard's model remains caught in the unstable tension that characterises our existing criminal practices: the real psychology of criminal law's persons, the limitations to freedom that can in fact arise given our psychology, and the social constraints that shape and limit our capacities, are taken into account at the sentencing and punishment stage, but these same features are suppressed at the conviction stage of criminal law's judgement of responsibility, 'detached blame'. Lacey and Pickard accept this compromise even while certain of their insights speak against it.

This is, I suspect, because they concede a crucial retributivist premise: that respect depends on holding responsible,[13] 'detached blame'; that anything else might reify or 'dehumanise' offenders,[14] treating them as mere things or animals rather than rational agents. That premise, though, presupposes a theory of agency and a moral psychology, both questionable, which are embedded in our existing holding responsible practices. Lacey and Pickard's acceptance of this retributivist premise prevents them from getting into view something that their own reflections on affective blame imply: that our moral emotions disclose the inappropriateness not only of punitiveness but of the categorial structure of our practice of holding criminally responsible, 'detached blame', itself.

Far from being uniquely placed to respect offenders as persons, the retributive practice of detached blame, of holding responsible and punishing, is

[11] See J Feinberg, 'The Expressivist Function of Punishment' (n 10); J Murphy and J Hampton (eds), *Forgiveness and Mercy* (Cambridge University Press, 1988). On expressivism, see C Reeves, 'What Punishment Expresses' (2019) 28 *Social and Legal Studies* 31, 31–57.

[12] MS Moore, *Placing Blame: A Theory of the Criminal Law* (Oxford University Press, 1997) chs 1–4.

[13] V Tadros, 'Poverty and Responsibility' (2009) 43 *Journal of Value Inquiry* 391.

[14] J Gardner, 'On the General Part of the Criminal Law' in RA Duff (ed), *Philosophy and the Criminal Law* (Cambridge University Press, 1998) 254.

incapable of doing so. Therapy can be reconciled with respect, not because therapy can be reconciled with the justice model, but because respect does not depend on the justice model at all. The justice model's austere conception of respect ignores the psychology of real persons and fictionalises them as autonomous beings abstracted from the constraints, limitations and privations of psychological reality. Lacey and Pickard's model is unable to follow through on its important insights into the normative significance of the real psychology of persons because it remains committed to a responsibility practice governed by such a fiction. In order to institute respect for criminal law's persons, a radically transformed responsibility practice would be necessary. Or so, at least, I shall argue. I begin by arguing that what undermines affective blame must undermine detached blame as well (section II), and then develop an account of what that might be (sections III–V), before considering the implications of this for our criminal responsibility practice, and some of the reasons why these might be resisted (sections VI–VII), concluding with a suggestion as to how to proceed from here (section VIII).

II. BLAME AND BLAMEWORTHINESS

The claim that we can and should preserve detached blame while rejecting affective blame, thereby reconciling the 'justice' – that is, retributive – model of detached blame with forgiving punishment presupposes that 'detached' and 'affective' blame are normatively separable: that there are phenomena which ground reasons which rationally undermine affective blame that do not also count against detached blame (where by 'rationally undermining' I mean reasons which are justifying and thereby psychologically efficacious). Only if this is so can it be consistent to disavow affective blame while endorsing detached blame, for only then can there be grounds which can move us to do so whose moving us is owed to their justifying us in doing so. And my immanent criticism of the model is quite straightforward: that this premise of normative separability turns out on inspection to be false. So in fact that which rationally undermines affective blame also rationally undermines detached blame.

Lacey and Pickard offer three kinds of reason said to rationally undermine affective blame, which correspond to the three rationality-conditions on blaming emotions that Pickard has elsewhere proposed,[15] and none satisfy the normative separability test. First, they propose subjective reasons, that is, reasons which focus on us and our wider aims and purposes. Basically, affectively blaming and the punitive practices it motivates in criminal justice will not do any good and may even frustrate our wider purposes – reduction of offending and public

[15] H Pickard, 'Irrational Blame' (2013) 73 *Analysis* 613, 624.

protection, rehabilitation and reintegration of offenders into the community, say.[16] Drawing on work in evolutionary psychology, they point out that

> [r]etributive punishment that stigmatises and gives license to expressions of affective blame may therefore serve to further alienate such offenders from society – in effect, increasing the divide between 'us' and 'them' and shifting an already marginalised and underprivileged faction of our community into a bona fide out-group, thereby confirming their belief that there can be no valuable relationship between society and them.[17]

If we want to reduce reoffending and protect the public, the best strategy is a reintegrative and reconciliatory approach to punishment through forgiveness rather than affective blame. At the same time, detached blame – holding criminally responsible – is claimed to actively further these wider aims.

These subjective reasons correspond to Pickard's condition on rational blame that it 'must not actively undermine rational ends'.[18] They are essentially strategic reasons concerning what it is instrumentally rational for us to feel and do given our wider aims. This sort of criticism of affective blame fits within the broader tradition of what Srinivasan has recently called a 'counterproductivity critique'.[19] But, as she points out, subjective, strategic reasons are merely extrinsic reasons for not feeling or expressing some emotion, which are tangential to the question of whether those emotions are intrinsically appropriate.

Indeed, it is odd that Pickard counts this sort of subjective strategic rationality as among the rationality-conditions for the moral emotions at all, for we can ask of anything whether it conflicts with our wider rational ends, but we would not entertain 'conduciveness to our wider rational ends' as one of the rationality-conditions of belief, say: we cannot, and generally should not even if we could, believe according to what suits our wider aims. Revising a belief just because holding it conflicts with our wider aims is a central case of doxastic irrationality: rationalisation.

Strategic rationality seems similarly to miss the point with the blaming emotions as well – as Srinivasan puts it, 'a shift of focus from intrinsic to instrumental justification for anger often comes across as a non sequitur (at best) and morally obtuse (at worst)'.[20] Though one can always ask about how anything fits with our wider aims, it is unclear that such extrinsic considerations properly belong to accounts of the rationality of rational phenomena. They appear to support the separability of the reasons bearing on detached and on affective blame only by side-stepping this more fundamental issue. That is, subjective,

[16] Lacey and Pickard, 'From the Consulting Room to the Courtroom?' (n 4) 21.
[17] ibid 22.
[18] Pickard, 'Irrational Blame' (n 15) 624.
[19] A Srinivasan, 'The Aptness of Anger' (2018) 26 *Journal of Political Philosophy* 123, 125.
[20] ibid 128.

strategic reasons do not seem to be the *right kind* of reasons for not affectively blaming.[21] In light of this it is unsurprising that, as Lacey and Pickard admit, such strategic considerations are not likely to cut the motivational mustard with the blaming emotions. We may see strategic reasons not to blame and yet remain, and rightly so, unmoved, because they are not reasons of the relevant sort.

Second, they propose intersubjective or relational reasons not to affectively blame, corresponding to Pickard's condition that 'blame must be appropriate to the nature of the relationship'.[22] Given the hardships many offenders have faced in life (trauma, abuse, neglect and deprivation of various kinds) that are typically connected to social injustices or failures of the community, we may think that

> [w]hen children grow up in our midst subject to such conditions, arguably we as a society bear some responsibility for the harm inflicted on them if we fail to intervene. Our responsibility, in turn, may undercut our moral standing to affectively blame the adults these children become.[23]

As a political community, our complicit responsibility deprives us of the standing to express or even feel affective blame toward offenders; the normative character of our relationship as a community to those of our members we have failed gives reasons in political morality against affective blame. But these, too, fail to underwrite normative separability: for it is unclear why our community's responsibility and complicity don't similarly undermine our standing to hold people responsible and punish them altogether. Is it not the case that, as Murphy argued, since 'just punishment rests upon reciprocity', and a feature of 'most existing communities [is] the absence of such reciprocity', that 'punishment is unjust in such a setting because it involves pretending (contrary to fact) that the conditions of justified punishment are met'?[24] And if we ask, in Duff's words, whether the community has 'the right to call [offenders] to account for their wrongs, with suitably clean collective hands and with clear consciences',[25] why should the same factors that allegedly vitiate affective blame not compel us to answer 'no'?

They assert that 'the appeal to adverse early environment and social inequality does not eliminate criminal responsibility or argue against accountability' because 'responsibility is attributed simply in virtue of agency',[26] but this is changing the subject. The relevant question here is not what the grounds of

[21] See P Hieronymi, 'The Wrong Kind of Reason' (2005) 102 *Journal of Philosophy*, 437–57; O Na'aman, 'The Fitting Resolution of Anger' (2020) 177 *Philosophical Studies* 2417.

[22] Pickard, 'Irrational Blame' (n 15) 624.

[23] Lacey and Pickard, 'From the Consulting Room to the Courtroom?' (n 4) 24.

[24] JG Murphy, *Retribution, Justice and Therapy* (Reidel, 1979) 80.

[25] RA Duff, *Answering for Crime: Responsibility and Liability in the Criminal Law* (Hart Publishing, 2007) 192.

[26] Lacey and Pickard, 'From the Consulting Room to the Courtroom?' (n 4) 24.

attribution of responsibility are, but whether we as a community have the standing to hold persons to account, to hold them responsible, and punish them, at all, given what Lacey and Pickard see as our community's complicity with the offender's hardships and offending. Indeed, they seem to concede the point when writing that 'the moral standing to hold to account is also arguably premised on relatively equal relationships, and is hence undermined in radically unequal societies such as ours'.[27] The obvious reply might be to insist, as Duff did in an earlier piece, that although our community is unjust and fails people, it is not so bad that it undermines our standing to hold them responsible.[28] This would save detached blame, but it will not underwrite normative separability, for the obvious rejoinder would be that if things are not so bad, they are presumably not so bad that we cannot affectively blame, either. For it is unclear why our standing to hold responsible at all should be any more resilient in the face of radical community failures than our standing to affectively blame. On normative separability, the intersubjective reasons fare no better than the subjective ones.

Now Lacey and Pickard accept that 'just as clinicians no doubt sometimes fail to keep affective blame at bay' despite the good subjective, strategic reasons to do so, in criminal justice as well the subjective reasons not to affectively blame will not necessarily be sufficient to motivate not affectively blaming, and suggest another strategy they think helps in clinical work and can do so in criminal justice as well: reflection on 'the whole of the person and the whole of their story',[29] the person's whole reality. This takes in reflection on that person's present psychological and social situation, and on their past experiences, life history. Reflection on a person's life narrative will typically reveal, in clinical and criminal justice contexts, histories of 'severe childhood psychosocial adversity'[30] and other social hardships and exclusions, connected to class-based, racialised and gendered domination and exclusion. Hence we should see the offender 'not only as one who harms, but as one who has been harmed', as 'both perpetrators and as victims', and doing so will help to motivate not affectively blaming: 'at least reducing, if not outright extinguishing, its force'.[31]

Now to the extent that reflection on the person's whole reality rationally undermines blaming emotions, that can only plausibly be because such reflection reveals objective reasons not to affectively blame – that is, reasons bearing on the intrinsic appropriateness of blaming emotions toward the person who is their potential object, in the whole context. Such reasons correspond to Pickard's

[27] ibid.

[28] RA Duff, 'Law, Language and Community: Some Preconditions of Criminal Liability' (1998) 18 *Oxford Journal of Legal Studies* 189. By 2007 Duff's position is more equivocal: see Duff, *Answering for Crime* (n 25) 192–93.

[29] Lacey and Pickard, 'From the Consulting Room to the Courtroom?' (n 4) 23.

[30] ibid 24.

[31] ibid 23.

third (objectivist) requirement, that the person blamed 'must be blameworthy and so justly deserve a hostile, negative response',[32] and it is now clear what the problem is: the objective rationality-condition for affective blame just is blameworthiness, that is, desert of detached blame, of being held responsible. The crucial consideration is the irreducible question of the intrinsic fittingness of the blaming emotions to the person who is their object, but this is the very same question as the question of detached blame, that is, of the intrinsic appropriateness of holding responsible itself. The responsiveness of our blaming emotions to reflection on the person's whole reality is an implicit judgement about blameworthiness itself, and thus puts in question not only blaming emotions but detached blame – holding criminally responsible – itself.

III. THE TYRANNY OF THE PAST

We might think the ethically relevant feature of the whole reality of the person is not the deprivations and hardships in the person's past per se, but rather the effects that those experiences have had on the person they now are. Lacey and Pickard, though, reason backwards from those effects rather than putting them centre stage: 'given the degree of psychiatric morbidity in the prison population, it is reasonable to conclude that many … are not only perpetrators, but also past victims'.[33] When we reflect on the often terrible hardships, trauma and suffering that is a typical feature of both patient and offender histories, this provokes 'compassion and understanding', and thereby dislodges blame.

Now, that someone has suffered in the past might make us feel compassion, but that does not on its own rationally undermine blame. The suggestion here might be we feel they have 'suffered enough'. But, as retributivists have often pointed out,[34] this inference seems implausible. In itself, past suffering does not cancel present blameworthiness. We do not blame someone less on finding out they had flu recently. Alternatively, it might be that such reflections motivate not affectively blaming because of some general determinist incompatibilist commitment: our blaming emotions subside in response to the thought that their crimes were caused (by their past suffering). But, as compatibilists have argued, that thought would not account for the specific focus on offenders' traumatic pasts. If everything is causally determined, and that fact undermines affective blame, then that should hold across the board, and the fact of psychosocial hardship should be neither here nor there.[35] Neither interpretation, then, can rationally explain the impact of someone's past hardship on our blaming emotions.

[32] Pickard, 'Irrational Blame' (n 15) 624.
[33] Lacey and Pickard, 'From the Consulting Room to the Courtroom?' (n 4) 24.
[34] eg, G Sher, *Desert* (Princeton University Press, 1987).
[35] eg, Moore (n 12) 487.

How, then, does the person's traumatic past bear on our moral emotions? It must be mediated by our appreciating not just that someone has suffered, but that their past suffering distinctively explains how they came to be as they now are. It is the link between their past and their present reality that is crucial. While Lacey and Pickard reason back from 'psychiatric morbidity' to presumed past victimhood, this gets the cart before the horse: what is important is not as such that they have been victims of harm, but the consequences of such past harms for their present psychological actuality. Lacey and Pickard gesture towards this thought when emphasising that such offenders 'have not only suffered terrible harm, but … have also not been given the opportunity to learn how to behave as moral citizens should'.[36] This situates the importance of the person's history in relation to a deeper understanding of who they have become and why they have acted as they have. Against this, Gary Watson suggests that when we only know about a wrongdoer's present situation, we have no grounds for not blaming them, but when we learn about their past and find a history of abuse and deprivation, we change our understanding: we now make sense of why they are that way, for anyone – we might think – who'd had their life might well have become much like them.[37] But this is to separate the person's present reality from their past in an unsustainable way, flattening out the different possible modes of our relation to our past and of its bearing on who we are in the present. In thinking that the person's present situation gives us no grounds for not blaming, Watson assumes that the present person is a product of their past only in the sense that anyone is, in a truistic and empty sense, a product of their past. In seeing no difference between this general sense in which we are all products of our past, and the distinctive ways in which someone who has suffered a life of neglect, trauma or abuse may be a product of their past, Watson is pushed towards thinking of the significance of a traumatic past as having to do with the general significance of an event-determinist metaphysics for responsibility.

Lacey and Pickard's remarks about the significance of the past lead them in a similar direction: the effect of a traumatised offender's past on them is not in kind different from the effect of anyone else's; it is just that their history has led them to being the kind of person who does not know how to be well-behaved. This view is inevitable if one assumes a certain implausible but widely accepted event-based metaphysics, but it is unviable because it collapses the distinction between the influence of the past and the tyranny of the past.[38]

As MacIntyre has recently pointed out, a view on which every 'adult life is equally shaped and controlled by the past' is one in which 'some of the crucial differences' between agents with certain sorts of psychopathology and rationally

[36] Lacey and Pickard, 'From the Consulting Room to the Courtroom?' (n 4) 24.

[37] G Watson, 'Responsibility and the Limits of Evil' in G Watson (ed), *Agency and Answerability: Selected Essays* (Oxford University Press, 2004).

[38] See R Wollheim, *The Thread of Life* (Cambridge University Press, 1986) ch 5.

healthy agents are 'obliterated'.[39] The sorts of traumatic life-histories typical of serious offenders can cause people deep and lasting psychological harm. It is not know-*that* but know-*how* that they've been denied the chance to learn: know-how consists not of propositional content, but of rational powers (or capacities). The developmental disruption, disturbance or privation of certain central rational powers is what is picked out by the concept of the tyranny of the past as distinct from the mere having of a past. Someone's traumatic past rationally bears on our emotional response because it deepens our understanding of their present by making comprehensible how they might be in the present tyrannised by what they have in the past undergone.

The relevance, then, of reflection on someone's past history lies in contextualising and deepening our understanding of the person they have become and the ways they have come to act. It is about not merely seeing the offender 'not only as one who harms, but as one who has been harmed', but seeing them as one who harms *because* they have been harmed, where the explanatory 'because' flows not through indiscriminately causally deterministic chains of events, but through the developmental privation – inhibition, suppression, distortion – of the person's rational powers. Life history is relevant to the extent that past experiences have blocked, distorted or undone the acquisition or development of rational powers that are essential to agency and necessary for what we may call, in the language of moral psychology, rational health,[40] or, in the language of moral philosophy, freedom, in the sense of autonomy. This is why attention to a person's past is important. My suggestion is that it is by generating an inchoate appreciation of this unfreedom or heteronomy, manifest in many cases of psychopathology and in many others that would not be clinically so described, that reflection on the person's whole reality rationally undermines affective blame by undermining its objective aptness, that is, by undermining blameworthiness.

IV. UNFREE AGENCY

In denying this, Lacey and Pickard must claim that the agentive capacities the norms of responsibility supposedly track are properly engaged even while affective blame would be inapt. They are the familiar 'volitional capacities' of 'choice and a sufficient degree of control', and those 'cognitive capacities' such that '[the person] know[s] what they are doing when they commit an offence'.[41]

The immediate problem here is that the concepts 'choice', 'control' and 'knowledge' are equivocal as to their referent, and this obscures the fact that

[39] A MacIntyre, *The Unconscious*, rev edn (Routledge, 2004) 9.

[40] See R Moran, *Authority and Estrangement* (Princeton University Press, 2001); E Harcourt, 'Containment and Rational Health' (2017) 26 *European Journal of Philosophy* 798.

[41] Lacey and Pickard, 'From the Consulting Room to the Courtroom?' (n 4) 2.

what is implicitly required by our holding responsible norms is something more than agency simpliciter: it is autonomous agency.

It is in one sense trivially true that agents 'exercise choice and control' and 'know what they are doing' in any particular action: if it is an action, something they do rather than something that merely happens to or in them, there are at least various choices the agent makes (whether reflectively or not) concerning precisely how to move their body, they exercise control over their body as it moves, and they know what they are doing under some true description. This is what is involved in the freedom of spontaneity, analytic to agency.[42] But this does not entail autonomy – choice, control and knowledge in the ethically relevant sense.

For choice over aspects of the particular action does not entail choice over the kind of action. And control of one's body does not entail control of one's actions: one may 'control one's body', that is, move one's body, without being in control of the kinds of actions one does. That requires agency with respect not merely to one's movements but to one's ends. But it is surely the kind of action, not the particular action, that matters for blameworthiness.[43] Spontaneity powers are not unimportant because they are essential to agency, but the engagement of autonomy powers, rational agency with respect to one's ends, is what counts for blameworthiness. And knowledge of what one is doing under some description is necessary to agency, but that minimal sort of knowledge does not entail the right kind of practical knowledge at the right level of description: the level of the end that is practically efficacious in it. That may not be known to the agent, either in the right way, or at all.

The sort of knowledge relevant here is a special kind of self-knowledge that is essentially first-personal, and the agent may not know the end that is practically efficacious and thereby realised in their action in this first-personal way. They may find their action, or the end they are pursuing in it, unintelligible; or they may find their act intelligible but only because they have distorted their apprehension of the world in which they act, so that the morally salient true descriptions under which they are acting are unavailable to them. In either case, they may properly be said to not know what they are doing in the relevant way, despite 'knowing what they are doing' in the minimal, spontaneity sense.

The kinds of choice, control and knowledge that is analytic to agentive spontaneity, then, do not entail autonomy. Persons are not necessarily autonomous; their actions may be fully actions, and yet unfree, heteronomous. And this – I want to suggest – is what is presupposed by, and explains, the way our moral emotions are affected by reflection on the person's whole reality.

Autonomy of action means that the action is the agent's own, but over what this amounts to there is deep dispute. Subjectivist accounts of autonomy

[42] H Steward, 'Fairness, Agency and the Flicker of Freedom' (2009) 43 *Noûs* 64.
[43] As Steward argues, ibid.

understand autonomy to be something to do with the internal coherence-relations within a person's psychological items or 'motivational set', and which connect autonomy to the phenomenological, such that it is constitutive of heteronomy that it shows up in the person's experience, as felt alienation. The most influential such 'hierarchical' accounts stipulate that autonomous actions are those flowing from effective desires (which move the agent to action) the agent is identified with, where that means the desires cohere with some special 'higher-order' mental items that 'speak for' the agent ('higher-order desires',[44] 'values',[45] the desire to be rational,[46] temporally projected 'plans and policies',[47] etc).

Such accounts turn out be inadequate to both our pre-theoretical intuitions and clinical practice. They insist that autonomy is purely internal to the psychology of a person so that only failures that show up phenomenologically for the agent can count as failures of autonomy, but that seems to fail to account for various cases where we would want to deny the person is autonomous, such as systematic brainwashing, sci-fi mental-state-manipulation,[48] or psychotic delusion. In such cases, that the person does not feel that their attitudes are awry, that they do not subjectively experience their heteronomy, seems only to compound, not cancel out, the problem.

But subjectivist accounts implicitly recommend such delusional states as a cure for heteronomy. For one way to cure a person's heteronomy, on such views, would be to manipulate their higher order desires/values etc, so that those corresponded with the hitherto alienated first-order desires. If heteronomy is merely subjective in that subjectively felt alienation is constitutive or essential to it, one could remedy heteronomy by manipulating the higher-order desires/values etc, whose conflict with those first-order desires makes for their alienation. On this view, psychosis could be a remedy for neurotic heteronomy: my alienation from my neurotic desires to perform what I see as irrational actions can be eliminated if I come to see them – falsely – as rational and valuable actions, as things worth wanting to do. A philosophical elucidation of the concept of autonomy that entails that you can avoid violating someone's autonomy by manipulating them more, or that you can escape the heteronomy of neurosis by regressing to psychosis, is hardly promising.

In response, others, such as John Christman, offer procedural qualifications, so that an agent is not autonomous if their effective desires are those which,

[44] H Frankfurt, 'Freedom of the Will and the Concept of a Person' in H Frankfurt (ed), *The Importance of What we Care About* (Cambridge University Press, 1988).

[45] G Watson, 'Free Agency' in G Watson (ed), *Agency and Answerability: Selected Essays* (Oxford University Press, 2004).

[46] D Velleman, 'What Happens When Someone Acts?' (1992) 101 *Mind* 461.

[47] M Bratman, 'Reflection, Planning and Temporally Extended Agency' in M Bratman (ed), *Structures of Agency* (Oxford University Press, 2007).

[48] As in Frankfurt-style examples.

even if they now identify with them, they would reject if they understood their genesis.[49] This is designed to ensure that desires brought about by manipulation or pathological irrationality are not counted as autonomous, regardless of whether or not the agent feels alienated from them. But it ultimately remains a form of coherentist subjectivism that runs into analogous problems in harder cases. The hypothetical conditional that, of a heteronomous desire (or belief, emotion, etc), the agent would not endorse it if they understood its causal history, only holds if the agent endorses appropriate procedural norms, such that they could recognise the normative force of procedural violations in such a way that they would be led to self-criticism by procedural scrutiny of their attitudes.[50]

Whether manipulation undermines someone's autonomy will thus depend on that person's normative conception of appropriate versus manipulative procedures, that is, on that person's conceptualisation of autonomy. One could thus avoid manipulating someone simply by ensuring that, in addition to whatever else in their motivational set you manipulated, you also manipulated their conception of autonomy, their normative understanding of the distinction between the procedurally appropriate and the manipulative. We could cure someone of their heteronomy by manipulating their commitments as to the appropriate procedural requirements for desire-formation or as to the relevance of procedural standards themselves to the question of whether they should endorse a desire. Similarly, psychosis could still be a remedy for neurosis as long as one's delusions included delusions about the nature of and procedural requirements for autonomy. The more sophisticated subjectivist accounts of autonomy and heteronomy become, it seems, the more insidious become the sorts of manipulation they recommend.

Of course, subjectivist accounts of autonomy articulate something which in many cases is valuable (internal harmony in a person's motivational set), but they cannot recognise that it is not always, in the abstract, valuable, nor explain why it is when it is. What such accounts lack is the ability to distinguish between those cases where the satisfaction of subjectivist criteria is a genuine mark of autonomy, and those cases where it may be a mark of greater heteronomy.

Now Pickard has elsewhere claimed that agency does entail autonomy – that spontaneity powers entail autonomy powers, so that choice, control and knowledge regarding one's body's particular movements entails choice, control and knowledge regarding one's ends as well.[51] But her argument there really shows only that on a certain dominant theory of action heteronomous action is incoherent. The theory of action (and thus the metaphysics) presupposed

[49] See J Christman, 'Autonomy and Personal History' (1991) 21 *Canadian Journal of Philosophy* 1; and the critical discussion in F Freyenhagen and T O'Shea, 'Hidden Substance' (2013) 9 *International Journal of Law in Context* 53.

[50] See Freyenhagen and O'Shea, ibid 63.

[51] H Pickard, 'Psychopathology and the Ability to Do Otherwise' (2015) 90 *Philosophy and Phenomenological Research* 135.

by subjectivist accounts – the so-called 'standard story'[52] – is on independent grounds inadequate. The standard story conceives of action as bodily movement that is *just caused* by desire (plus belief), and heteronomous actions as bodily movements that are just caused – by alienated desires, desires that are in conflict with the higher-order desires (values, etc) that supposedly 'speak for' the agent. Since it is, in this picture, the higher-order desires that represent the agent's role in their action that a heteronomous action is caused without and contrary to the agent's higher-order desires means that it occurs without the agent's own participation. But we cannot make sense of heteronomous agency by appeal to the idea that such actions are just caused without the agent's participation, for then it is unclear how those 'actions' are really actions at all.[53]

But it does not follow from that that agency entails autonomy, that the concept of heteronomous action is incoherent. What Pickard's account misses is that the standard story of action with its event-causal metaphysical presuppositions does just as bad a job of making sense of autonomous as of heteronomous action.[54] If the standard story cannot make sense of autonomous action anyway, its failure to make sense of heteronomous action says nothing against the reality of heteronomous action itself. The proper conclusion to draw is not that agency is necessarily autonomous, but that the standard story is inadequate to the task of rendering action, autonomous or heteronomous, intelligible.

Heteronomous action must consist in an alien structure in the agent's relation to the ends they themselves realise in their actions. But this cannot be a merely subjective affair; since subjectivist accounts are systematically unable to articulate what is valuable in subjective autonomy, only some form of objectivist account will do. Christman's position contains an element that is genuinely objectivist, in his stipulation that the process of desire-formation must not have involved 'manifestly inconsistent' desires or beliefs,[55] objectivist because it does not depend on whether or not the agent subjectively recognises the relevance of manifest inconsistency. But why, once we accept that something objective like this can undermine autonomy, should we stop there?

A robustly objectivist account of autonomy would make autonomy track responsiveness to real reasons.[56] Autonomy then refers to an ideal wherein the

[52] Velleman (n 46).

[53] M Alvarez, 'Actions, Thought-experiments and the Ability to Do Otherwise' (2009) 87 *Australasian Journal of Philosophy* 61; H Steward, *A Metaphysics for Freedom* (Oxford University Press, 2012).

[54] For a recent, persuasive argument to this effect see A Hinshelwood, 'The Relations Between Agency, Identification and Alienation' (2013) 16 *Philosophical Explorations* 243.

[55] Christman (n 49) 15.

[56] See S Wolf, 'Sanity and the Metaphysics of Responsibility' in F Schoeman (ed), *Responsibility, Character, and the Emotions* (Cambridge University Press, 1987); P Benson, 'Feminist Intuitions and the Normative Substance of Autonomy' in JS Taylor (ed), *Personal Autonomy* (Cambridge University Press, 2005). Freyenhagen and O'Shea (n 49) and F Freyenhagen, 'Autonomy's Substance' (2015) 34 *Journal of Applied Philosophy* 114 – to which the last few paragraphs are heavily indebted – recently defend the objectivist view.

powers of practically rational agency are properly developed and engaged. In autonomous action practically self-conscious thought is efficacious:[57] in acting, the agent knows the end they are striving to realise 'under the aspect of the end',[58] that is, they apprehend the end they are realising first-personally or from the inside, *qua* end, viz as something valuable, good, worth realising, and they apprehend what they are doing as issuing from their apprehension of the end. Hence the autonomous agent is in a position to answer Anscombe's distinctive sense of the question 'why?' by giving their reasons for action, which they apprehend, as such from the inside.[59] When this is so, the agent's relevant motivational states are 'transparent'[60] but *for the right reasons*: they are an expression of the agent's rational powers of responsiveness to the world. This conception underpins libertarian accounts of a Kantian or Sartrean character which claim that agency is necessarily autonomous, a view Pickard seems to endorse. But such libertarian accounts assert the ideal as an actuality – they assert the necessary practical efficacy of reason. Yet reflection on what we know about the real psychology of persons suggests otherwise – that though autonomous action, practically self-conscious thought, is a real possibility, it is not a necessary feature of agency. It is rather an aspiration and an accomplishment that can fail or break down because autonomy-powers can be prevented from developing or engaging properly.

V. THE MORAL PSYCHOLOGY OF HETERONOMY

What is at stake in thinking about autonomy and heteronomy is, to put it in Aristotelian terms, the possibility of a harmonious relation between the rational and non-rational natures in the soul.[61] And psychoanalysis, as Lear has argued, is a taking up of this Aristotelian question that rejects the picture of reason and nature sitting alongside one another as unrelated principles in the soul, and reconceives their relation as one of interpenetration.[62] This move allows it not only to further our understanding of how autonomy might in practice be realised, but deepens our appreciation of the ways it can go awry, and thus of why it should be a difficult accomplishment at all. Let me consider two such ways.

First, in subjective unfreedom/heteronomy, the end the agent realises in action is not one they apprehend 'under the aspect of the end': although it is moving

[57] See M Boyle and D Lavin, 'Goodness and Desire' in S Tenenbaum (ed), *Desire, Practical Reason, and the Good* (Oxford University Press, 2010); M Haase, 'Practically Self-Conscious Life' (MS); S Rodl, *Self-consciousness* (Harvard University Press, 2007).

[58] T Aquinas, *Summa Theologiae* La, question 6, art 2.

[59] See E Anscombe, *Intention* (Harvard University Press, 2000).

[60] In Moran's sense in Moran (n 40).

[61] See J Lear, *Wisdom Won From Illness* (Harvard University Press, 2017) ch 1.

[62] This is not something that cognitive psychology has been able to do, though I cannot defend this claim here.

them to action, and so they know that it is their end, they cannot make sense of it as their end. They see it as not sufficiently worth pursuing, but this evaluation does not have the result of dislodging or dissipating its power, its draw. The person's evaluative reason has become, with respect to a certain region of inner life, inert, because that region has been insulated from reason's power by a forcefield of unintelligibility. And this means reason has ceased, within this region of their life, to be practically efficacious. The agent knows, as if third-personally, what the end pursued in their action as a matter of fact is, but they cannot avow it as their end. It seems to them alien, and their alienation manifests a crisis of self-intelligibility. Such a structure has often been thought characteristic of neurotics and unwilling addicts 'helplessly violated' by their desires,[63] and of other even more troubling cases. Wollheim recounts the serial murderer Dennis Nilsen's thinking to himself, as he prepared to execute his latest victim, 'here I go again', and remarks that here 'he is thereby revealing … [that] His murderousness surprises him as much as us'.[64] Though 'we are very unlikely to be able to see why … he desires what he desires … [he] is likely to be in exactly the same position'.[65]

This is the sort of heteronomy that subjectivist accounts recognise, but as we have seen they are not able to explain why it is heteronomous, nor how such heteronomous action is even possible. But a certain sort of psychoanalytic account is promising on both scores, because it brings into view how desire may be organised by our non-rational nature – *unconscious phantasy* – through unconscious symbolic links, so that our rational powers of evaluation and practical deliberation are rendered impotent. As Lear has argued, Freud's conception of unconscious phantasy replaces the canonical conception of a simply irrational part of the soul with a non-rational form of mental functioning that is not simply chaotic but has an inner *logos* of its own, though a fundamentally different, archaic and infantile one which is metaphorical, wishful and bodily.[66] Phantasies can be thought of as emotionally and affectively charged implicit narrative or dramatic structures that organise conscious experience like an emotional *a priori* structure. Through symbolic associations and substitutions, unrealistic unconscious phantasy can get overlaid onto the world in distorting ways, such that the person is consciously motivated to pursue some end that is incomprehensible to them as an end. They cannot see any point or worth in it, and that is because, as a conscious end in the world, there *is* no point to it. It is really just a metaphorical stand-in for some archaic relic, an ossified infantile wish that can make no sense to adult, conscious comprehension, or is so unacceptable to their conscious reflection that they cannot get it into view.

[63] Frankfurt (n 44).
[64] Wollheim, *The Mind and Its Depths* (n 2) 124.
[65] ibid.
[66] See Lear (n 61).

Thus, phantasy can give rise to a desire that is 'imperious'[67] because it is unintelligible, and so untestable and unrevisable: acting on it does not promise any comprehensible satisfaction, not only as we see it, but as the agent themselves sees it; it becomes an entrenched bit of unreason. Such imperious desires are manifestations not of rational powers, but of the subversion of those powers by unconscious phantasy. This is why they lack transparency. They are not non-transparent in quite the way Moran seems to envisage the paradigm case, but although the agent first-personally apprehends their imperious desire in the distinctive way in which desire is felt from the inside, and thus apprehends from the inside the end as the end they are pursuing, they are not able to first-personally apprehend that end *as* an end, 'under the aspect of' the end': it is not intelligible to them as something worth pursuing. It is because the distorting influence of unconscious phantasy, rather than the agent's rational powers, is the source of the desire that its 'force' is so divorced from its 'importance'.[68] An agent's acting on an unimportant and unintelligible, alien desire appears inexplicable only until we grasp that what is explanatorily crucial is not the desire they are acting on, but the phantasy the agent is 'acting out'. Because they cannot apprehend nor comprehend this unconscious phantasy first-personally, nor the fact of their acting it out, they are not in a position to subject either to practical reflection, revision or restraint. If this is right, Freud's concepts of unconscious phantasy and of 'acting out' help elucidate subjective unfreedom as a real psychological possibility for us.

Second, objective unfreedom or heteronomy. The action is in pursuit of an end that the person apprehends from the inside not only as their end but as *an* end. The desire which motivates them is thus, at the time of acting, transparent in Moran's sense: the person comprehends their desire from the inside and takes it to be tracking what is worth desiring. There is, at the time, no first-personal gap between force and importance. Objectively heteronomous action is thus subjectively, phenomenologically, indistinguishable from autonomous action. What distinguishes it from autonomous action is what it is that explains the transparency of the desire. In autonomous action the desire is transparent for the right reasons: it is transparent because it is the expression of the person's rational powers in shaping their own inclinations in accordance with their appreciation of what is worth wanting. Objectively unfree actions are motivated by desires that are transparent for the wrong reasons: they are rooted in unconscious phantasy, like imperious desires, but that phantasy has reorganised – distorted – not only their desires but also their view of the world and of themselves, their view of external and internal reality.

The direction of fit is the wrong way round here: desire has not been brought into line with reason; reason – including perceptual and introspective

[67] Wollheim, *The Thread of Life* (n 38) 120.
[68] See Wollheim, *The Mind and Its Depths* (n 2) 123.

interpretation – has been brought into line with desire, because both have been conditioned non-rationally by unconscious phantasy. There is, then, no immediately available subjective foothold by which the person can get into view either sort of distortion. If such distortion is, unusually, deep and stable, we call it brainwashing or psychosis, but more localised and transient distortions of this kind are commonplace, figuring centrally in some types of personality disorder, and more commonly still at lower levels in everyone.

Subjective unfreedom is thus an advance on objective unfreedom, because it manifests the person's capacity to avoid distorting the world to fit the desire, which, with the world undistortedly in view, is encountered as simply unintelligible instead.[69] Hence the arachnophobe's inefficacious awareness that British spiders are harmless contrasts favourably with the psychotic delusion that, say, a cover-up is suppressing the facts about the actual deadliness of British spiders. More familiarly, anxiety, anger or affection may distort our experience of persons and situations rather than being shaped by those experiences, and when this happens our experience is prefabricated by unconscious phantasy rather than being a rationally responsive apprehension of the world.

The power to distinguish what is coming from inside and what is coming from outside is what Bion called the capacity to 'contain' bits of mental life,[70] and it is something that must be acquired through the right intersubjective experiences, with, to begin with, the parents. The more developed the capacity to contain, the more a person will be able to avoid unconscious distortions of the world in experience. Uncontained phantasy will often be localised, transient or oscillating: the person may think to themselves that their earlier anger was quite irrational given the context but be unable to retain this thought first-personally the next time it happens. Outside the immediate grip of the phantasy, they apprehend the temporary transparency of those motives as itself an illusion, but in the moment such insight is unavailable. Phantasies may be activated by events and then pass away so that temporary distortions of experience wax and wane.

Through the concepts of unconscious phantasy and of containment, then, psychoanalysis also helps elucidate the possibilities of mundane objectively unfree action.[71]

VI. THE ANTINOMY OF RESPONSIBILITY

This account of heteronomy elucidates the possibility of unfree agency, which explains the pervasiveness of the tyranny of the past that is, I have claimed,

[69] See Harcourt (n 40).

[70] W Bion, 'Attacks on Linking' in W Bion (ed), *Second Thoughts* (Karnac, 1984).

[71] For readers wary of psychoanalytic vocabulary, the points I have just made could be roughly articulated in the terms of the contemporary cognitive-neuroscientific paradigm – though not without loss.

the true object of reflection on the whole reality of the person. We now have an explanation of why attention to the whole reality of the person rationally undermines affective blame, objectively, such as to undermine blameworthiness and thus the normative structure of our holding criminally responsible practice itself.

The upshot, I want to claim, is that our practice of holding responsible is fundamentally inadequate to the real psychology of criminal law's persons. The task for the philosophy of criminal law is to engage in concrete utopian reflections on the possibility of a different responsibility practice in a changed form of ethical life that would be more adequate to the real psychology of persons.

This is not, of course, the conclusion Lacey and Pickard reach. Instead, we saw, they insist that the sensitivity of our moral emotions to the whole reality of the person has no bearing on the validity of the normative structure of our practice of holding criminally responsible, 'detached blame'. But Lacey and Pickard individually have very different conceptions of what sort of thing our practice of holding responsible is, and together they seem to follow Pickard's view of responsibility norms as embodying timeless metaphysical truths about agency, just the kind of view which Lacey has elsewhere criticised.[72] But this means they have to assert that our existing responsibility norms track capacities that are properly exercised in wrongdoing even where affective blame is not apt. And this overlooks the distinction, considered above, between agency simpliciter (spontaneity), and autonomous agency. It ignores the actuality of the category of unfree agency and the real moral psychology of heteronomy.

Elsewhere, Lacey has argued that privations in rational capacities undermine autonomy in ways the criminal law's norms fail properly to recognise, and in ways she thinks deprive many offenders of a fair opportunity to conform their behaviour to the criminal law.[73] But these same factors become, in the Lacey and Pickard position, irrelevant to the norms of holding criminally responsible. Lacey's independent arguments suggest that the Lacey and Pickard account of detached blame – that 'responsibility tracks agency' – is inadequate. She has railed against retributivists like Moore for advancing the view that responsibility tracks metaphysical truths about agency, but the 'responsibility without blame' model seems to endorse just that sort of view of the norms of our practice of holding criminally responsible.

Moreover, the 'responsibility tracks agency' view is, as they admit, a rather simplified story, for it says nothing about how the central excuses such as duress operate, but it is clear that duress does not rest on the fact that the person's agency was not engaged, that their actions were not fully actions; duress

[72] See N Lacey, 'Responsibility and Modernity in Criminal Law' (2001) 9 *Journal of Political Philosophy* 249; N Lacey, 'In Search of the Responsible Subject' (2001) 64 *Modern Law Review* 350.

[73] N Lacey, 'Socializing the Subject of Criminal Law: Criminal Responsibility and the Purposes of Criminalization' (2016) 99 *Marquette Law Review* 541.

excuses by negating the voluntariness of action, not of movement. If we are to understand our current conception of the bounds of voluntariness as being more than merely decisionistic, we will need to see it as recognising – albeit in certain very limited circumstances – the fragility and contingency of autonomy, the vulnerability of our rational powers to inner and outer circumstance: the real psychology of persons, and the social context in which that develops and in which people act. But then the 'responsibility tracks agency' view must be wrong. Responsibility norms already implicitly recognise (albeit in limited ways) both that responsibility depends on autonomy, and that agents are not necessarily autonomous.

Lacey and Pickard resist this conclusion because, I suspect, they worry that the only alternative to holding responsible is not holding responsible, exculpating. That alternative is unattractive because to simply exculpate heteronomous wrongdoing would be ethically unserious. This is already a difficulty for Lacey's account in 'Socializing the Subject', for she there also links her 'socializing' of the criminally responsible subject to a vision of 'criminal law and its surrounding processes' as 'aspir[ing] to foster positive goals such as integration, reform, and even forgiveness',[74] but it is unclear how these could be pursued if responsibility norms exculpate heteronomous wrongdoing in the ways she envisages (whether through more contextual *mens rea* standards or defences).[75] Within the binary logic of our practice of holding criminally responsible, not holding responsible, exculpating, marks the end of the matter. And that would surely fail to do justice to the person's relationship to their past wrongdoing and to the community's relationship to that and to the person in light of it.[76]

Both the Lacey and Pickard position which asserts that 'responsibility tracks agency' and that our practice of holding responsible is unscathed by the critique of affective blame, and the alternative that Lacey endorses in 'Socializing the Subject', which entertains not holding responsible in recognition of individual heteronomy, fail to carve at the joints of moral reality. What motivates each is the inadequacy of its opposite. Neither holding responsible nor exculpating is satisfactory, and yet there seems to be no other alternative: this I call the *antinomy of responsibility*.

What are we to make of it? Lacey and Pickard side with holding responsible followed by forgiving and reparative dialogue, and that is certainly a more attractive compromise than we have in practice at the moment, but a compromise it still is, and an unstable one. This becomes explicit when Lacey and Pickard

[74] ibid 556.

[75] Lacey prefers more sensitive fault standards, while others have favoured special defences: D Delgado, 'Rotten Social Background Should the Criminal Law Recognise a Defence of Severe Environmental Deprivation?' (1985) 3 *Law and Inequality* 9.

[76] The alternative of a 'bar to trial' defence (see Duff, *Answering for Crime* (n 25) 192–93; Duff, *Punishment, Communication, and Community* (n 9) ch 5) would have the same result and seems no less ethically unserious.

concede that, as they are seeing things, holding responsible sits in tension with reparative dialogue and change.[77]

The categorial straitjacket that forces us into the antinomy of holding responsible or not holding responsible is the artefact of a concrete, contingent form of ethical life. The alternative to compromise would be to reject the choice our existing responsibility practice imposes on us: that is inadequate to the moral reality that our moral emotions intimate and a realistic philosophical psychology elucidates. If we are willing to put that practice in question – to see it as merely the form of ethical life that we happen to have – then we can see that not holding responsible does not entail exculpating after all: it only entails exculpating within the categorial terms of our existing practice. A radically different responsibility practice might make possible a response which is neither holding responsible nor exculpating.

The question, then, is whether a different form of ethical life is possible, whether a different responsibility practice informed by the real psychology of persons that could recognise heteronomy and institute realistic respect for unfree agents is possible. I see no convincing grounds for maintaining that our ethical life is in principle the most desirable one possible, that it could not conceivably change to take on a very different, more realistic and truthful shape, or for insisting on a pragmatism, whether Wittgensteinian or Hegelian, that renders the idea of radical ethical criticism of our form of ethical life itself unintelligible. That way lies, as Williams put it, 'an undiscriminating acceptance of whatever conceptual resources of [our] society actually exist'.[78] Our efforts should be turned to the task of thinking through what such a different responsibility practice, a more realistic and truthful form of ethical life, might look like and what resources for its development might be identified in what we already know about the as-yet only partially actualised human life-form.[79]

VII. RESPONSIBILITY, REIFICATION AND RESPECT

I began by noting the influential *reification objection*: retributivists have often suggested that any alternative to our existing practice of holding responsible must reify agents, treating them as if they were a mere thing and thus depriving them of the respect that is owed to persons. As Strawson put it, 'the humanity of the offender himself is offended' by not holding responsible.[80] Arguments in these terms have been commonplace since: not to hold responsible would be

[77] Lacey and Pickard, 'To Blame or to Forgive?' (n 4) 690.

[78] B Williams, 'Pluralism, Community and Left Wittgensteinianism' in B Williams (ed), *In the Beginning Was the Deed* (Princeton University Press, 2005) 36.

[79] See C Reeves, 'Beyond the Postmetaphysical Turn' (2016) 16 *Journal of Critical Realism* 217.

[80] Strawson (n 5) 62.

to 'objectify',[81] 'disrespect'[82] or 'dehumanise'[83] the person, to deprive them of the status of persons. Channelling the 1970s anti-psychiatry zeitgeist, Murphy wrote:

> Practices of punishment and responsibility are compatible with human dignity in that they place a premium upon the status of persons as choosing beings. One alternative to this is coercive therapy ... [involving] perhaps a total restructuring of the personality [as in] *A Clockwork Orange* [or] *One Flew Over the Cuckoo's Nest*.[84]

Murphy echoes a contrast pressed earlier by Strawson,[85] and, though presented as *an* alternative, its rhetorical force flows from the tacit suggestion that a reifying system of treatment in which crime is 'regarded as a symptom', a 'happening with a causal explanation rather than an action for which there were reasons',[86] is the *only conceivable* alternative to our existing practice of holding responsible. Any practice that departed fundamentally from our practice of holding responsible would be one in which the 'distinction between mere events or happenings and human actions is erased',[87] reifying people and thus failing to respect them as agents or persons with dignity and rights.

Now this reificatory denial of respect is, so the objection goes, entailed by the acknowledgment of heteronomy. Once we admit that someone acted heteronomously, we are effectively admitting that they are not agents or persons at all, at least in respect of the relevant conduct. And once that move is made, the individual's rights, their entitlement to be treated as a person, have been obliterated, for, as a bit of mere causal nature, there is no reason not to coercively treat them, as we might a dangerous animal. Any alternative to holding responsible that countenances the heteronomy of criminal law's persons is bound to regard someone, as Moore puts it, 'as an in-itself rather than as a for-itself'.[88]

Yet the objection rests on an inadequate conception of the object of respect, real persons, and in turn on an austere and unrealistic conception of respect for persons. It is rooted, as Moore's Sartrean jargon indicates, in the Kantian dualism of things and persons, where heteronomy belongs to the realm of things, mere causal nature, whereas respect attaches to persons conceived as necessarily autonomous, rational wills.[89] With that dualism in place, to view someone as heteronomous entails a shift to seeing them as a mere thing, because the hallmark of personhood is rational autonomy.

[81] Moore (n 12) 546.
[82] Tadros (n 13) 392.
[83] Gardner (n 14) 254.
[84] Murphy (n 24) 134–35.
[85] Strawson (n 5).
[86] H Morris, 'Persons and Punishment' in H Morris (ed), *On Guilt and Innocence* (University of California Press, 1976) 36.
[87] ibid 37.
[88] Moore (n 12) 546.
[89] See I Kant, *Groundwork of the Metaphysics of Morals* (trans H Paton, Harper and Row, 1964) 65 and 428. I discuss this point in more detail in C Reeves, 'Adorno, Freedom and Criminal Law' (2016) 27 *Law and Critique* 323.

Retributivism accurately registers the fact that our existing responsibility practices are deeply embedded in this dualism, so that within its conceptual constraints, to not hold responsible is to reify. But this implication arises only because of the way in which our responsibility practices and their underlying conceptual order shoehorn the ethical phenomena into a false dilemma between autonomous persons and heteronomous things. Since this Kantian picture rules out heteronomous agency, it confines respect to autonomous agents. The question of the normative standing of heteronomous, unfree agents simply does not arise. And under the influence of this picture, it is supposed that there is no alternative to our practice of holding responsible that would not be reifying.

But if agency can be unfree, heteronomous, in the ways I have suggested, then the picture is false; it ought to be abandoned. The forms of heteronomy I have considered do not undermine agency: recognising them does not imply a view of actions as indistinguishable from mere happenings, symptoms; they do not turn someone into a mere thing or mere animal, a bit of causal nature. Rather, they work through agency and action: heteronomy is a privation in the exercise of agency, not a negation of it. Heteronomy does not obliterate agency; it is intelligibly predicated only of agency. And this means there should be no temptation to insist that heteronomous agents are mere things that do not warrant respect.

Indeed, if we are all, to a greater or lesser extent and in differentiated and particular ways, heteronomous agents, heteronomous agency should be seen as the norm and the paradigm case of a rights-bearing agent. Moreover, autonomy and heteronomy are not all-or-nothing. Heteronomy is typically localised, selective and specific. Regions of heteronomy in a person's life, rather than heteronomy across the board, are the norm. Such regions do not render a person wholly unintelligible to us as an ethical interlocutor. Rather, they render certain regions of that person's life – their desires, beliefs, emotional responses, in some areas – unintelligible to us: just the same regions that are (in subjective heteronomy) or should be (in objective heteronomy) unintelligible to them.

Consider, then, Gardner and Macklem's claim that 'self-respecting defendants' have reason to refuse excuses based on 'rationally incapacitating conditions' because they

> have an interest in being accorded their status as fully-fledged human beings, ie as creatures whose lives are rationally intelligible even when they go off the rails, and who can therefore give a rationally intelligible account of how they came to do so.[90]

This implicitly denies the possibility of heteronomy. As MacIntyre writes,

> individuals afflicted by neurosis resort to psychoanalysis [because] they have found themselves doing things that they have no good reason to do or good reason not to

[90] J Gardner and T Macklem, 'Compassion Without Respect? Nine Fallacies in *R v Smith*' (2001) *Criminal Law Review* 623, 627.

> do, they have tried to reason with themselves and then have discovered that their reasoning has been flawed by phantasy, or ... has been practically ineffective. They have become to some degree unintelligible to themselves.[91]

Certainly, we want to be accorded 'our' status as 'fully-fledged human beings', and to be such is to aspire to being a creature whose life is 'rationally intelligible'. But this is as a matter of fact frequently not what our lives are actually like: we are endemically liable to fall short of that aspiration. But this does not mean we cease thereby to be fully-fledged human beings, becoming non-rational animals, or, even, mere things, our actions mere happenings. It is internal to being a fully-fledged human being that one is a creature whose life is not necessarily and always rationally intelligible.

In cases of objective unfreedom, the person is, at the time, unable to see their own heteronomy. Under such conditions, an agent's seemingly 'rationally intelligible account' of their conduct may be false, and systematically so. The drive to be the sort of creature that can give a rational self-account may, under conditions of objective heteronomy, feed mere rationalisation and thus entrench objective heteronomy. After all, the tendency to render intelligible what is in fact unintelligible lies at the heart of objective heteronomy itself, and surely our interest is in being able to give a genuine rationally intelligible account of ourselves rather than a mere rationalisation.

With subjective unfreedom, the person is aware of their unfreedom, because they are aware of the objective unintelligibility of their alien end. Here, the agent will not be able to give a 'rationally intelligible account' of themselves at all. Relative to objective heteronomy this is an advance, but it still manifests a privation *qua* rational animal. Yet, such self-unintelligibility is not a failure to be fully a person; it is a possibility of privation immanent to personhood.

Unfree agency occupies a space between autonomous self-intelligible agency and arbitrary causal nature, where transparent, rational self-intelligibility is an essential aspiration, but not a given. The reification objection is premised on an austere and unrealistic psychological and metaphysical picture that is unable to make space for this thought. In the equation of 'fully-fledged human being' with 'rationally self-intelligible creature', it, like our practice of holding responsible, is guilty of over-rationalising the psychology of real persons. This over-rationalising of the person goes hand-in-hand with an under-rationalising of heteronomy: recall that unconscious phantasy is not remotely mere causal nature, but rather an idiosyncratically meaningful drama with a certain narrative and bodily *logos* of its own.

The conceptual dualism of our holding responsible practices tracks the organising opposition of persons and things and forces us to fit the facts into one of these categories. But it is wrong to think that this dilemma is itself basic

[91] MacIntyre (n 39) 13.

and unavoidable rather than the artefact of the moral practices we happen to have. Lacey and Pickard wrongly concede that the only way to institute respect is by holding responsible, and this obscures the more radical implications of their thought that reflection on the whole reality of the person (rationally) undermines affective blame. They endorse our existing holding responsible practice because they see that as the only alternative to reification. But this dilemma itself presupposes the categorical frame of our existing responsibility practice – the modern metaphysics of things and persons – and the austere conception of what persons would have to be like to warrant the respect that that entails. Lacey and Pickard's position really points to the need for radically changed, psychologically realistic and ethically serious responsibility practices instituting real respect for persons comprehended as potentially free but often unfree agents.

VIII. THE GRAMMAR OF TAKING RESPONSIBILITY

One promising avenue is suggested by Lacey and Pickard's remark that 'it is a presumption of effective treatment that patients have choice and a significant degree of control over their behaviour and can therefore be asked to take responsibility for it, as we naturally say'.[92] Now asking someone to take responsibility is not the same as holding them responsible. And the grammar of taking responsibility may, it seems to me, contain the conceptual seeds for a changed responsibility practice that would be truthful and ethically serious, that could institute genuine respect for persons apprehended as rational animals for whom privation and heteronomy are pervasive possibilities, and that could be more in tune than our existing practice is with the reparative and reconciliatory aspirations that animate Lacey and Pickard's account.

That grammar of taking responsibility is at the core of therapeutic action – not the cognitive therapy on which Pickard focuses, but the psychoanalytic conversation, in which 'two people actively interact with each other, each in the process (among other things) of trying to understand each other and themselves'.[93] In asking someone to take responsibility within the psychoanalytic process, the analyst aims to cultivate in someone self-intelligibility-for-the-right-reasons, which is to say, rational health, real autonomy, but this necessarily involves their transforming their relationship to their own mental life and to what they have been and have done. This undertaking necessarily involves a commitment to openness to truthfulness, to the reality of others, and to potential change. It builds into its presuppositions humility in the face of one's vulnerability as well as the aspiration to and courage for a painful transformative self-emancipatory

[92] Lacey and Pickard, 'From the Consulting Room to the Courtroom?' (n 4) 13.
[93] Lear (n 61) 179.

process. That is, it offers a more psychologically realistic and ethically serious answer to the question, in Lear's words, of what it would involve for someone to become 'able to reconcile themselves to their past'.[94]

Whereas the grammar of holding responsible is that of theoretical attribution of a status, a being, and is essentially second-personal, the grammar of taking responsibility is that of a dynamic, practical process of becoming, and is essentially first-personal. So while holding oneself responsible is essentially an internalised second-personal theoretical judgement in which the self is a passive object, taking responsibility is an active practical judgement in which the 'I' figures as an agent of a self-transformation. Holding someone responsible is to ask them to hold themselves responsible, to internalise a second-personal static, theoretical judgement; asking someone to take responsibility is to ask them to undertake a process of change towards truthfulness and increased freedom.

The grammar of taking responsibility thus presupposes neither that someone is a necessarily heteronomous, passive mere thing, which would make emancipatory change impossible, nor that they are a necessarily autonomous person, which would make emancipatory change unnecessary. Rather, it presupposes that they are a realistically conceived 'fully-fledged human being', that is, a potentially autonomous but actually (partially) heteronomous person, one whose unfree passivities are themselves possible objects of their own self-emancipatory agentive activity.

On this view, it seems to me, Lacey and Pickard's rejection of affective blame – which I have so far accepted – would have to be revisited. For within the framework of taking responsibility, rather than holding responsible, the possibility opens up for a different kind of 'affective blame' – a different kind of anger – that is distinct from the kind that is bound up with holding responsible. It would be a kind of anger that is tied to the recognition of someone as a complex, messy whole person in a complex, messy context, quite opposed to the sort of anger that is involved in the affective blame that Lacey and Pickard rail against. Such anger, insofar as it is embedded in a practical relation to the other as a contextualised, complex whole person might be not only acceptable but required.

A premise of psychoanalysis is that a person needs the right sort of conversation with another in order to take responsibility in this way. If the psychoanalytic conversation is to help the person take responsibility, the analyst must be able to engage truthfully, that is, they must be able to take responsibility themselves as well. The grammar of taking responsibility, then, is genuinely dialogical, governing a shared intersubjective undertaking that presupposes humility and courage and a willingness to be truthful and an openness to change

[94] Lacey and Pickard, 'To Blame or to Forgive?' (n 4) 690.

on both sides. If the grammar of taking responsibility were to be instituted practically in a form of ethical life, it would require that in asking someone to take responsibility the community also be willing to take responsibility, that is, to engage truthfully with what it has been doing and to seriously undertake to change. Needless to say, this implies a level of political maturity that seems to be beyond the modern *polis*.

9

Implicit Bias, Self-Defence and the Reasonable Person

JULES HOLROYD AND FEDERICO PICINALI

THE REASONABLE PERSON standard is used in adjudicating claims of self-defence. In US law, an individual may use defensive force if her beliefs that a threat is imminent and that force is required are beliefs that a reasonable person would have. In English and Welsh law, it is sufficient that beliefs in imminence and necessity are genuinely held; but the reasonableness of so believing is given an evidential role in establishing the genuineness of the beliefs. There is, of course, much contention over how to spell out when, and in virtue of what, such beliefs are reasonable.

In this chapter, we identify some distinctive issues that arise when we consider that implicit racial bias might be implicated in the beliefs in imminence and necessity. Considering two prominent interpretations of the reasonable person standard, we argue that neither is acceptable. On one interpretation, we risk unfairness to the defendant – who may non-culpably harbour bias. On another, the standard embeds racist stereotypes. Whilst there are formulations of the defence that may serve to mitigate these problems, we argue that they cannot be avoided in the presence of racist social structures.

I. INTRODUCTION

In this chapter, we explore the impact that the findings from social psychology about cognitive bias should have on the concept of 'person' in the criminal law.[1] More precisely, our focus is on the reasonable person standard. As we will show, the finding that we are beset by cognitive biases might be thought to undermine,

[1] For another recent exploration of the impact of findings about implicit bias on conceptions of responsibility in criminal law, see N Lacey, 'Socializing the Subject of Criminal Law: Criminal Responsibility and the Purposes of Criminalization' (2016) 99 *Marquette Law Review* 541, 551–53.

on at least some occasions, the extent to which we are reasonable. What implications does this have for the application of the standard?

Our enquiry is narrowed in two ways. First, whilst the reasonable person standard appears at various points in criminal law, we focus our attention on its role in the claim of self-defence in both US law and English and Welsh law. Second, we focus on implicit racial biases; in particular, on the related phenomena of weapons bias, shooter bias and perceptions of aggression. This is because these phenomena are directly relevant to the beliefs and actions at issue in claims of self-defence. It is an open question that we leave here unaddressed whether other cognitive biases pose similar challenges for this or other parts of the law.

We proceed as follows. First, we outline the phenomena of weapons bias and shooter bias. Second, we articulate and modify a much discussed test case of self-defence. This allows us to import the phenomena of racial bias into a hypothetical scenario in which the claim of self-defence is at issue. Third, we consider how the defence, as formulated in US law and English and Welsh law respectively, would apply to our test case – with particular attention to the different role that the reasonable person standard plays in the two jurisdictions. In the course of our discussion of the defence, we employ a distinction introduced by Meir Dan-Cohen between rules of conduct (directed to the public and regarding how to act) and decision rules (directed to officials and regarding how to respond to a putative violation of a legal norm). This distinction helps us to better articulate the tensions that arise when the reasonable person standard is applied to individuals harbouring implicit biases. We argue that plausible ways of construing the reasonable person standard in light of implicit racial bias face either the charge of being unfair towards the biased individual, or of stigmatising the group targeted by the bias. The bottom line is that insofar as the reasonable person serves as a normative ideal, this ideal is not one that can be met easily whilst our agency is embedded in unjust social relations.

II. UNREASONABLE PERSONS AND BIASED BELIEFS

A huge research programme in social psychology has revealed that individuals frequently display a range of cognitive biases. These include confirmation bias – the disposition to more readily believe evidence consistent with one's prior beliefs; familiarity bias – the disposition to make preferential judgements of things with which we are familiar; anchoring bias – the disposition to be swayed in our judgements by an arbitrary fixed point, to which our subsequent judgements are anchored. All of these biases are grounded in modes of automatic thinking that are often useful: they provide fast automatic cognitive short-cuts that enable us to avoid cognitively demanding processing. For example, confirmation bias means that we do not have to deliberate from scratch about the full set of evidence available, for or against that belief, on each occasion we have to form a new belief. But whilst often useful, these 'habits of cognition' may sometimes distort our reasoning.[2] A feature of these cognitions which makes us particularly ill-placed to identify these distortions is that their operation is often difficult to detect (perhaps because they operate for the most part automatically); it is fast (because automatic), and so is difficult to exert control over. These cognitive biases are often called 'implicit cognitions'.

Certain kinds of implicit cognition have garnered a great deal of attention from psychologists and philosophers, and with good reason.[3] These are the cognitions that encode information about social identity, such as race, gender, age, sexuality and associated characteristics. Our social cognitions may encode problematic associations that link stereotypical characteristics with social group membership, despite our explicit disavowal of those stereotypes. For example, our cognitions might associate men more strongly with leadership qualities than women.[4] Or we might associate white people more strongly with intellectual constructs than Black people.[5] These associations have been widely detected by a number of indirect measures, such as the Implicit Association Test (IAT).[6] To discover that there are aspects of our cognition that we may repudiate is itself troubling; but worse, they appear to have a role in producing discriminatory judgements and behaviours.[7] For example, these biases have been found to correlate with differential evaluations of the same CV, and differential judgements of suitability for hiring, when the only variable is the gender or race of the person to whom the CV belongs (as indicated by the name at the top of the CV).[8] Medical practitioners harbouring implicit racial biases make different prescription recommendations for patients reporting the same symptoms but who differ with respect to race.[9] And white individuals' 'micro behaviours' – non-verbal indicators of tension or discomfort – have been found to differ in

[2] See P Devine et al, 'Long-term Reduction in Implicit Race Bias: A Prejudice Habit-breaking Intervention' (2012) 48 *Journal of Experimental Social Psychology* 1267.

[3] See J Jost et al, 'The Existence of Implicit Bias is Beyond Reasonable Doubt: A Refutation of Ideological and Methodological Objections and Executive Summary of 10 Studies that no Manager Should Ignore' (2009) *Research in Organisational Behaviour* 39; C Lai et al, 'Reducing Implicit Racial Preferences: I. A Comparative Investigation of 17 Interventions' (2014) 143 *Journal of Experimental Psychology: General* 1765.

[4] V Valian, *Why So Slow? The Advancement of Women* (MIT Press, 1999).

[5] D Amodio and P Devine, 'Stereotyping and Evaluation in Implicit Race Bias: Evidence for Independent Constructs and Unique Effects on Behaviour' (2006) 91 *Journal of Personality and Social Psychology* 652.

[6] Indirect measures access cognitions via means other than self-report, which is notoriously unreliable. See G Nosek and M Banaji, 'The Implicit Association Test at Age Seven: A Methodological and Conceptual Review' in J Bargh (ed), *Automatic Processes in Social Thinking and Behaviour* (Psychology Press, 2007) for a review of indirect measures, including the Implicit Association Test (IAT).

[7] Of course, there are other important explanatory considerations, such as social structure and institutional design (see S Haslanger, 'Distinguished Lecture: Social Structure, Narrative and Explanation' (2015) 45 *Canadian Journal of Philosophy* 1).

[8] J Dovidio et al, 'Why Can't We Just Get Along? Interpersonal Biases and Interracial Distrust' (2002) 8 *Cultural Diversity and Ethnic Minority Psychology* 88.

[9] A Green et al, 'Implicit Bias Among Physicians and its Prediction of Thrombolysis Decisions for Black and White Patients' (2007) 22 *Journal of General Internal Medicine* 1231, 1238.

interracial interactions, where greater signs of tension and lesser attentiveness are displayed by white interlocutors.[10] Insofar as one maintains that gender or race should be irrelevant to the evaluation of the quality of an applicant's materials, or irrelevant to the disposition to prescribe treatment, or irrelevant to the quality of one's interactions with others, these biases can be said to have a distorting effect on judgement and behaviour.

The research literature on implicit bias is vast (see Jost for a comprehensive, but already out-of-date literature survey),[11] and dismayingly indicates that we are at risk of these distortions far more often than we might otherwise have supposed. Here we want to focus on two particular instances in which implicit biases might impact on beliefs or actions. We then turn to the relevance of these cases for the reasonable person standard in criminal law.

A. Biased Perceptual Judgements

A number of studies have revealed 'weapons bias': the tendency to associate weapons more readily with Black males.[12] When asked to identify ambiguous objects, experimental participants are more likely to identify an object as a weapon when they have been primed with a Black male's face, than in the condition in which the primes are white males' faces. The hypothesis is that individuals more strongly associate with weapons – particularly guns – Black males than white males. Whilst not statistically supported, these associations may be entrenched by media presentations that promote racial stereotypes. The problematic outcome is that this has an impact on individuals' perceptual judgements of material objects. This finding garners further support in 'shooter bias' tasks.[13] Experimental participants are presented with scenes in which Black or white males are depicted holding ambiguous objects (which, in fact, are guns, mobile phones, drink cans) and told that their time-limited task is to press 'shoot' or 'do not shoot' depending on whether the individual before them is armed. The finding (that has been replicated not only in US, but also UK populations) is that individuals more readily make the error of shooting an individual who is not armed when that individual is Black. The hypothesis, again, is that individuals form mistaken perceptual judgements of ambiguous objects.[14] Perceptual judgements under normal circumstances are thought

[10] Dovidio et al (n 8).

[11] Jost et al (n 3).

[12] K Payne, 'Weapon Bias Split-second Decision and Unintended Stereotyping' (2006) 15 *Current Directions in* Psychological Science 287.

[13] J Glaser and E Knowles, 'Implicit Motivation to Control Prejudice' (2008) 44 *Journal of Experimental Social Psychology* 164.

[14] A competing hypothesis is that individuals' motor responses are readier for action when faced with a potentially armed Black male than a potentially armed white male. K Payne, Y Shimizu and L Jacoby, 'Mental Control and Visual Illusions: Toward Explaining Race-biased Weapon

to provide reason for belief; but in these cases, perception provides misleading evidence. What misleads, here, is our own cognition – implicit racial biases. This is a phenomenon that philosophers have called 'cognitive penetration', whereby one's own prior cognitions taint one's perceptual evidence.[15]

To clarify the problem, let's take the belief g: 'that there is a gun'. In the case in which an individual is unarmed, and implicit racial bias distorts perceptual judgement, the belief g would be formed more readily if the individual is Black. Many of us rightly balk at the idea that we might form such perceptual judgements on the basis of race and take such beliefs to violate an important moral ideal (which might be cashed out in terms of respect, or equality). But the belief would also be in bad epistemic shape, since it would violate a fairly uncontroversial epistemic norm, such as that 'perceptual judgements influenced by distortive biases do not provide justification for belief'.[16] The difficulty, of course, is in knowing when one's perceptions are distorted in this way.[17] The point at this stage is not to make a judgement about the reasonableness or otherwise of making these mistakes (more on this later), but rather to point out that the resulting beliefs can readily be identified as defective: as violations of an uncontroversial epistemic norm.[18] Yet many of us may well harbour such weapons biases (indeed, fair-minded undergraduate students at the University of Sheffield manifested these biases).[19]

Misidentifications' (2005) 41 *Journal of Experimental Social Psychology* 36, found some support for this, but on other occasions, they found that the error was one of mistaken perceptual judgement.

[15] S Siegel, 'Cognitive Penetrability and Perceptual Justification' (2012) 46 *Noûs* 201. Siegel discusses the problems that the 'cognitive penetration' of belief pose for the epistemic status of perceptual evidence, including cognitive penetration of perception by implicit bias.

[16] In a much lower stakes example of this: perceptual judgements of length in Müller-Lyer illusions do not provide justification for belief. However, consider that epistemic norms may be violated also if the belief turns out to be true. If founded in bias, the belief would not be appropriately evidentially sensitive (*cf* A Madva, 'Why Implicit Attitudes are (probably) Not Beliefs' (2016) 193 *Synthese* 2659; N Levy, 'Neither Fish nor Fowl: Implicit Attitudes as Patchy Endorsements' (2015) 49 *Noûs* 800.

[17] See J Saul, 'Scepticism and Implicit Bias' (2013) 5(37) *Disputatio* 243, for the worry that insofar as we are ill-positioned to detect when we are influenced by biases, this generates a radical kind of scepticism that she calls 'bias-induced doubt'.

[18] See J Holroyd and K Puddifoot, 'Implicit Bias and Prejudice' in M Fricker et al (eds), *The Routledge Handbook of Social Epistemology* (Routledge, 2019) for various specifications of this epistemic norm, under all of which the norm is violated by beliefs based on implicit biases. However, some have argued that base rate information provides useful support for our beliefs and, especially, that implicit biases may provide evidential support for belief by encoding such information (see TS Gendler, 'On the Epistemic Costs of Implicit Bias' (2011) 156 *Philosophical Studies* 33). This supposes that implicit biases are the kind of mental state that can represent precise statistical data. But it is unlikely that implicit biases accurately represent such information, insofar as they are crudely associative (see K Puddifoot, 'Dissolving the Ethical/Epistemic Dilemma over Implicit Bias' (2017) 20 *Philosophical Explorations* 73) and are not appropriately evidentially sensitive (see Madva (n 16); Levy (n 16)). It is for these reasons that we endorse the claim that the phenomenon of statistical discrimination is distinct from implicitly biased behaviour (see also RM Blank, M Dabady and CF Citro (eds), *Measuring Racial Discrimination* (The National Academies Press, 2004).

[19] R Scaife et al, 'To Blame? The Effects of Moralized Feedback on Implicit Racial Bias' (2020) 6(1) *Collabra: Psychology* 30.

Consider also the following set of studies that focused on distorting biases, but this time on perceptions of aggression. The first focuses on aggression as expressed in Black and white faces. Hugenberg and Bodenhausen found that white individuals more readily identified faces as expressing anger and hostility when the faces were Black, rather than white.[20] Individuals who showed greater anti-Black implicit bias (ie, stronger associations – measured with IATs – between Black people and negative terms, than white people and negative terms) were more ready to judge an ambiguous Black face as hostile. Again, such perceptual judgements appear to be distorted by implicit racial biases, and so any resulting belief (about the degree of hostility manifested) lacks adequate perceptual justification.[21]

We have reason to believe that such implicit biases and their distortive effects are widespread. It is likely that many of us have biases of this kind. Simply possessing such biases is widely thought to be non-culpable: they are frequently formed on the basis of exposure to associations in our environment, independently of whether individuals endorse or subscribe to the problematic stereotypes that they encode.[22] And, some have argued that since it may be difficult to be aware of such implicit biases, until such awareness is gained we are not culpable for failing to take steps to rid ourselves of these biases.[23]

It is tempting to immediately conclude that individuals who harbour implicit biases and form perceptual judgements and beliefs under the influence of implicit bias (hereafter 'bias-based beliefs'), are necessarily unreasonable. Certainly, there is nothing to be said to condone such patterns of cognition,

[20] K Hugenberg and GV Bodenhausen 'Facing Prejudice: Implicit Prejudice and the Perception of Facial Threat' (2003) 14 *Psychological Science* 640.

[21] This recent study corroborates an older one: in B Duncan, 'Differential Social Perceptions and the Attribution of Intergroup Violence: Testing the Lower Limits of Stereotyping of Blacks' (1976) 34 *Journal of Personality and Social Psychology* 590, participants were asked to evaluate ambiguous behaviour (described as 'a shove'). When participants observed this behaviour perpetrated by Black against white individuals, it was judged to be an act of violent hostility. When perpetrated by white against Black individuals, it was evaluated as 'playing around'. Note that this study was conducted in 1976, when racial attitudes may have been somewhat different from those prevailing now, so it is less clear that these conclusions generalise to us, here and now.

[22] P Devine et al, 'The Regulation of Explicit and Implicit Race Bias: The Role of Motivations to Respond Without Prejudice' (2002) 82 *Journal of Personality and Social Psychology* 835; Saul (n 17).

[23] N Washington and D Kelly, 'Who is Responsible for this?' in M Brownstein and J Saul (eds), *Implicit Bias and Philosophy* (Oxford University Press, 2016). Full disclosure: one of us has argued that we may be blameworthy for discriminatory behaviour due to implicit bias (J Holroyd, 'Responsibility for Implicit Bias' (2012) 43 *Journal of Social Psychology* 274; J Holroyd, 'Implicit Bias, Awareness and Imperfect Cognitions' (2014) 33 *Consciousness and Cognition* 511; J Holroyd and D Kelly, 'Implicit Bias, Character and Control' in J Webber and A Masala (eds), *From Personality to Virtue* (Oxford University Press 2016); J Holroyd, 'What do we Want from a Model of Implicit Cognition?' (2016) 116 *Proceedings of the Aristotelian Society* 153). However, if interpersonal blame is not a suitable analogue for state punishment (J Holroyd, 'The Retributive Emotions: Passions and Pains of Punishment' (2010) 39 *Philosophical Papers* 343), and the conditions for responsibility in interpersonal relations differ from those necessary for criminal liability, the arguments made there cannot be carried over to this context).

and they are clearly defective and damaging. In some pre-theoretical sense, it seems quite clear that such biases generate unreasonable patterns of inference and resultant belief. However, the task ahead of us is to consider how the reasonable person standard, as it is invoked in criminal law, could or should deal with such patterns of inference and belief.

III. RACISM AND SELF-DEFENCE

In this section, we draw attention to a case – 'the case of the mistaken racist' – which has received much attention in the scholarly literature.[24] For our purposes, this case provides a helpful model that we can modify to envisage the role that implicitly biased action might play in cases of self-defence. The primary role of this case here is to animate the implicit biases introduced in the previous section. Garvey presents the following example, modelled on the *Goetz* case[25] (we paraphrase):

> The case of the mistaken racist: G is riding public transport, when he is approached by two young Black males. From their perceived demeanour and repeated demand for money, in conjunction with his past experience of being mugged on the subway – also by Black men – G forms the belief that he faces a threat of serious physical harm, and perhaps mortal danger. He believes he may be killed and that lethal force is needed to defend himself. G pulls out a concealed weapon, shoots and kills one of the men, before fleeing (later to turn himself in).[26]

Much of the discussion surrounding the case (including Garvey's description of Goetz and G as racist) supposes that G endorses repugnant racist stereotypes, or even feelings of racial animosity, and that these are behind the beliefs that he is in mortal danger and that lethal force is required. We hold that beliefs based in explicit racism are obviously unreasonable.[27] However, importing into this scenario the empirical findings from the previous section, we face a rather different set of concerns when considering the question of reasonableness:

> The case of the mistaken implicitly biased individual: B is riding public transport, when he is approached by two young Black males. Like many of us, B has implicit

[24] See S Garvey, 'Self-Defense and the Mistaken Racist' (2008) 11 *New Criminal Law Review: International and Interdisciplinary Journal* 119; G Fletcher, *A Crime of Self-Defense: Bernhard Goetz and the Law on Trial* (University of Chicago Press, 1988).

[25] *People v Goetz* 68 NY 2d 96 (1986).

[26] See Garvey (n 24) 123–25. This case differs in some important respects from the real Goetz case, in which all four of the men were wounded, one of whom after what seemed like premeditated action. Significantly, Goetz had also previously been attacked and wounded on the subway, which was appealed to in support of the claim that his belief in imminent attack was reasonable.

[27] Though see Garvey (n 24) for an extended discussion of whether this renders the defence unavailable. However, consider that the presence of explicit racist beliefs raises doubt as to whether the agent acted in order to defend herself or for some other unlawful purpose. *cf* A Ashworth and J Horder, *Principles of Criminal Law*, 7th edn (Oxford University Press, 2013) 122.

racial biases, which inform his perceptual judgements both of the degree of hostility manifested, and of the presence of a weapon in the hand of one of the men. On the basis of the distorted perceptual judgements of the young men's demeanour and behaviour, B forms the belief that he faces a threat of serious physical harm, and perhaps mortal danger. He believes he may be killed and that lethal force is needed to defend himself. B deploys potentially lethal force to repel the perceived danger.

In jurisdictions such as the US or England and Wales, we would expect individuals such as B to be charged with attempted murder or murder, and to try to establish that they acted in self-defence.[28] If they succeed, the outcome of the trial is an acquittal. A successful claim of self-defence may show that the individual's conduct was in fact justified: in a nutshell, that the use of such force was necessary to avert criminal harm to themselves (or to others). Alternatively, the defence may serve to excuse. For the time being, though, our focus is on the justificatory role of self-defence, as it is in this context that the problems raised by implicit bias are most evident. In section VII we return to the excusatory role of self-defence.[29] The availability of the defence in the US and in England and Wales rests on whether the defendant (B) can show that she has met a distinctive set of conditions. Each set of conditions makes reference to standards of reasonableness to which individuals are held, though these standards are somewhat differently deployed in each of the two jurisdictions. So, it is instructive for our purposes to consider how the qualifying conditions for self-defence would deal with implicit bias in each case.

Notably, the few treatments of the research findings on implicit bias in relation to self-defence have operated on the assumption that the bias-based belief is unreasonable. For example, Lee takes seriously the observation that 'most individuals would be more likely to "see" a weapon in the hands of an unarmed Black person than an unarmed White person'.[30] But she is mainly concerned that if this observation is true of jurors, they 'may also be more likely to find that an individual who says he shot an unarmed Black person in self-defence because he believed the victim was about to kill or seriously injure him acted reasonably'.[31] She finds this problematic as she assumes that this belief of the

[28] NB: under English and Welsh law the defendant only has to bear an evidential burden with respect to the issue of self-defence. If the burden is discharged, it will then be for the prosecution to disprove self-defence according to the standard of proof for conviction. We are leaving aside the question as to whether a partial defence (eg, of provocation or loss of control) may be available and may be put forward in such cases. However, to the extent that such a defence relies on an assessment of reasonableness the considerations that we make here may apply to it as well. To be sure, the 'new' English and Welsh defence of loss of control does not include a reasonable person standard but appeals to the notion of a 'normal degree of tolerance and self-restraint' (see the Coroners and Justice Act 2009, s 54(1)(c)). A test based on this notion seems problematic if implicit biases are the norm. Note also that whilst we focus on murder or attempted murder, in English and Welsh law a claim of self-defence can be made for any instance of intentional use of force against the person.

[29] Another variable that we consider there is the distinction between full and partial defence.

[30] C Lee, 'Making Race Salient: Trayvon Martin and Implicit Bias in a Not Yet Post-racial Society' (2013) 91 *North Carolina Law Review* 1555, 1584.

[31] ibid 1585.

individual is unreasonable. Attention to the judgement of juries is of course important. But Lee's assumption requires careful consideration. Whilst we have no interest in defending the claims that such biased-based belief is reasonable, we must consider further precisely what characterisation of the reasonable person standard supports the conclusion that such a belief is indeed unreasonable, and whether that characterisation is independently defensible.

A. A Useful Device for Thinking about Self-Defence

Deploying a heuristic device introduced by Dan-Cohen,[32] we can say that self-defence does double duty both as a rule of conduct and a decision rule. Rules of conduct are addressed to the general public, conveying information about what behaviours are permissible or prohibited. In the case of self-defence, the rule conveys the message that the use of force is permissible, subject to certain conditions being met. In contrast, decision rules are directed to officials in the criminal justice system (judges, jurors etc), and convey instructions regarding how to deal with individuals charged with violating a rule of conduct. In the case of self-defence, the instructions are that individuals should not be punished if their use of force meets certain conditions. One and the same legal norm may be intended and/or perceived as both a rule of conduct and a decision rule – as in the case of self-defence. However – as Dan-Cohen argues – this 'double duty' can create tensions and mixed messages: decision rules may generate 'side-effect' messages pertaining to conduct, for example.[33] The distinction between the two types of rule – or the two dimensions of the same rule – is helpful to us: it brings to light some of the tensions that emerge in the ways that implicit bias may be dealt with by different versions of the reasonable person standard, as deployed in the claim of self-defence in US law and in English and Welsh law.

IV. US LAW AND THE 'REASONABLE-BELIEF RULE'

In US law, for the defence of self-defence to be available to individuals such as B, it is not sufficient that B believed that there was imminent lethal danger and that potentially lethal force was required to avert the threat.[34] The relevant

[32] M Dan-Cohen, 'Decision Rules and Conduct Rules: On Acoustic Separation in Criminal Law' (1984) 97 *Harvard Law Review* 625.

[33] Dan-Cohen discusses the case of duress, where a norm intended to guide the decision-maker is likely to be understood by citizens as a norm guiding behaviour – thus undermining the force of important criminal law prescriptions. See Dan-Cohen (n 32) 632–34.

[34] We are well aware that speaking of 'US law' as if it were a single and coherent legal system is at best imprecise. Not only may the federal criminal law and the state criminal law differ; the penal codes of the different states present important differences as well. Theoretical works sometimes refer to the Model Penal Code as providing an approximate indication of the state of the criminal

beliefs must also be reasonable, irrespective of whether they are in fact true. Following Baron, the question of reasonableness may be framed in terms of whether a reasonable person might believe as B did, and so act as B did, in the same circumstances.[35]

As has been much discussed, the answer to this formulation of the question depends in part on what features are built into the reasonable person – what are the 'relevant particulars' of the individual that we suppose are shared with the reasonable person.[36] In other words, what background beliefs, dispositions, cognitive processes should we hold fixed in deciding whether the individual in that circumstance believed reasonably? The key question in our case concerns whether a reasonable person might be supposed to share with B – and indeed, with many of us – the implicit biases that distorted perceptual judgement, causing the beliefs that threat was imminent and force required. Let us consider some (more or less) promising ways of articulating the reasonable person standard,[37] what they might indicate with respect to this question, and what the further implications of such construals might be.[38]

A. The Reasonable Person as the Ordinary or Typical Person

One way of construing the reasonable person is as the ordinary or typical person.[39] According to this interpretation, if the average or ordinary person would believe as B did, then B's belief is reasonable. As we have seen, since implicit biases

law in the US. Whether this strategy is appropriate or not, the Model Penal Code is not our focus here, given that it does not require that the beliefs relevant to self-defence be reasonable. As far as federal law is concerned, our point of reference is the case of *United States v Peterson* 483 F 2d 1222 (1973). At the state level, instead, we refer to the Penal Code of the State of New York – which was the relevant code in the Goetz case. Both Peterson and the New York code require reasonableness as a feature of the beliefs that are relevant to self-defence.

[35] See M Baron, 'The Standard of the Reasonable Person in Criminal Law' in RA Duff et al (eds), *The Structures of Criminal Law* (Oxford University Press, 2011) 15–16. Baron argues that the better framing of the standard is this, rather than in terms of what the reasonable person would have believed or done, since the phrasing in the text makes clearer that there is latitude: that reasonable people may disagree or come to different conclusions.

[36] ibid 17.

[37] The construals of the reasonable person that we address here are prominent in the literature, but by no means the only interpretations possible. As will become apparent, though, the tension that we discuss in the chapter does not hinge on the particular interpretations of the reasonable person standard at issue, but rather on the fact that in the context of implicitly biased behaviour both the choice of affording the defence and that of denying it are unpalatable.

[38] To the reader: if your interest is only in English and Welsh law, these discussions of unreasonableness may seem irrelevant. But as we will see, assessments of reasonableness are not wholly absent from the English and Welsh law of self-defence – so the following discussion will pay off when we come to consider this law in section VI. See also the previous note.

[39] M Kelman, 'Reasonable Evidence of Reasonableness' (1991) 17 *Critical Inquiry* 798, 800; Baron (n 35) 26–30; J Gardner, 'The Many Faces of the Reasonable Person' (2015) 131 *Law Quarterly Review* 563, 564–66; M Moran, *Rethinking the Reasonable Person: An Egalitarian Reconstruction of the Objective Standard* (Oxford University Press, 2003) 13–16.

are pervasive, most likely the ordinary or typical person would have the cognitive biases to which B is susceptible, and so would have the distorted perceptual judgements that lead to the beliefs that B had. On this construal of the reasonable person, B believed reasonably, and so the defence of self-defence would be available; thus, B's use of potentially lethal force would be justified.[40]

This is an uncomfortable line of reasoning. Recall that we noted that the distorted perceptual judgement did not provide adequate justification for the belief that threat was imminent and lethal force required. Yet, this process may be entirely typical and ordinary. If the reasonable person standard is construed as the ordinary person, and what they would believe, then what it is reasonable to believe may – as in this case – lack justification. For those who see the reasonable person as the – in the relevant respect – justified person this is untenable.[41] And, as many authors have noted,[42] it is manifestly true that what is ordinary or typical is often unjustified, defective, or even repugnant in some ways. Baron references the 1896 US Supreme Court ruling that racially segregated travel arrangements were deemed reasonable, a judgement made with reference to ordinary and established conduct.[43] So much speaks against taking what is reasonable to be coextensive with what is ordinary or typical. This holds in the case of implicit bias as much as in the case of more familiar beliefs or preferences.

B. The Reasonable Person as Having a 'Reasonable Basis' for Belief

Baron draws attention to the construal of 'reasonableness' that the New York Court of Appeals gave in justifying their decision in the *Goetz* case.[44] The crucial part is the Court's claim that a determination of reasonableness must be based on the defendant's circumstances, which encompass 'any prior experiences he had which could provide a reasonable basis for a belief that another person's intentions were to injure … him or that the use of deadly force was necessary'.[45]

[40] *cf* J Armour, 'Race Ipsa Loquitur: Of Reasonable Racists, Intelligent Bayesians and Involuntary Negrophobes' (1994) 46 *Stanford Law Review* 781, 787 ff, strongly criticising the concept of the 'reasonable racist'. According to the 'reasonable racist standard', reasonableness exclusively depends on typicality. Assuming that the 'typical American' believes that 'Black people are prone to violence' – hopefully, an assumption that was already dubious at the time when the article was written – it may well be judged reasonable for defendants such as G or B to harbour the relevant beliefs in imminence and necessity. Notice that the argument of the reasonable racist is framed in terms of beliefs rather than implicit biases. In this respect, it is weaker than the argument offered here – given that the following considerations of fairness towards the defendant (see section V.A) do not arise in the case of racist beliefs.

[41] Gardner (n 39).

[42] Kelman (n 39); Baron (n 35); Gardner (n 39); Armour (n 40); Moran (n 39).

[43] Baron (n 35) 27.

[44] *People v Goetz* (n 25).

[45] ibid 114.

On this view, the reasonable person is modelled as having reasonable bases for her beliefs. Therefore, the defendant's past experiences are built into the reasonable person insofar as those experiences provide a reasonable basis for belief. Accordingly, the reasonable person may have false or mistaken beliefs, informed by inferences from the defendant's past experiences, so long as those experiences provide a reasonable basis for such beliefs. In the *Goetz* case, his past experiences of assault by Black males were considered and it was asked whether they should be part of the relevant circumstances in the sense articulated above. The conclusion was that they should not, since they were not found to provide a reasonable basis for his belief that these individuals pose an imminent threat – this sort of race-based inference was not considered a reasonable basis for belief.

In the case of implicit bias, then, we might say that whilst the ordinary person may well believe as B did, B wouldn't be reasonable insofar as her belief is bias-based, since – as we noted above – the bias-based distorted perceptual judgements are not within the circumstances that provide a reasonable basis for belief. This is because, as we saw earlier, such distorted perceptions violate an uncontroversial epistemic norm. On this construction of the reasonable person, individuals such as B are unreasonable, and the claim of self-defence is unavailable to them.

C. The Reasonable Person as the Non-Culpable Person

An alternative reading of the reasonable person is as the person who may be mistaken or inaccurate, but non-culpably so. For example, Kelman offers a picture of the reasonable person as 'not blameworthy', such that even if her beliefs are mistaken, they are not due to missteps that result from any fault on the part of the agent.[46] Likewise, Baron suggests that 'the fact that the belief is unreasonable should matter only if the individual is culpable for the belief'.[47] The idea is that even unreasonable beliefs should not be taken to reflect badly on the agent – and should not be beliefs she is held accountable for – if she is not culpable for arriving at those unreasonable beliefs. This adds an additional layer of evaluation into the reasonable person standard, and one that appears well motivated when we consider cases such as the implicitly biased individual. This view may seem to present a natural way of making sense of the individual, such as B, who believes that threat is imminent and lethal force is required, but believes this on the basis of distorted perceptual judgements; such an individual may suffer such distortions through no fault of her own.[48] This reading of the

[46] Kelman (n 39) 801.

[47] Baron (n 35) 26–27.

[48] Of course, if the individual does not disavow the biases and/or intentionally cultivates them, we may consider her culpable for harbouring them.

reasonable person standard makes the defence available to B, since it permits the conclusion that a person is reasonable if her beliefs, though unreasonable, are not culpably held. What is interesting about this construal is that, in fact, the reasonable belief requirement of US law drops out. The focus shifts to epistemic culpability, rather than whether the belief is reasonable.

We have, then, three versions of the reasonable person standard: the 'ordinary person standard', according to which the bias-based belief is reasonable; the 'reasonable basis for belief standard' according to which the bias-based belief is unreasonable; and the 'non-culpable standard', according to which what matters is not so much the unreasonableness of the belief, but whether the agent is culpable for holding it. In the following subsection, we consider the ramifications of applying the latter two standards to bias-based belief. Since the 'ordinary person' standard is widely regarded as problematic, we set this aside.

V. EVALUATING THE REASONABLE PERSON STANDARDS

Our task in this section is to evaluate the relative merits and challenges that may face each of these formulations of the reasonable person standard. To recap, one option is the reading according to which bias-based beliefs are not reasonable (the reasonable basis for belief standard), so the claim of self-defence is unavailable to individuals such as B; another is the reading according to which, whilst bias-based beliefs are unreasonable, the agent is not culpable for having them and, therefore, is not unreasonable. Under the latter standard B's claim of self-defence may succeed. One way of proceeding with the comparative evaluation of these readings may be to consult our intuitions about reasonableness. But such intuitions are likely differing and flimsy, as evidenced by the inconsistencies characterising the literature and the case law. Instead, we can proceed by considering the wider ramifications of a legal system that endorses one or the other of these standards. It is at this point that Dan-Cohen's heuristic device, introduced earlier, comes to our aid.[49]

A. Reasonable Basis for Belief as a Decision-Rule

A reasonable person standard that requires that individuals have a reasonable basis for belief is not met by defendants with bias-based beliefs; officials (judges instructing jurors, jurors themselves) would thus be guided by a standard designed to exclude from the realm of reasonableness the beliefs in the imminence of a threat and the necessity of force, where those beliefs are based on biased perceptual judgements – as in the case of B. In this respect, the standard

[49] Dan-Cohen (n 32).

tells officials to reject as unreasonable beliefs that are based in biases. This looks like a defensible standard, insofar as it asks officials to construe as unreasonable beliefs that have the hallmarks of defective, irrational or repugnant cognitions.

However, in considering such biased-based beliefs as unreasonable, and therefore excluding that individuals harbouring them can avail themselves of the claim of self-defence, this decision-rule may face various objections, each rooted in considerations of fairness. Considerations of fairness have been given (albeit brief) treatment by Lee in her discussion of implicit bias and self-defence: she considers the possibility that it is unfair to hold an individual liable 'for acting on a sincere belief that he was about to be killed … even if his beliefs stemmed from racially biased assumptions'.[50] One might support this line of thought, she remarks, by appealing to Garvey's claim that such a belief 'is one that only a saint or a fool would ignore'.[51] Garvey's point is that the state should not demand that anyone who genuinely believes that she is in great danger fails to heed that belief. Lee rejects this argument, on the assumption that allowing a claim to self-defence based on any sincere belief, irrespective of its reasonableness, is deeply problematic – we defer this issue to section VI, where we discuss English and Welsh law. Lee also considers Garvey's suggestion that it would be illiberal for the state to punish citizens for having state-disapproved beliefs – for example, racist beliefs – and that, therefore, the state cannot deny citizens a defence grounded upon such beliefs. However, Lee remarks that Garvey's position is not supported by the case law of the US Supreme Court.[52]

Whatever the merits of these responses to Garvey's sweeping claim that any sincere belief – even if explicitly grounded in racist stereotypes – should be a ground for self-defence, Lee's remarks do little to help us evaluate the fairness or otherwise of not accepting a claim of self-defence grounded in bias-based beliefs. Her remarks do not target the particular features of such beliefs which seem to make the charge of unfairness particularly apt. These features are as follows.

First, perceptual judgements influenced by implicit bias are difficult to avoid. This is especially so if individuals lack any knowledge of such biases, or have never considered that perceptual judgements themselves might be distorted by aspects of their cognition of which they are unaware.[53] Second, even if

[50] Lee (n 30) 1604.

[51] Garvey (n 24) 126. Garvey's reasoning is that it may be problematic to deny the defence on the basis of bias-based beliefs since denying the defence to individuals such as B essentially makes individuals liable to punishment for certain attitudes they hold (eg, implicit racial biases). Garvey worries that it is highly illiberal for the state to punish individuals on such a basis; or to hold them liable to punishment for failing to take sufficient steps to rid themselves of such attitudes. Note, though, that the criminal justice system often takes into account the attitudes of individuals both as evidence of guilt (see bad character evidence) and as constitutive of guilt (negligence).

[52] Lee (n 30) 1606.

[53] *cf* Washington and Kelly (n 23).

individuals are cognisant of such dispositions to bias, it is unclear that conditions of 'fair avoidability' are met, since bias mitigation methods are not yet reliably successful.[54] Even an individual who took considerable measures to rid herself of biases could not be guaranteed success. Of those interventions that are successful, many are short-lived, with little evidence of any intervention being successful in the long term. As such, it may seem that individuals who use force due to bias-based beliefs may be unable to avoid any such erroneous beliefs, even when putting diligent effort into this task. A third and pressing line of concern with denying an individual the defence on the basis of biased beliefs is the extent to which this places liability upon an individual for what is effectively a collective failing. The concern here is that current understandings in social psychology attribute the causes of implicit biases to broader social and structural problems – prevalent stereotypes and inequalities that we may, as individuals, disavow. Insofar as this is the case, there is something problematic about holding an individual responsible – and accordingly, liable to punishment for intentional killing – on the basis of what is, essentially, a collective failure.

So, even if we were to agree with Lee in denying that any honest belief could per se ground a claim to self-defence, there are features of bias-based beliefs that make it particularly unfair to deny their reasonableness for the purposes of self-defence.

B. Reasonable Basis for Belief as a Rule of Conduct

Consider a conduct rule that demands that people ensure a reasonable basis for the beliefs that are relevant to self-defence. We are bound to conclude that it would be a violation of such a rule for someone to act in self-defence on the basis of bias-based beliefs. As a result, she is not permitted to use force. Individuals should conduct themselves with caution in instances in which there is reason to believe that bias may guide perception, belief, and – potentially lethal – action. Imposing a requirement to ensure a reasonable basis for belief resonates with the option favoured by Kelman – who does not, however, deal explicitly with implicit bias. He writes that in setting such a rule, 'we ask those who make at least partly race-based judgement of a person's violent intentions to use "alternative screening devices" … [B]asically, we ask them to wait until an actor makes his violent intentions clearer'.[55] The costs of doing so, he argues, are likely less than the costs of accepting race-based beliefs as reasonable for the purposes of self-defence. In any case, the conduct rule at issue would send a clear signal that force on the basis of bias-based beliefs is impermissible. It is valuable that the legal system conveys such strong anti-racist norms.

[54] Lai et al (n 3).
[55] Kelman (n 39) 816.

However, one might have doubts about the efficacy of such a rule of conduct in informing action, in particular when implicit biases are at play. First, the situations in which individuals deploy self-defence are most likely not situations in which careful deliberation is also deployed.[56] Second, as noted above, in the absence of knowledge about implicit bias, the efficacy of such a conduct rule is further reduced. Unless individuals are aware that their perceptions may be distorted by racial bias, an exhortation to wait until violent intentions are made clear may fail to receive uptake. After all, the bias distorts precisely those perceptions which represent violent intentions. Absent more widespread knowledge of implicit bias, then, concerns of fair avoidability arise. Moreover, even if the individual has knowledge of being biased, the automatic operation of the bias makes it extremely difficult for her to distinguish between biased and unbiased perceptions and to act only based on the latter. Perhaps an individual may train herself to distinguish those perceptions based in bias from those which are undistorted; but the current state of knowledge and research does not reliably afford us such training techniques.[57]

C. Summary So Far

Deployment of the 'reasonable basis for belief' interpretation of the reasonable person standard yields the conclusion that individuals who have bias-based beliefs in imminence and necessity are not reasonable, and therefore cannot avail themselves of the claim of self-defence. We have seen that various considerations of fairness arise in relation to the deployment of such an interpretation *qua* decision rule. And, *qua* conduct rule, whilst clear directives would be given by the law about the importance of avoiding race-based beliefs, current knowledge about implicit bias means that individuals are not well placed to guide their conduct in accordance with these directives. Let us now consider the alternative interpretation of the reasonable person standard, which permits mistaken and even unreasonable beliefs, so long as they are non-culpably held.

[56] *cf* Richard Restak, 'The Fiction of the Reasonable Man' *Washington Post* (17 May 1987), available at: www.washingtonpost.com/archive/opinions/1987/05/17/the-law-the-fiction-of-the-reasonable-man/15dea8f3-521a-48d0-aba8-9e361774450e/, making the rather strong claims that 'there are no reasonable people under conditions in which death or severe bodily harm are believed imminent' and that '[t]o expect reasonable behaviour in the face of perceived threat, terror and rage is itself a most unreasonable expectation'. Depending on how one construes the reasonable person standard, she may agree or disagree with either or both of Restak's claims. In any case, even if it were true that as a standard of conduct reasonableness could not serve as a deliberative guide in such contexts, this is not to say that the reasonable person standard has no role, eg, in providing the contents of a decision rule to criminal justice officials and in setting wider social expectations.

[57] Lai et al (n 3).

D. Non-Culpable Unreasonable Belief as a Decision-Rule

Under this interpretation of the reasonable person standard, the bias-based belief may well be unreasonable without undermining the reasonableness of the belief-holder. What matters, for the assessment of reasonableness of the belief-holder, is not the unreasonableness of the belief per se, but whether the individual is culpable for the unreasonable belief. On one common line of thought, to the extent that biases are pervasive, contingent upon social environment, not widely known of, and difficult to expunge from our cognitions, the distorted perceptual judgements and attendant beliefs are not culpable. The deployment of this reading of the standard as a decision rule would mean that the claim of self-defence would be available to individuals such as B.[58] The considerations of fairness aired above may speak in favour of this decision rule: even if the beliefs are unreasonable, the individual could not avoid the distorted judgement – at least, not without extraordinary measures – and wider patterns of social inequality or cultural stereotype are implicated in the individual's biases. The circumstances of the person are such that any of us may be similarly disposed to believe unreasonably. This construction of the standard instructs officials not to punish if the individual is guilty of no greater fault than most of the rest of us – namely, harbouring biases we disavow.

E. Non-Culpable Unreasonable Belief as a Rule of Conduct

Recall that the claim of self-defence does double duty as a decision rule and a conduct rule. The defence serves as a justification, and so also conveys to the general public messages about how it is permissible to act.[59] If the claim of self-defence is successful in the case of bias-based belief, what conduct rule is thereby transmitted? The normative message conveyed would be that it is permissible to (attempt to) inflict harm or intentionally kill on the basis of bias-based beliefs. This seems deeply troubling for obvious reasons. First, it contains and conveys a disrespectful normative message. The message is that individuals

[58] Note that thus construed, it would make more sense for the claim of self-defence to function as an excuse, given that the relevant beliefs would be unreasonable. We address this option in section VII.

[59] Note that the concerns raised in this section could not be avoided even if the defence was not explicitly intended as a conduct rule, since conduct rules may be transmitted as unintentional side-effects of decision rules (*cf* Dan-Cohen (n 32)). Moreover, if the non-culpable unreasonableness standard were understood as transforming self-defence into an excuse, rather than a justification, these concerns would not go away. True, the state would not say that it is permissible to act on such bias-based beliefs, but merely that doing so is excusable. But this would still convey – albeit perhaps with a lesser force – the problematic messages outlined below. More on this in section VII below. Finally, note that on any rendering of the standard according to which bias-based beliefs are reasonable these concerns will arise with even greater force.

may permissibly use potentially lethal force based on distorted perceptions that encode racist stereotypes. This devalues the lives of Black citizens, allowing the reliance on distorted perceptions to outweigh their right to be protected by the state. Second, in maintaining that it is permissible to use force on the basis of bias-based beliefs, the state sanctions the deployment of racist stereotypes, permitting reliance on mistaken associations between Black people and weapons to govern behaviour. Third, in sanctioning these stereotypes, the state plays a role in perpetuating and entrenching the very biases that distort cognition in the ways we have described. Fourth, the consequences of the pervasive knowledge of such a message may have an impact on the extent to which Black citizens feel safe in making use of their freedoms: Kelman puts this in terms of being 'stigmatized, excluded from participation in generally available activities … [and] subjected to the demeaning supposition that others know a lot about them when who they truly are as individuals is wholly misassessed'.[60]

One might observe that the role of such a conduct rule is limited – indeed that rule may be utterly ineffective in guiding conduct – because the contexts in which it is deployed, contexts where threat appears imminent, are not those in which deliberative thought and reflection on the directives of the law are generally gone in for. This does nothing to deflect the above worries. The conduct rule is troubling not because individuals in self-defence scenarios will deliberatively govern their conduct accordingly, but because of the evaluative presuppositions of such a rule: at its starkest, that Black lives do not matter, that racist stereotypes are a legitimate basis for action.

Nor are these worries mitigated by noting that the reasonable person standard exemplifies a strategy of 'selective transmission'. According to Dan-Cohen, strategies of selective transmission are deployed – intentionally or otherwise – to send different messages, respectively, to decision-makers and the general public (to whom rules of conduct apply).[61] Vagueness is one such strategy. Leaving a standard imprecisely specified may be one of the methods by which decision rules are insulated from the general public so as to avoid transmitting conduct rules which convey problematic normative messages.[62] The imprecision of a standard such as the reasonable person standard means that the law can withhold from explicitly committing to the claim that bias-based beliefs are a legitimate basis for the use of lethal force. This 'vagueness' may serve to cloak some of the more

[60] Kelman (n 39) 816.

[61] Dan-Cohen (n 32) 635. Here is Dan-Cohen's example of a case in which selective transmission is useful (Dan-Cohen (n 32) 646): the conduct message 'ignorance of the law is no excuse' is well known and serves a useful function in setting a certain standard for conduct. But in practice, the decision rules deployed in determining whether conduct carried out in ignorance of the law is in fact punishable permit many exceptions. He argues that it is useful if these exceptions are not transmitted to the public but remain embedded in the case law and in the legal scholarship surrounding it.

[62] As an example of how vagueness operates as a strategy of selective transmission, Dan-Cohen discusses the defence of duress. See Dan-Cohen (n 32) 639–40.

problematic aspects of a decision rule for determining reasonableness, and so may mitigate the problematic normative messages otherwise conveyed to the public.

Perhaps selective transmission is a possibility under certain circumstances, but it does not seem realistic in these cases. As a matter of empirical fact, great media attention is paid (and rightly so) to the outcomes of trials such as those of *Goetz* and those like our imaginary B. This is precisely because of concerns about racism in society and in criminal justice.[63] In any case, even if it were possible to deploy effective strategies of selective transmission, it seems to us that there is something sinister in the extreme about the law embedding an interpretation of a standard that sanctions racism, whilst concealing or attempting to conceal this from the general public. That the law deploys a legal construct which embeds racist messages, irrespective of whether they are heard loud and clear, is itself objectionable. Even if in general selective transmission strategies may be reconciled with rule of law requirements of clarity and publicity,[64] in this instance selective transmission is especially problematic.

F. Summary So Far

This interpretation of the reasonable person standard allows the claim of self-defence to succeed in the case of bias-based beliefs, a result that appears to be supported by considerations of fairness towards the defendant. However, when we heed the implications that this rendering of the defence has in terms of rules of conduct (either explicitly, or as implied side-effects of the decision rule), we see that this construal of the reasonable person standard is deeply problematic and implicates the law in various racist evaluative stances.

The foregoing discussion, then, brings to light some deep tensions on either reading of the reasonable person standard. In short, a reading of the standard that denies self-defence – for example, based on the consideration that implicit biases are not a reasonable basis for beliefs – faces deep concerns about fairness, at least given the current understanding of the cognitive phenomena at issue. On the other hand, a reading of the standard that permits the defence – based on the consideration that the relevant beliefs are non-culpably unreasonable – generates deeply problematic normative messages which entrench stereotypes and devalue the lives of Black citizens. If the criminal law's reasonable person standard accommodates bias, racist normative messages are embedded in the law. If the criminal law's person is not biased, considerations of fairness arise in its treatment of citizens who, almost unavoidably in this historical moment, are so.

[63] See, eg, C Light, *Stand Your Ground: A History of America's Love Affair with Self-Defense* (Beacon Press, 2017) for work on the selective use of 'Stand Your Ground' laws in ways that favour white males.

[64] Dan-Cohen (n 32) 665–77.

VI. ENGLISH AND WELSH LAW AND THE GENUINE BELIEF RULE

All of the above discussion is framed within the context of US law and focuses on the reasonableness or otherwise of the beliefs that a threat is imminent, and that potentially force is required to deflect the threat. One might think that these concerns are avoided in English and Welsh law, according to which: 'The question whether the degree of force used by D was reasonable in the circumstances is to be decided by reference to the circumstances as D believed them to be' (Criminal Justice and Immigration Act 2008, section76(3)).[65]

Crucially, the individuals' beliefs (that they are facing a threat and that force is required) do not have to be reasonable, but just genuinely held (the subjective element of the defence).[66] The requirement of reasonableness applies only to the degree of force used given the individual's subjective apprehension of the situation (the objective element).

English and Welsh law, then, focuses on what the individual genuinely believed, and asks what force would be reasonable given that belief. In order to establish whether the use of force was reasonable, consideration is given to the fact that the individual, such as B, 'had only done what he honestly and instinctively thought was necessary'.[67] The issue that arises, given our present concern, is that we have reason to suppose that on at least some occasions, what individuals 'honestly and instinctively' believe to be necessary is the result of distorted perceptual judgements. An individual might believe that force is necessary on the basis of the belief that there is a threat, and that belief – in the presence of a weapon, or in the degree of hostility manifested – may be based on distorted perceptual judgements.

A. Evaluating the 'Genuine Belief' Standard

Avoiding an assessment about the reasonableness of the belief does not resolve the tensions outlined in section V. On the face of it, as a decision rule, the English and Welsh standard directs officials to maintain that even unreasonable

[65] See also *R v Gladstone Williams* (1984) 78 Cr App R 276.

[66] The European Court of Human Rights claimed that a genuine belief is not sufficient; the belief must also be held 'for good reason' (see *McCann v United Kingdom* (1996) 21 EHRR 97, para 200). Notably, the Court only dealt with cases of preventative force under Art 2 of the European Convention on Human Rights (Right to life), thus cases involving the killing of an individual on the part of enforcement officers. In any case, notwithstanding that it had the opportunity to do so, the Court has not remarked on the incompatibility between the Convention and the English and Welsh law on self-defence.

[67] Criminal Justice and Immigration Act 2008, s 76(7)(b). *cf Palmer v The Queen* [1971] AC 814, para 832: 'If a jury thought that in a moment of unexpected anguish a person attacked had only done what he honestly and instinctively thought was necessary that would be most potent evidence that only reasonable defensive action had been taken'.

but genuinely held beliefs are compatible with the availability of the defence. Accordingly, the genuine belief standard renders acting on bias-based beliefs justified, so long as the force used was reasonable, given such beliefs. So understood, the genuine belief standard would appear to face all the problematic ramifications outlined above: conveying disrespect; sanctioning cognitions that deploy racist stereotypes; entrenching those stereotypes, and the demeaning consequences of stigmatisation for those individuals targeted by them. Yet, avoiding these consequences would require refinement of the genuine belief standard. One might either creatively interpret the standard so as to deny that such bias-based beliefs could be 'honestly and instinctively' held; there is something inherently dishonest about such biased beliefs, one might say. Alternatively, one could simply hold that such bias-based beliefs are insufficient for the purposes of self-defence; even honest belief, when based in bias, cannot justify defensive force. Either of these refinements, though, faces the fairness concerns for the defendant, as raised above. So, the very same tension discussed earlier seems to play out in the context of the genuine, rather than reasonable, belief rule. However, there are additional complexities in the way that English and Welsh law deals with self-defence that are worth addressing.

B. The Re-Emergence of the Reasonable Person

Whilst the focus of the English and Welsh defence is on genuine belief, the notion of reasonableness re-emerges in the instructions regarding how one might ascertain genuineness of belief. Section 76(4) of the Criminal Justice and Immigration Act 2008 indicates that:

> If D [the defendant] claims to have held a particular belief as regards the existence of any circumstances –
>
> (a) the reasonableness or otherwise of that belief is relevant to the question whether D genuinely held it.[68]

Thus, officials are instructed that certain inferences may be made from normative standards to the existence of cognitive states. That a belief is reasonable may be evidence that the individual held it; that it is unreasonable may be evidence that the belief was not honestly held. The reasonable person standard re-emerges as a decision rule, in particular, with an evidential role. That a reasonable person may have believed *p* is said to provide evidential support for the fact that the defendant did genuinely so believe. This raises again the issue

[68] *cf* CPS Legal Guidance, 'Self-Defence and the Prevention of Crime: S76 of Criminal Justice and Immigration Act 2008', available at: www.cps.gov.uk/legal/s_to_u/self_defence/#rachel which also emphasises the evidential role of reasonableness. Crucially, these guidelines also suggest that 'the more unreasonable the belief, the less likely it is that the court will accept it was honestly held'.

as to what a reasonable person might believe – in particular, whether she may form bias-based beliefs.

Given the pervasive disposition to bias-based beliefs, this evidential directive seems warranted only if the model of a reasonable person is construed as incorporating the sorts of implicit biases outlined in section II. But as we have seen, to endorse such a model is to face the objections raised in section V. This is so, even if provision 4(a) above is explicitly indicated as a decision-rule: as we observed earlier conduct rules may be generated as a side effect, conveying the normative message that it is reasonable to hold and act on bias-based beliefs. Admittedly, given that this decision rule would be evidential rather than substantive in nature – in particular, it would not identify a fact that is relevant for criminal responsibility, but only a fact that is relevant to prove one such fact – it is plausible to argue that the rule would be less powerful in sending the negative messages discussed earlier, as it would play a less visible role in adjudication. Accordingly, this evidential role may be an effective method of 'selective transmission', by which the problematic messages embedded in the evidential directive are at least in part prevented from conveying problematic messages about permissible conduct. However, as we argued earlier a legal construct which embeds racist assumptions is itself objectionable and covering it up is no remedy.

On the other hand, a model of the reasonable person which does not accommodate within the circumstances of the reasonable person such biases, undermines the evidential role that reasonableness should play according to section 76(4). Under this reading, the fact that a belief is reasonable gives little evidential support to the claim that it was genuinely held, since we know that dispositions to bias pervasively influence our cognition. A model of the reasonable person that excludes implicit bias, then, considerably weakens the epistemic warrant for this particular decision rule.

VII. A PALLIATIVE SOLUTION

The tension we have identified is between fairness towards the defendant and the sanctioning of racist stereotypes. This arises most starkly in judicial systems in which the only options facing court officials are to convict an individual for an intentional infliction of (or attempt to inflict) harm, or to accept the justification of self-defence, and thus acquit. As Lee notes, a middle ground may be to resort to a partial defence of imperfect self-defence in a case of genuine but unreasonable belief.[69] This avenue is followed in several US jurisdictions. Such a

[69] Lee (n 30). The other main proposals that Lee considers are ways of 'making race salient' in the criminal trial, since empirical evidence suggests that doing so is an effective means to reducing racism (1586–1600). For example, mock jurors encouraged to consider race directly across various scenarios avoided judgements that expressed racial bias, compared with those for whom race was not made salient. Whilst there is much of interest in here for criminal justice systems and theorists

defence may serve to reduce the charge – for example, from murder to voluntary manslaughter.[70] This partial defence could provide a model for the treatment of self-defence claims in cases of non-culpably unreasonable belief. It could then be available to individuals who use force due to bias-based beliefs.

Lee's proposal is instructive because it allows us to identify one variable that is relevant to the tensions articulated above: partial versus full defence. The merit of a partial defence, in our case of bias-based belief, is that it mitigates the problematic messages that a full defence may send to the public, whether directly or as a side effect. However, the partial defence still apportions punishment – perhaps severe – to the defendant, so that concerns of fairness in the face of non-culpable mistake remain. Grave concerns persist about punishing individuals – albeit with a more lenient sentence – for intentional harm perpetrated on the basis of cognitions they not only repudiate but inherited from a social context shaped by a state whose institutional structures and dynamics have demonstrated a disregard for racial equality.

There is a second independent variable that is not made explicit in Lee's discussion of the imperfect defence: excuse versus justification.[71] As observed at the start, self-defence may function as a justification; that is, it renders the conduct permissible. If the defence functions as an excuse, instead, it does not have this implication; the conduct is treated as wrongful notwithstanding the defence. The merit of excusing over justifying in the case of bias-based belief, then, is that the defence sends a qualitatively different message to the public. It conveys the message that individuals are not permitted to act on racial biases, although they are excused for doing so. Note, though, that from a perspective of dissatisfaction with a society infected by racism and with the role of criminal justice within it, this message remains inadequate. It communicates that intentionally killing someone due to racist stereotypes is excusable. Such a message would legitimately be met with outrage.[72] This is especially the case

to consider, Lee's proposal to deploy such strategies in self-defence cases is based on the assumption that bias-based beliefs are obviously unreasonable and, therefore, that they could not ground self-defence. This stance, however, does not address the distinctive considerations of unfairness that we raised in section V.

[70] Lee (n 30) 1603–04. A somewhat similar approach is taken in the Model Penal Code, notwithstanding the absence of any mention of reasonableness. *cf* the Model Penal Code, s 3.09(2), stating that if the belief is recklessly or negligently mistaken and if recklessness and negligence suffice to establish culpability for the relevant crime, the defendant should be convicted as if she acted recklessly or negligently. This looks like a legal fiction, given that in cases such as B's the agent acts intentionally.

[71] For a discussion of this variable in the context of self-defence, see A Norrie, *Crime, Reason and History: A Critical Introduction to Criminal Law*, 4th edn (Cambridge University Press, 2014) 292–94; and G Fletcher, *Basic Concepts of Criminal Law* (Oxford University Press, 1998) 130–38, 158–63.

[72] One might think that this message could be nullified by accompanying the application of the defence with an explicit pronouncement, disavowing such stereotypes. But it appears manifestly inadequate to disavow racial stereotypes at the same time as embedding a concept that deploys them.

where the criminal justice system itself is deeply implicated in entrenching racial inequality.[73]

Any of the options available within this two-variable framework, then (consider, for instance, a partial excuse), may lessen but do not resolve the tensions that we have articulated. The best that this framework can offer is a schema of palliative responses to the problems that implicit racial biases generate in the case of self-defence.[74]

VIII. CONCLUDING REMARKS

We set out with a hypothetical – but all too likely – scenario where implicit racial biases are implicated in perceptual judgements, on the basis of which beliefs about the imminence and gravity of a threat are formed and acted upon. Is the criminal law's person someone who would form such bias-based beliefs? We have argued that there are costs in either way of settling this question. If the criminal law's reasonable person is not susceptible to implicit biases, a distinctive question of fairness arises. The fact is that such biases may influence all of us despite our best efforts. Under these circumstances it is unfair to punish individuals for acting in accordance with bias-based beliefs. Yet if the criminal law's reasonable person is susceptible to such implicit biases, the system embeds racist stereotypes. This communicates problematic normative messages about the legitimacy of deploying racial stereotypes and devalues Black lives.

It is important to note that this tension is not atemporal and irresolvable. Here the challenges to an adequate model of the criminal law's person are distinctive. They differ from those arising from lines of argument to the effect that all agents lack the requisite form of agency to ever be criminally responsible – because of some metaphysical thesis of determinism, or because of neurological features that show our agency to be mechanistic and beyond our control. Rather – and by way of final diagnostic remarks – we propose that this tension arises from the following two features of our relationship to criminal

[73] M Alexander, *The New Jim Crow: Mass Incarceration in the Age of Color Blindness* (The New Press, 2010).

[74] Someone may raise issues concerning the implementation of any proposal that would require ascertaining the role of implicit bias in the defendant's action. For instance, she may contend that it would be infeasible to provide evidence not only that the defendant was implicitly biased, but also that these biases influenced her beliefs at the time of acting. However, one can provide evidence of the presence of a bias – as has been done millions of times over online – with use of the IAT (or commensurate measure) – especially if the tests are deployed across a range of contexts and occasions. See Project Implicit: implicit.harvard.edu/implicit/. Also, one proxy indicator of the bias' causal role in action could be the strength of the association measured. Finally, it seems to us that the problems raised by this objection are not qualitatively different from problems that beset other defences with a long-standing legal pedigree: consider defences of insanity, loss of control, diminished responsibility and intoxication. It is arguable that the expert evidence that would be available to establish the facts relevant to the defence discussed here is on no less solid footing than the (expert or non-expert) evidence often relied upon in order to establish these other defences.

law. The first is contingency: actual human agency, its functioning, and what can reasonably be expected of us all, is contingent upon our social context. We are susceptible to bias because our cognitions are shaped by a racist history and environment; but our cognisance of these psychological and social phenomena and our strategies in addressing them are not yet sufficiently developed that we may reasonably be expected to avoid such defective agency. However, the contingent facts of our racist social context make all the more pressing the need to fashion a criminal justice system that does not perpetuate further stigmatising stereotypes. Of course, the criminal law could not and should not be the only tool through which to expunge implicit biases or secure racial equality; but, at least, it should not embed racist presuppositions, fuel implicit biases and perpetuate racist stigmatisation.

The second feature that gives rise to the tension we have identified is the dual role that we ask the notion of the person in criminal law to perform. This notion is sometimes invoked as a normative ideal, setting standards to which we should strive in our conduct. Sometimes, however, the notion aims to accommodate the many ways in which, perhaps through no fault of our own, we may be defective.[75] Our discussion points to the somewhat pessimistic conclusion that where our agency is embedded in socially unjust relations, the normative ideal is a rather distant, perhaps unachievable one.

[75] This is most evident when the criminal law's person is construed based on the (problematic) notion of normality and on the traits of the agent. A clear example of this is the English and Welsh law on loss of control. See, in particular, s 54(1)(c) of the Coroners and Justice Act 2009. For a critical assessment of the tension between the reasonable person standard as normative ideal and its descriptive/exculpatory content see Moran (n 39) 301–07.

Index

www.ingramcontent.com/pod-product-compliance
Ingram Content Group UK Ltd.
Pitfield, Milton Keynes, MK11 3LW, UK
UKHW020815290926
15470UKWH00003B/1177

9 781509 923748